Hello! 365 Chocolate Candy Recipes

(Chocolate Candy Recipes - Volume 1)

Best Chocolate Candy Cookbook Ever For Beginners

Ms. Ibarra

Ms. Ingredient

Copyright: Published in the United States by Ms. Ingredient/ © MS. INGREDIENT

Published on January, 18 2020

All rights reserved. No part of this publication may be reproduced, stored in retrieval system, copied in any form or by any means, electronic, mechanical, photocopying, recording or otherwise transmitted without written permission from the publisher. Please do not participate in or encourage piracy of this material in any way. You must not circulate this book in any format. MS. INGREDIENT does not control or direct users' actions and is not responsible for the information or content shared, harm and/or actions of the book readers.

In accordance with the U.S. Copyright Act of 1976, the scanning, uploading and electronic sharing of any part of this book without the permission of the publisher constitute unlawful piracy and theft of the author's intellectual property. If you would like to use material from the book (other than just simply for reviewing the book), prior permission must be obtained by contacting the author at msingredient@mrandmscooking.com

Thank you for your support of the author's rights

Content

CONTENT 3

INTRODUCTION 8

LIST OF ABBREVIATIONS 10

365 AMAZING CHOCOLATE CANDY
RECIPES.. 11

1. Alexander's Chocolate-covered Peanuts ... 11
2. Almond Coconut Candies 11
3. Almond Crunch... 12
4. Amazing Healthy Dark Chocolate 12
5. Angel Food Candy 12
6. Angel Food Christmas Candy 13
7. Apricot Cashew Clusters............................ 13
8. Aunt Rose's Fantastic Butter Toffee.......... 14
9. Aunt Teen's Creamy Chocolate Fudge...... 14
10. Austrian Chocolate Balls....................... 15
11. Bacon-pecan Chocolate Truffles........... 15
12. Baked Fudge.. 16
13. Banana Cream Chocolate Truffles 16
14. Basic Truffles 17
15. Best Ever Fudge 17
16. Best Peppermint Bark 17
17. Birch Pretzel Logs.................................. 18
18. Bird's Nest Treats................................... 18
19. Bittersweet Chocolate-orange Truffles. 19
20. Bittersweet Double Chocolate Truffles 20
21. Blueberry, Coconut, And Pistachio
Chocolate Bark.. 21
22. Brazilian Brigadeiro-filled Chocolate
Easter Egg.. 21
23. Brigadeiro.. 22
24. Buckeye Balls II 22
25. Bugle Cones 23
26. Bunny Tails.. 23
27. Butter Cream Easter Egg Candies......... 24
28. Butterscotch Fudge................................. 24
29. Butterscotch Peanut Candy 24
30. Candied Lemon Peel................................ 25
31. Candy Bar Fudge..................................... 25
32. Candy Cane Reindeer 26

33. Caramel Peanut Fudge............................ 26
34. Caramel Pretzel Bites 27
35. Cashew Caramel Fudge 28
36. Chef John's Chocolate Bark 28
37. Cherry Blossom Fudge 29
38. Cherry Chocolate Bark 29
39. Cherry-pistachio Bark 30
40. Chestnut Truffles..................................... 30
41. Chewy Chocolate Candies....................... 31
42. Chewy Chocolate Logs 31
43. Chocolate Almond Bark.......................... 32
44. Chocolate Almond Brittle 32
45. Chocolate Almond Popcorn.................... 32
46. Chocolate Amaretto Fudge..................... 33
47. Chocolate Angel Food Candy 34
48. Chocolate Basket 34
49. Chocolate Billionaires 35
50. Chocolate Candy Clusters 35
51. Chocolate Caramel Candy....................... 36
52. Chocolate Caramel Corn......................... 36
53. Chocolate Caramel Turkey Legs............. 37
54. Chocolate Cheese Candy.......................... 37
55. Chocolate Cherries 38
56. Chocolate Cherry Candies....................... 38
57. Chocolate Cherry Fudge.......................... 39
58. Chocolate Cherry Truffles 39
59. Chocolate Chews 40
60. Chocolate Chip Cookie Dough Fudge .40
61. Chocolate Chip Cookie Dough Truffles
41
62. Chocolate Chow Mein Clusters 41
63. Chocolate Cinnamon Mud Balls............ 41
64. Chocolate Clusters................................... 42
65. Chocolate Covered Cherries................... 42
66. Chocolate Covered Easter Eggs 43
67. Chocolate Covered Marshmallows........ 43
68. Chocolate Covered Pecans 44
69. Chocolate Covered Potato Chips 44
70. Chocolate Cream Bonbons..................... 44
71. Chocolate Crunch Patties....................... 45
72. Chocolate Crunchies 45
73. Chocolate Easter Eggs............................. 46
74. Chocolate Fish Lollipops 46
75. Chocolate Fudge...................................... 46
76. Chocolate Haystacks................................ 47
77. Chocolate Hazelnut Truffles 47
78. Chocolate Islands 48

3

79. Chocolate Krisps 48
80. Chocolate Marshmallow Candy Squares 49
81. Chocolate Marshmallow Peanut Butter Squares 49
82. Chocolate Mascarpone Truffles 49
83. Chocolate Mint Candy 50
84. Chocolate Molasses Taffy 50
85. Chocolate Mousse Balls 51
86. Chocolate Nut Balls 51
87. Chocolate Nut Candies 51
88. Chocolate Nut Fudge 52
89. Chocolate Nut Fudge Rolls 52
90. Chocolate Orange Bites 53
91. Chocolate Orange Fudge 53
92. Chocolate Peanut Brittle 54
93. Chocolate Peanut Butter Balls 54
94. Chocolate Peanut Butter Bars 55
95. Chocolate Peanut Butter Candies 55
96. Chocolate Peanut Butter Cups 55
97. Chocolate Peanut Butter Fudge 56
98. Chocolate Peanut Clusters 56
99. Chocolate Peanut Sweeties 57
100. Chocolate Pecan Bark 57
101. Chocolate Pecan Candies 58
102. Chocolate Pecan Caramels 58
103. Chocolate Peppermint Bark 58
104. Chocolate Peppermint Candies 59
105. Chocolate Pizza Heart 59
106. Chocolate Pomegranate Candies 60
107. Chocolate Pralines, Mexican Style 60
108. Chocolate Pretzel Rings 61
109. Chocolate Pretzel Treats 61
110. Chocolate Pretzels 62
111. Chocolate Raisin Truffles 62
112. Chocolate Rum Truffles 62
113. Chocolate Salami 63
114. Chocolate Sour Cream Fudge 63
115. Chocolate Spiders 64
116. Chocolate Spoons 64
117. Chocolate Truffle 64
118. Chocolate Truffles 65
119. Chocolate Turtles 65
120. Chocolate Turtles® (the Candy) 66
121. Chocolate Walnut Fudge 66
122. Chocolate Zebra Clusters 67
123. Chocolate, Peanut & Pretzel Toffee Crisps 67
124. Chocolate-coated Pretzels 67
125. Chocolate-covered Apricot-pecan Pretzels 68
126. Chocolate-covered Chips 68
127. Chocolate-covered Coffee Beans 69
128. Chocolate-covered Pomegranate Seeds 69
129. Chocolate-covered Praline Chews 69
130. Chocolate-dipped Apricots 70
131. Chocolate-dipped Candy Canes 71
132. Chocolate-dipped Peanut Nougat 71
133. Chocolate-dipped Pretzel Rods 71
134. Chocolate-dipped Pretzels 72
135. Chocolate-dipped Treats 72
136. Chocolate-peanut Butter Keto Cups 73
137. Chocolaty Peanut Clusters 73
138. Christmas Bark Candy 74
139. Christmas Chocolate Bark 3 Ways: Pistachio, Pink Peppercorn, And Currant Bark . 74
140. Coconut Almond Candy 75
141. Coconut Chocolate Delights 75
142. Coconut Chocolate-covered Cherries ... 76
143. Coconut Cream Eggs 76
144. Coconut Joys 77
145. Coconut Snacks 77
146. Coconut Yule Trees 77
147. Coffee Shop Fudge 78
148. Cookie Balls 78
149. Cookie Dough Truffles 78
150. Cookies & Cream Truffle Balls 79
151. Cookies 'n' Cream Fudge 79
152. Cookies 'n' Creme Fudge 80
153. Cookies-and-cream Truffles 80
154. Cow Pies Candy 81
155. Cranberry Almond Bark 81
156. Cranberry Fudge 81
157. Creamy Orange Fudge 82
158. Create-a-bark 82
159. Crunchy Chocolate Cups 83
160. Crunchy Chocolate Eggs 83
161. Dairy State Fudge 83
162. Dandy Caramel Candies 84
163. Dark Chocolate Almond Rocks 84
164. Dark Chocolate Orange Truffles 85
165. Dark Chocolate Popcorn 85
166. Dark Chocolate Pumpkin Truffles 85
167. Dark Chocolate Raspberry Fudge 86

168. Dark Chocolate-covered Berries, Almonds, And Pretzel Crisps® 86
169. Delectable Maple Nut Chocolates......... 87
170. Double Chocolate Fudge 87
171. Double Chocolate Walnut Fudge.......... 88
172. Duo-chocolate Fudge 88
173. Easter Creme Egg® Rocky Road.......... 89
174. Easter Eggs... 89
175. Easy Chocolate Clusters...................... 90
176. Easy Chocolate Drops............................ 90
177. Easy Chocolate Truffles 91
178. Easy Mint Chocolate Truffles 91
179. Easy Oreo Truffles 92
180. Easy Rocky Road Fudge 92
181. English Toffee Bars 92
182. Erika's "frango" Mints............................ 93
183. Extra Easy Fudge 93
184. Famous Coconut-almond Balls 94
185. Festive Holiday Bark.............................. 94
186. Fondant-filled Candies 94
187. Fried Egg Candy...................................... 95
188. Fudge-topped Brownies.......................... 95
189. Fudgy Buttons... 96
190. Fudgy Christmas Wreath 96
191. Fudgy Coconut Squares 97
192. Gaye's Microwave Fudge 97
193. German Chocolate Fudge....................... 98
194. German Christmas Nougatkugeln (nougat Balls)... 98
195. Gianduja.. 99
196. Giant Homemade Almond Butter Cups 99
197. Gingerbread Truffles 100
198. Gobbler Goodies 100
199. Golf Balls 101
200. Gooey Peanut Treats 101
201. Graham Cracker Fudge.........................102
202. Halloween Chocolate Spiders 102
203. Hogs And Kisses....................................103
204. Holiday Bark 4 Ways: Green Tea And Sea Salt Bark..103
205. Holiday Bark 4 Ways: Orange Pistachio Bark 104
206. Holiday Bark 4 Ways: Peppermint Bark 104
207. Holiday White Chocolate Fudge 105
208. Homemade Candy Bars 106

209. Homemade Caramels With Dark Chocolate And Sea Salt.......................... 106
210. Homemade Chocolate Easter Eggs ... 107
211. Homemade Melt-in-your-mouth Dark Chocolate (paleo) 107
212. Homemade Peanut Butter Cups......... 108
213. Homemade Valentine's Chocolates.... 108
214. Hot Chocolate Truffles 109
215. Ice Cream Sundae Caramels 109
216. Irish Cream Truffle Fudge 110
217. Jan's Chocolate Coffee Bean Bark...... 110
218. Janaan's Fudge.. 111
219. Layered Mint Chocolate Fudge.......... 111
220. Layered Peanut Butter Chocolate Fudge 112
221. Lemon Cream Bonbons 112
222. Lemon Drop Bark 113
223. Les Truffles Au Chocolat.................... 113
224. Light Chocolate Truffles 113
225. Liquor-infused Chocolate Strawberries 114
226. Luscious Chocolate Truffles................ 114
227. Made-in-minutes No-cook Fudge 115
228. Maine Potato Candy.............................. 115
229. Mamie Eisenhower's Fudge................. 116
230. Maple Cream Bonbons......................... 116
231. Maple Peanut Delights.......................... 116
232. Maple-bacon White Chocolate Fudge 117
233. Marbled Almond Roca 117
234. Marian's Fudge....................................... 118
235. Marshmallow Chocolate-covered Cherries118
236. Marshmallow Flowers........................... 119
237. Marshmallow Puffs 119
238. Martha Washington Candy 120
239. Marzipan Harvest Table Topper 120
240. Melt In Your Mouth Toffee 121
241. Microwave Mint Fudge 121
242. Microwave Truffles 122
243. Milk Chocolate Raspberry Truffles ... 122
244. Milk Chocolate Fudge.......................... 123
245. Milk Chocolate Truffles 123
246. Million Dollar Fudge............................. 123
247. Million-dollar Chocolate Fudge 124
248. Mint Chocolate Bark............................ 124
249. Mint Chocolate Cookie Crunch.......... 125
250. Mint Chocolate Fudge 125

251. Mint Truffles 126
252. Minty Chocolate Crackles 126
253. Mocha Truffles 127
254. Morgan's Amazing Peppermint Bark .127
255. Mounds Balls 128
256. My Christmas Fudge 128
257. Nana's Rocky Road Fudge 129
258. Neapolitan Fudge 129
259. Never-fail Fudge 130
260. No Fail Chocolate Fudge 130
261. No-bake Chocolate Cookie Triangles 131
262. No-bake Cookie Dough Truffles 131
263. No-bake Fudge Bar 132
264. No-cook Never-fail Fudge 132
265. No-fuss Truffles 133
266. Nut Fruit Bark 133
267. Nutty Chocolate Caramels 133
268. Nutty Chocolate Fudge 134
269. Nutty Chocolate Marshmallow Puffs .134
270. Nutty Chocolate Peanut Clusters 135
271. Nutty Chocolate Truffles 135
272. Nutty White Fudge 135
273. Old Fashioned Fudge 136
274. Old-time Butter Crunch Candy 136
275. One Bowl Chocolate Fudge 137
276. One Bowl Chocolate Fudge With Pecans 137
277. One Two Three Fudge 138
278. Orange Chocolate Meltaways 138
279. Orange Flavored Fudge 138
280. Orange-almond Chocolate Logs 139
281. Orange-fruit Nut Truffles 139
282. Oreos And Candy Cane Chocolate Bark 140
283. Oreo™ Cookie Bark 140
284. Peanut Butter And Banana Chocolate Truffles 141
285. Peanut Butter Candy Bars 141
286. Peanut Butter Chocolate Balls 141
287. Peanut Butter Chocolate Bark 142
288. Peanut Butter Chocolate Cups 142
289. Peanut Butter Chocolate Fudge 143
290. Peanut Butter Clusters 143
291. Peanut Butter Cocoa Fudge 144
292. Peanut Butter Honeybees 144
293. Peanut Butter Truffles 145
294. Peanut Choc-scotch Fudge 145

295. Pecan Carmel Clusters 146
296. Pecan Chocolate Candies 146
297. Pecan Delights 146
298. Pecan Fudge 147
299. Peppermint Candy 147
300. Peppermint Fudge 148
301. Peppermint Mocha Chocolate Bark ... 148
302. Peppermint Pretzel Dippers 149
303. Perfect Peppermint Patties 149
304. Popcorn And Peanut Truffles 150
305. Potato Chip Clusters 150
306. Pretzel Sparklers 150
307. Pretzel Turtles® 151
308. Pumpkin Truffles 151
309. Raspberry Truffle Fudge 152
310. Raspberry Truffles 152
311. Raspberry-mocha Chocolate Bark 153
312. Raw Strawberry-filled Chocolate Truffles 153
313. Ribbon Fantasy Fudge 154
314. Rich Candy Bar Fudge 154
315. Rich Truffle Wedges 155
316. Rocky Road Candies 155
317. Rocky Road Fudge 156
318. Salted Caramel And Toasted Pecan Truffles 156
319. Shortcut Fudge 157
320. Simple And Amazing Peanut Butter-chocolate Fudge 157
321. Simple Macadamia Nut Fudge 157
322. Soda Cracker Candy 158
323. Soda Cracker Chocolate Candy 158
324. Speculoos Cups 159
325. Speedy Oven Fudge 159
326. Spiced Chocolate Truffles 160
327. Spook-tacular Chocolate-dipped Pretzels 160
328. Stovetop Dark Chocolate Popcorn 161
329. Strawberry Chocolate Truffles 161
330. Stuffed Cherries Dipped In Chocolate 161
331. Sugar-free Chocolate Fudge 162
332. Surprise Chocolate Fudge 162
333. Swedish Chocolate Balls (or Coconut Balls) 163
334. Sweet Pretzel Stacks 163
335. Sweet Tooth Treats 164

336.	Sweetheart Fudge	164
337.	The Best White Chocolate Almond Bark 165	
338.	The Ultimate Chocolate Bar	165
339.	Three-chip English Toffee	166
340.	Three-chocolate Fudge	166
341.	Tiger Butter Candy	167
342.	Toasted Coconut Truffles	167
343.	Toffee Squares	168
344.	Trail Mix Clusters	168
345.	Trio Of Chocolate Truffles	169
346.	Triple Chocolate Fudge	169
347.	True Love Truffles	170
348.	Truffle Acorns	170
349.	Truffle Cherries	171
350.	Truffle Cups	171
351.	Truffle Topiary	172
352.	Turtles® Candies	172
353.	Twilight Dark Chocolate Truffles	173
354.	Vegan Almond Truffles	173
355.	Vegan Chocolate Truffles	174
356.	Vegan Truffles - Toasted Coconut	174
357.	White Chocolate Cranberry Fudge	175
358.	White Chocolate Easter Eggs	175
359.	White Chocolate Fudge	176
360.	White Chocolate Grapes	176
361.	White Chocolate Jingle Candy	176
362.	White Chocolate Marshmallow Fudge	177
363.	White Chocolate Peppermint Bark	177
364.	White Chocolate Peppermint Crunch	178
365.	White Christmas Candy	178

INDEX **179**

CONCLUSION **185**

Introduction

***

Why I Love Cooking

Hi all,

Welcome to MrandMsCooking.com—a website created by a community of cooking enthusiasts with the goal of providing books for novice cooks featuring the best recipes, at the most affordable prices, and valuable gifts.

Before we go to the recipes in the book "Hello! 365 Chocolate Candy Recipes", I have an interesting story to share with you the reason for loving cooking.

My mom would always tell me:

Cooking is an edible form of love…

As a young kid, I helped my mom cook. She would always cook any dish I liked. Observing how she cooked motivated me to try cooking. Ten years later, I'm sharing with you my cooking inspiration as well as the reasons why I love it.

1.   Trying something different

Various cuisines of the world use different kinds of ingredients. You can download and share a lot of recipes on the internet. Even so, you can add your own unique twists to recipes and experiment with various versions and styles.

Trying out new recipes and ingredients isn't bad when cooking, as long as you produce something edible…

2.   Enjoyment

Whomever you cook for— family, friends, or even yourself—you'll surely have fun doing it. It's satisfying to see how the combination of various spices, meat, and vegetables yield an awesome flavor. From cutting to cooking them, the whole process is nothing but pure joy.

3.   Receiving wonderful feedback

Don't you get a sense of pride, joy, and accomplishment when people love the dish you've cooked and let you know their thoughts? You'll definitely savor the moment when you hear someone praise your cooking skills.

Each time someone tells me, "This has a great flavor" or "This is insanely delicious!" I get more motivated to become a better cook…

4.   Healthy eating

Rather than consuming processed food, using fresh ingredients for your dishes makes them good for the body. Cook your own meals so that you can add more fresh vegetables and fruits to your diet. Cooking also allows you to discover more about the different nutrients in your meals.

Because you prepare your meals yourself, having digestive problems will be the least of your worries…

5.   Therapeutic activity

Based on my experience, cooking calms the mind. Finding food in the fridge, gathering the ingredients, getting them ready, and assembling everything together to create a yummy dish are more relaxing than just spending idle time on the couch watching TV. Cooking never makes me stressed.

My mother would always tell me: Cooking is an edible way to make your loved ones feel loved…

Keeping Up Your Passion for Cooking

Cooking is not for everyone. But people who are passionate about cooking and their families are fortunate indeed. It spreads happiness around. Do you love cooking? Sustain your passion—it's the best feeling ever!

When combined with love, cooking feeds the soul…

From my unending love for cooking, I'm creating this book series and hoping to share my passion with all of you. With my many experiences of failures, I have created this book series and hopefully it helps you. This Ingredient Recipes Series covers these subjects:

- Cheese Recipes
- Butter Recipes
- Red Wine Recipes
- Cajun Spice Recipes
- Mayonnaise Recipes
- ...

I really appreciate that you have selected "Hello! 365 Chocolate Candy Recipes" and for reading to the end. I anticipate that this book shall give you the source of strength during the times that you are really exhausted, as well as be your best friend in the comforts of your own home. Please also give me some love by sharing your own exciting cooking time in the comments segment below.

List of Abbreviations

C👩‍🍳👨‍🍳King LIST OF ABBREVIATIONS	
tbsp(s).	tablespoon(s)
tsp(s).	teaspoon(s)
c.	cup(s)
oz.	ounce(s)
lb(s).	pound(s)

365 Amazing Chocolate Candy Recipes

***

1. Alexander's Chocolate-covered Peanuts

"It can make for 28 servings."
Serving: 28 | Prep: 15m | Ready in: 1h17m

Ingredients

- 18 oz. white almond bark, broken into pieces
- 2 cups chocolate chips, or more to taste
- 24 oz. lightly salted peanuts, or more to taste

Direction

- In a slow cooker, add almond bark. On High, stir from time to time until mostly melted, for about 2 minutes. Reduce the heat to Low. Mix in chocolate chips until thoroughly dark, for about 30 seconds. Add the peanuts.
- Drop the peanut clusters onto a parchment paper-lined countertop by a spoonful to test if they are chunky and thick. Mix in more chocolate chips and peanuts if it is too runny and loose.
- Use parchment paper to line 4 to 5 baking sheets. Use a melon baller to put spoonfuls of the peanut clusters on top. Let harden for about 1 hour.

Nutrition Information

- Calories: 286 calories;

- Total Carbohydrate: 21.2 g
- Cholesterol: 0 mg
- Total Fat: 22.8 g
- Protein: 7.7 g
- Sodium: 199 mg

2. Almond Coconut Candies

"The combination of deep dark chocolate, almonds, and coconut in this candy recipe is irresistible."
Serving: 5 dozen. | Prep: 25m | Ready in: 25m

Ingredients

- 4-1/2 cups confectioners' sugar
- 3 cups sweetened shredded coconut
- 1 cup sweetened condensed milk
- 1/2 cup butter, melted
- 1 tsp. vanilla extract
- 60 whole unblanched almonds
- FROSTING:
- 1-1/2 cups confectioners' sugar
- 1/2 cup baking cocoa
- 1/2 cup butter, melted
- 3 tbsps. hot coffee

Direction

- Mix the first 5 ingredients together in a large mixing bowl. Form mixture into balls about 1 inch; arrange balls on lightly greased baking sheets. Pat an almond on top of each ball. Refrigerate for 60 minutes.
- Mix frosting ingredients together until no lumps remain; instantly frost over the candies. Refrigerate until frosting is solid. Keep chilled in the fridge.

Nutrition Information

- Calories: 123 calories
- Total Carbohydrate: 18 g
- Cholesterol: 10 mg
- Total Fat: 6 g
- Fiber: 0 g
- Protein: 1 g

- Sodium: 50 mg

3. Almond Crunch

"This recipe is often requested whenever I serve it. Be sure to have a working candy thermometer and use quality ingredients. Avoid using margarine in place of butter because the water content is very high."
Serving: 16 | Prep: 15m | Ready in: 2h20m

Ingredients

- 1 cup blanched slivered almonds
- 1 cup butter
- 1 1/4 cups white sugar
- 2 tbsps. light corn syrup
- 2 tbsps. water
- 2 cups milk chocolate chips

Direction

- Preheat an oven to 190 degrees C (375 degrees F). Place almonds in a baking sheet in a single layer. Then toast in oven for about 5 minutes until browned lightly.
- Line foil onto a jelly roll pan.
- Mix water, corn syrup, sugar, and butter in a heavy saucepan. Over medium heat, cook while stirring continuously until the mixture is boiling. Let boil without stirring to hard crack stage, 150 degrees C (300 degrees F). Transfer from the heat.
- Mix in almonds, working quickly and transfer the mixture to the jelly roll pan lined with foil. Spread the candy evenly in pan by tilting pan from side to side. Drizzle chocolate chips atop candy brittle. Allow to sit for about five minutes or until soft and shiny. Evenly spread the chocolate atop the candy. Let to cool to lukewarm and then chill for one hour. Cut into small pieces.

Nutrition Information

- Calories: 317 calories;
- Total Carbohydrate: 32.6 g
- Cholesterol: 35 mg

- Total Fat: 21 g
- Protein: 3 g
- Sodium: 84 mg

4. Amazing Healthy Dark Chocolate

"This chocolate is tasty and healthy with 3 superfoods as its ingredients. You can serve this as the following: dip fruit into it, refrigerate and roll to make truffles, press into mold and frying pan or prepare hot chocolate."
Serving: 24 | Prep: 5m | Ready in: 5m

Ingredients

- 1 cup coconut oil, melted
- 1 cup unsweetened cocoa powder
- 1 cup maple syrup

Direction

- In a bowl, combine maple syrup, cocoa powder, and coconut oil until evenly blended.

Nutrition Information

- Calories: 121 calories;
- Total Carbohydrate: 10.8 g
- Cholesterol: 0 mg
- Total Fat: 9.6 g
- Protein: 0.7 g
- Sodium: 2 mg

5. Angel Food Candy

"This chocolate coated candy is crunchy."
Serving: 30 | Prep: 20m | Ready in: 1h15m

Ingredients

- 1 cup white sugar
- 1 cup dark corn syrup
- 1 tbsp. vinegar
- 1 tbsp. baking soda
- 1 lb. chocolate confectioners' coating

Direction

- Butter a 9x13 inch baking dish.
- Mix vinegar, corn syrup and sugar over medium heat in a medium saucepan. Cook while stirring until sugar is dissolved. Without stirring, heat to 300-310°F (149- 154°C), or until when you drop a small amount of syrup into cold water, it forms hard, brittle threads.
- Take out of the heat; stir in baking soda. Transfer into buttered pan; do not spread. (Mixture should not fill the pan). Let cool completely.
- Melt coating chocolate while stirring frequently until smooth over a double boiler or in a microwave. Break cooled candy into bite-sized pieces and coat with melted candy coating. Allow to set on waxed paper. Keep covered tightly.

Nutrition Information

- Calories: 129 calories;
- Total Carbohydrate: 22.2 g
- Cholesterol: 0 mg
- Total Fat: 6 g
- Protein: 1.2 g
- Sodium: 135 mg

6. Angel Food Christmas Candy

"It was my father who motivated me to initially have a go at making this sweet."
Serving: 1-1/2 lbs.. | Prep: 5m | Ready in: 30m

Ingredients

- 1 cup sugar
- 1 cup dark corn syrup
- 1 tbsp. white vinegar
- 1 tbsp. baking soda
- 1 lb. milk chocolate candy coating, melted

Direction

- Mix the vinegar, corn syrup and sugar in a heavy saucepan. Cook over medium heat,

constantly mixing until sugar is dissolved. Cook without mixing until reaching 300 ° (hard-crack stage) on a candy thermometer. Don't overcook.
- Take away from heat then mix in the baking soda quickly. Pour into a 13x9-inch pan coated with butter. Don't spread the candy; the blend won't fill the pan.
- Break into pieces bite-size when cool. Dip into the melted chocolate; put onto waxed paper until chocolate is firm. Keep the candy covered tightly.

Nutrition Information

- Calories: 337 calories
- Total Carbohydrate: 63 g
- Cholesterol: 0 mg
- Total Fat: 11 g
- Fiber: 1 g
- Protein: 1 g
- Sodium: 356 mg

7. Apricot Cashew Clusters

"A fruity surprise in these scrumptious nut candies."
Serving: 2-1/2 dozen. | Prep: 30m | Ready in: 30m

Ingredients

- 1 package (11-1/2 oz.) milk chocolate chips
- 1 cup chopped dried apricots
- 1 cup chopped salted cashews

Direction

- Liquefy the chocolate chips in a double boiler or microwave; mix till smooth. Mix in cashews and apricots. On waxed paper-lined baking sheets, drop by rounded tablespoonfuls. Refrigerate for 15 minutes till set. Keep in an airtight container.

Nutrition Information

- Calories: 93 calories
- Total Carbohydrate: 11 g

- Cholesterol: 2 mg
- Total Fat: 5 g
- Fiber: 1 g
- Protein: 2 g
- Sodium: 41 mg

8. Aunt Rose's Fantastic Butter Toffee

""MY family's favorite toffee recipe.""
Serving: about 2 lbs. | Prep: 25m | Ready in: 40m

Ingredients

- 2 cups unblanched whole almonds
- 11 oz. milk chocolate, chopped
- 1 cup butter, cubed
- 1 cup sugar
- 3 tbsps. cold water

Direction

- Set the oven at 350° and start preheating. Toast almonds in a shallow baking pan, stirring occasionally, 5-10 minutes, till golden brown. Allow to cool. In a food processor, pulse chocolate till finely ground (do not overprocess); move into a bowl. In the food processor, pulse almonds till coarsely chopped. Scatter 1 cup of almonds onto the bottom of a 15x10x1-in. pan coated with grease. Sprinkle 1 cup of chocolate over.
- Stir water, sugar and butter in a heavy saucepan. Cook while stirring occasionally over medium heat till a candy thermometer reads 290° (soft-crack stage)
- Transfer the mixture over chocolate and almonds in the pan immediately. Sprinkle the remaining almonds and chocolate on top. Refrigerate till set; break into pieces.

Nutrition Information

- Calories: 177 calories
- Total Carbohydrate: 14 g
- Cholesterol: 17 mg

- Total Fat: 13 g
- Fiber: 1 g
- Protein: 3 g
- Sodium: 51 mg

9. Aunt Teen's Creamy Chocolate Fudge

"It takes only 15 minutes to make this heart melting fudge."
Serving: 48 | Prep: 10m | Ready in: 30m

Ingredients

- 1 (7 oz.) jar marshmallow creme
- 1 1/2 cups white sugar
- 2/3 cup evaporated milk
- 1/4 cup butter
- 1/4 tsp. salt
- 2 cups milk chocolate chips
- 1 cup semisweet chocolate chips
- 1/2 cup chopped nuts
- 1 tsp. vanilla extract

Direction

- Use aluminum foil to line one 8 x 8 inch pan. Set aside.
- Mix salt, butter, evaporated milk, sugar, marshmallow cream in a large saucepan on medium heat. Bring to a full boil, cook and stir constantly for 5 minutes.
- Get the pan off heat then add milk chocolate chips and semisweet chocolate chips to pan. Stir till chocolate is melted and the mixture becomes smooth. Put in vanilla, nuts and stir. Transfer the mixture into the prepared pan. Keep in the fridge to chill for 2 hours or till it becomes firm.

Nutrition Information

- Calories: 124 calories;
- Total Carbohydrate: 18.2 g
- Cholesterol: 5 mg
- Total Fat: 5.5 g

- Protein: 1.4 g
- Sodium: 26 mg

10. Austrian Chocolate Balls

"Top these dark chocolate balls with a delicious dark chocolate glaze."
Serving: 42 | Prep: 15m | Ready in: 45m

Ingredients

- 2 (1 oz.) squares unsweetened chocolate
- 1/3 cup butter
- 1 cup white sugar
- 1 egg
- 1 egg yolk
- 1/2 tsp. almond extract
- 1 1/3 cups all-purpose flour
- 1/2 cup finely chopped walnuts
- 1 (1 oz.) square unsweetened chocolate
- 1 tbsp. butter
- 1/4 tsp. vanilla extract
- 1 cup confectioners' sugar
- 3 tbsps. milk

Direction

- Melt 1/3 cup butter and 2 squares of chocolate over low heat in a small saucepan. Whisk constantly until melted; turn off the heat, and put to one side to cool. Turn oven to 350°F (175°C) to preheat.
- Combine egg and egg yolk in a medium bowl together with almond extract and sugar until fluffy and light. Mix in melted chocolate. Combine walnuts and flour; mix into the batter just until incorporated. Form dough into 3/4-inch balls, and arrange them 1 inch apart on unbuttered cookie sheets. If the dough feels too sticky, chill for half an hour before making balls.
- Bake for 8 to 12 minutes in the preheated oven until firm to the touch. Immediately remove to wire racks, and put aside to allow to cool.
- Melt 1 tbsp. butter and 1 square of chocolate together over low heat in a small saucepan, whisking often until no lumps remain. Put off the heat, and whisk in confectioners' sugar and vanilla until incorporated. Beat in milk, 1 tbsp. at a time, until glaze reaches desired thickness. Immerse top of the cookies into the glaze; let dry entirely before putting into an airtight container to store.

Nutrition Information

- Calories: 82 calories;
- Total Carbohydrate: 11.5 g
- Cholesterol: 14 mg
- Total Fat: 4 g
- Protein: 1.1 g
- Sodium: 15 mg

11. Bacon-pecan Chocolate Truffles

"Bacon flavored truffles."
Serving: 3-1/2 dozen. | Prep: 40m | Ready in: 45m

Ingredients

- 1 package (12 oz.) dark chocolate chips
- 6 tbsps. butter, cubed
- 1/3 cup heavy whipping cream
- 8 bacon strips, cooked and finely chopped
- COATING:
- 1 cup white baking chips
- 1/2 cup heavy whipping cream
- 1/2 tsp. maple flavoring
- 1-3/4 cups chopped pecans, toasted

Direction

- Put dark chocolate chips in small bowl. Heat cream and butter just to simmer in small saucepan. Put on chocolate; mix till smooth. Mix bacon in; cool to room temperature, occasionally mixing. Refrigerate for 1 1/2 hours till firm enough to shape, covered.
- Coating: Put baking chips in small bowl. Put cream to just a boil in small saucepan. Put on baking chips; use whisk to mix till smooth.

Mix maple flavoring in; completely cool, occasionally mixing, for 1 1/2 hours.

- Form dark chocolate mixture to 1-in. balls. In maple mixture, dip truffles; let excess drip off. Roll into pecans; put on 15x10x1-in. waxed paper-lined baking pan. Refrigerate till set. Keep between waxed paper layers in airtight container in the fridge.

12. Baked Fudge

"This recipe is wonderful."
Serving: 12 | Prep: 10m | Ready in: 1h10m

Ingredients

- 2 cups white sugar
- 1/2 cup all-purpose flour
- 1/2 cup unsweetened cocoa powder
- 4 eggs, beaten
- 1 cup butter, melted
- 2 tsps. vanilla extract
- 1 cup chopped pecans

Direction

- Set the oven to 300°F (150°C) and start preheating.
- Sift together cocoa, flour and sugar in a large bowl. Add eggs. Add pecans, vanilla and melted butter. Transfer to an 8x12-inch baking pan.
- Using a damp kitchen towel, line a roasting pan. Put a baking dish on towel, inside roasting pan; transfer roasting pan onto oven rack. Pour boiling water into the roasting pan to reach halfway up the sides of the baking dish. Bake until firm or for 50-60 minutes.

Nutrition Information

- Calories: 380 calories;
- Total Carbohydrate: 40.7 g
- Cholesterol: 102 mg
- Total Fat: 24.1 g
- Protein: 4.3 g
- Sodium: 159 mg

13. Banana Cream Chocolate Truffles

"This amazing truffle recipe is a combination of my imagination and ripe bananas."
Serving: about 4 dozen. | Prep: 35m | Ready in: 35m

Ingredients

- 1 package (14.3 oz.) Golden Oreo cookies
- 1 package (8 oz.) cream cheese, softened
- 2 tsps. banana extract
- 1/3 cup mashed ripe banana
- 1 lb. milk chocolate candy coating, melted
- Dried banana chips, coarsely crushed

Direction

- In a food processor, blend cookies into fine crumbs. Beat cream cheese with extract in a mixing bowl until incorporated. Whisk in banana. Mix in cookie crumbs. Cover and freeze, about 2 hours, until solid enough to shape.
- Form mixture into balls about 1 inch. Immerse the balls in candy coating; arrange coated candies on baking sheets lined with waxed paper. Instantly sprinkle top with banana chips.
- Chill for about half an hour until firm. Keep chilled in a covered container in the fridge.

Nutrition Information

- Calories: 110 calories
- Total Carbohydrate: 13 g
- Cholesterol: 5 mg
- Total Fat: 6 g
- Fiber: 0 g
- Protein: 1 g
- Sodium: 45 mg

14. Basic Truffles

"Basic truffle filling recipe that you may use to fill chocolate shells or roll it into balls on sprinkles, cocoa or powdered sugar."
Serving: 35 | Prep: 10m | Ready in: 1h50m

Ingredients

- 12 oz. bittersweet chocolate, chopped
- 1/3 cup heavy cream
- 1 tsp. vanilla extract

Direction

- Mix together the cream and chocolate in a medium saucepan on medium heat. Let it cook and stir until the mixture becomes smooth and the chocolate melts. Take it out of the heat and whisk in the flavoring. Pour it into a small dish and let it chill in the fridge for 1 1/2 to 2 hours until it becomes set, yet not hard. Form it into balls and roll it in the toppings or use it to fill the candies.

Nutrition Information

- Calories: 62 calories;
- Total Carbohydrate: 5.6 g
- Cholesterol: 4 mg
- Total Fat: 4.1 g
- Protein: 0.7 g
- Sodium: 1 mg

15. Best Ever Fudge

"This simple and tasty fudge is our tradition for every Christmas. It can be prepared in advance and store frozen for a maximum of 3 months.""
Serving: 24

Ingredients

- 2 cups white sugar
- 1 cup milk
- 1 tsp. vanilla extract
- 1 cup butter

- 25 marshmallows, quartered
- 2 cups milk chocolate chips
- 2 cups semi-sweet chocolate chips
- 2 (1 oz.) squares unsweetened chocolate
- 1 cup chopped pecans

Direction

- Lightly coat an 11x16-inch jelly roll pan with oil. Put aside.
- Combine butter vanilla, milk, and sugar in a large, heavy saucepan. Boil, whisking occasionally. Allow mixture to boil for 2 minutes.
- Take off from the heat; put in unsweetened chocolate, milk chocolate chips, semi-sweet chocolate chips, and marshmallows. Mix until melted and no lumps remain. Mix in nuts until incorporated.
- Transfer mixture to the prepared pan. Allow fudge to sit for at least 1 day before slicing into squares. Chill for easier cutting.

Nutrition Information

- Calories: 346 calories;
- Total Carbohydrate: 42.8 g
- Cholesterol: 24 mg
- Total Fat: 20.5 g
- Protein: 3.3 g
- Sodium: 65 mg

16. Best Peppermint Bark

""This is my take on the dish using Oreos®""
Serving: 40 | Prep: 25m | Ready in: 1h45m

Ingredients

- 12 peppermint candy canes
- 1 (15.5 oz.) package chocolate sandwich cookies (such as Oreo®), crushed
- 2/3 cup confectioners' sugar
- 1/2 cup margarine, melted
- 1 (12 oz.) package vanilla-flavored confectioners' candy coating

Direction

- Put aluminum foil around jelly roll pan.
- In a resealable plastic bag, put candy canes and place the bag over folded kitchen napkins and gently break with a hammer the candy canes in little chunks.
- In a bowl, mix in confectioners' sugar and chocolate cookie crumbs until the crumbs are covered. In the cookie crumbs, add in melted margarine.
- In the bottom of the jelly roll pan that is prepared, press evenly the cookie crumb mixture.
- For 50 seconds, on full power in a microwave, heat the confectioners' candy coating. Mix and resume heating until melted, smooth and hot, mixing every 15 seconds while mixing. Using a spatula, spread the candy on top of cookie crumbs until smooth top is achieved. Set aside for 10 minutes allowing the layer of candy to become firm.
- S, put the crushed candy canes on top of the confectioners' coating. Let sit for 2 minutes. Using a cut of waxed paper, gently press the candy cane pieces into the coating. For about an hour, set the peppermint bark to freeze. Take the bark from the foil and cut into chunks. Put in the refrigerator to store.

Nutrition Information

- Calories: 158 calories;
- Total Carbohydrate: 23.2 g
- Cholesterol: 2 mg
- Total Fat: 7.1 g
- Protein: 1.1 g
- Sodium: 90 mg

17. Birch Pretzel Logs

"Make your own version of a chocolate-dipped pretzel, or sometimes called "logs". Most pretzels are too costly in some shops, so better to make your own and serve some "log" stacks at any of your party gatherings. You can also tie some ribbons on the logs and give them away for Christmas."
Serving: about 2 dozen. | Prep: 30m | Ready in: 30m

Ingredients

- 1 lb. white candy coating, coarsely chopped
- 1 package (10 oz.) pretzel rods
- 1/2 cup semisweet chocolate chips
- 1 small heavy-duty resealable plastic bag

Direction

- Melt candy coating in microwave and stir until smooth. Place it in an 8-inch square pan or in a tall glass. Coat the pretzels by dipping or rolling; do not coat the part where you're holding the pretzel or at least 1 inch of it. Drip off some excess before placing in a baking pan that is lined with a waxed paper. Let them rest.
- Melt the chocolate chips in a microwave oven. Stir the chips until smooth. Place in a small zip locked plastic bag. In the bottom corner of the plastic bag, cautiously cut a tiny hole. Mark some stripes on the pretzel rods so they look like birch trees. Let them set before storing in a closed or sealed container.

18. Bird's Nest Treats

"The easy-prep recipe is delicious."
Serving: 1 dozen. | Prep: 25m | Ready in: 40m

Ingredients

- 1/4 cup butter, cubed
- 4-1/2 cups miniature marshmallows
- 1/4 cup creamy peanut butter
- 1/4 cup semisweet chocolate chips
- 4 cups chow mein noodles

- 1 cup jelly beans or candy eggs

Direction

- Melt marshmallows and butter until smooth while stirring occasionally over medium heat in a large saucepan. Add chocolate chips and peanut butter; heat while stirring until smooth, about 2 minutes. Take out of the heat; stir in chow mein noodles until coated well.
- Transfer to 12 mounds on a baking sheet lined with waxed paper. Form each into a nest with fingers; press an indentation in the nest's center. Fill 3-4 candy eggs or jelly beans into each nest. Cool.

Nutrition Information

- Calories: 296 calories
- Total Carbohydrate: 46 g
- Cholesterol: 10 mg
- Total Fat: 12 g
- Fiber: 1 g
- Protein: 3 g
- Sodium: 149 mg

---

19. Bittersweet Chocolate-orange Truffles

"Although the orange adds an exotic flavor to these candies, much of the flavor comes from the chocolate. Go for a bittersweet or semisweet with a flavor and level of sweetness you love. This recipe yield a huge batch of truffles. Best when served after resting at room temperature for about 5 minutes although they should be kept in the fridge."
Serving: 48 | Ready in: 12h

Ingredients

- ¾ cup whipping cream
- 1 tsp. freshly grated orange zest
- 2½ tbsps. orange juice
- 2 tbsps. superfine sugar, (see Note)
- 1 tbsp. Grand Marnier, Triple Sec or other orange-flavored liqueur, or 2 tsps. vanilla extract

- 8 oz. bittersweet or semisweet chocolate (45-65% cacao), coarsely chopped
- ½ cup (approximately) Dutch-process cocoa powder, sifted after measuring
- 8 oz. bittersweet or semisweet chocolate (50-75% cacao), coarsely chopped

Direction

- To prepare the ganache: Line foil onto an 8-inch-square pan and let it to overhang two opposing sides slightly. Use cooking spray to coat lightly.
- In a microwave-safe bowl or 2-cup glass measure, mix cream, orange liqueur (or vanilla), sugar, orange zest, and orange juice. Heat in microwave on High for about 1 minute until steaming. Keep watching to prevent boiling over. (Alternatively, mix in a small saucepan and then heat using medium-low heat until steaming.) Mix until sugar has dissolved. Reserve for 10 minutes.
- Put 8 oz. of chocolate in a medium microwave-safe bowl. (See Tip for another option). Heat for one minute in microwave on High. Microwave on Medium while stirring after every 20 seconds until mostly melted. Reserve.
- Place back cream mixture into the microwave (or stove) and then heat in microwave on High (or heat over medium-low) until steaming once again. Strain mixture through a fine sieve that is set onto chocolate and push down to force through as much liquid as you can. Avoid stirring the chocolate. Leave to rest without stirring for two minutes. Gently mix the cream mixture with a clean, dry spoon into chocolate until smoothly incorporated. In the beginning, the ganache will seem separated but it will slowly stick together after a few minutes of stirring. (In case there's any unmelted chocolate, place the bowl back into the microwave and heat on Medium for 30 seconds. Mix until smooth completely). Transfer to the pan prepared. Rap it a few times to make the surface even. Set aside for 3 to 4 hours until cooled completely. Cover and chill at least 6 hours and up to 2 days until firm and cold. (In case ganache isn't very firm

when pressed, put it in a freezer for up to one hour. If it's rock-hard, take it out from the fridge and allow to warm up for a few minutes.)

- To shape the truffles: Line foil onto a large baking sheet. Place ganache into a cutting board. Remove the foil. Chop the slab into quarters with a large sharp knife. Use foil to wrap each quarter separately and freeze for about 30 minutes until firm. Chop into 12 equal pieces (thirds lengthwise and fourths crosswise) while working with one quarter at a time. Form every piece into a rough round, and then roll it into a ball in between your palms. They need not to be perfect. Ensure you don't over handle the balls and use paper towels to wipe off the chocolate buildup onto your hands. Transfer the balls onto the pan prepared. Repeat this with the rest of the quarters. Cover using plastic wrap and freeze for about 1 hour until chilled thoroughly.
- To coat the truffles: Pour the cocoa into a small deep bowl. Pour eight oz. of chocolate into another small microwave-safe bowl and heat for 1 minute in microwave on High. Combine well. Continue heating in microwave on Medium while stirring after every 20 seconds until mostly melted. Mix until remaining chocolate has melted completely.
- Line foil onto another large baking sheet. Take out a dozen balls from freezer. Quickly submerge one ball at a time into the chocolate and turning with a fork to completely coat them. Use the fork to lift the ball out and tap a few times against the side of bowl to get rid of the excess chocolate. (You just need the ball covered with a thin layer of chocolate.) Immediately mix the truffle into the cocoa and swirl the bowl until truffle is coated evenly. Place into the pan prepared. Repeat this with remaining balls of chocolate until they're all coated and stir the chocolate often. In case chocolate cools and hardens, heat for 10 to 15 seconds in microwave on Medium and mix before you continue. Chill truffles until chilled properly.

Nutrition Information

- Calories: 61 calories;
- Total Carbohydrate: 7 g
- Cholesterol: 5 mg
- Total Fat: 4 g
- Fiber: 1 g
- Protein: 1 g
- Sodium: 1 mg
- Sugar: 5 g
- Saturated Fat: 2 g

---

20. Bittersweet Double Chocolate Truffles

"This soft and moist dessert has both a bittersweet flavor and a milk chocolate sweetness. This makes a perfect gift."
Serving: 1-1/2 dozen. | Prep: 30m | Ready in: 30m

Ingredients

- 1 cup 60% cacao bittersweet chocolate baking chips
- 3/4 cup whipped topping
- 1/4 tsp. ground cinnamon
- 1 cup milk chocolate chips
- 1 tsp. shortening
- Optional toppings: crushed peppermint candies, sprinkles and chopped nuts

Direction

- Heat bittersweet chips in a small saucepan over low heat until melted. Pour into a bowl and allow to cool for about 7 minutes until lukewarm.
- Beat cinnamon and whipped topping into the mixture. Freeze until firm enough to shape into balls, 15 minutes. Form into balls of an inch.
- Microwave shortening and milk chocolate chips until melted; stir until the mixture is smooth. Dunk truffles in chocolate and put on baking sheets lined with waxed paper. Add a sprinkle of preferred toppings immediately.

Chill in the refrigerator to firm up. Keep refrigerated in an airtight container to store.

Nutrition Information

- Calories: 105 calories
- Total Carbohydrate: 12 g
- Cholesterol: 2 mg
- Total Fat: 6 g
- Fiber: 1 g
- Protein: 1 g
- Sodium: 8 mg

---

21. Blueberry, Coconut, And Pistachio Chocolate Bark

""This beautiful chocolate bark can be made with a variety of berries to bring up of your choice.""
Serving: 8 | Prep: 10m | Ready in: 57m

Ingredients

- 3 (4 oz.) bars dark chocolate, chopped, divided
- 3 tbsps. shelled unsalted pistachios, coarsely chopped
- 3 tbsps. dried blueberries
- 1 tbsp. coconut chips
- 2 tsps. grated orange zest (optional)

Direction

- Microwave 8 oz. chocolate in a microwaveable ceramic or glass bowl for 1-3 minutes, stirring every 15 seconds. When chocolate is almost melted with chunks remaining still, take out of the microwave and mix until fully smooth. Put in the rest of 4 oz. unmelted chocolate. Whisk thoroughly until chocolate is completely melted.
- On a flat work surface, spread out a big piece of parchment paper. Transfer melted chocolate to parchment paper and use a spatula to thinly spread out into an even layer. Before the chocolate sets, quickly sprinkle orange zest, coconut chips, dried blueberries and pistachios on top.

- Allow to sit for 45 minutes until completely set. Beak into uneven pieces and keep in a tightly sealed container to store.

Nutrition Information

- Calories: 255 calories;
- Total Carbohydrate: 28.6 g
- Cholesterol: 2 mg
- Total Fat: 15.5 g
- Protein: 3.1 g
- Sodium: 4 mg

---

22. Brazilian Brigadeiro-filled Chocolate Easter Egg

"This great recipe is for those that love the famous Brazilian chocolate brigadeiro. Made with chocolate eggs filled with brigadeiro and then covered with chocolate sprinkles."
Serving: 8 | Prep: 1h | Ready in: 1h40m

Ingredients

- Brigadeiro Filling:
- 2 (14 oz.) cans sweetened condensed milk
- 6 tbsps. cocoa powder
- 2 tbsps. unsalted butter
- 1/2 cup 35% heavy whipping cream, or more as needed
- Chocolate Eggs:
- 3 (7 oz.) bars good-quality milk chocolate, chopped
- 2 large (1-lb.) plastic Easter egg molds
- 1/2 cup chocolate sprinkles

Direction

- In a pot, mix butter, cocoa powder and condensed milk and then bring the contents to boil, stirring constantly, on top of medium heat. Cook the mixture until it starts to pull away from the sides and bottom of the pan. Take out from the heat source and mix in cream. Use a whisk to beat well until smooth.

In case the filling is too firm, pour in extra cream, 1 tbsp. at a time.

- Put the milk chocolate on top of a double boiler that is over simmering water. Stir regularly while scraping down the sides using a rubber spatula for about 5 minutes, to prevent scorching, until chocolate is about 80% melted.
- Place the chocolate on top of a clean and smooth surface, ideally granite or marble, and then spread and temper with a spatula or knife. Check the temperature of chocolate by bringing a toothpick dipped in the chocolate to your lips, the chocolate should be cold on the lips. Continue to cool and checking if it's too hot. Into a bowl, place the tempered chocolate.
- Into the Easter egg mold halves, spread a layer of chocolate evenly and then chill for 10 minutes. Take out from the fridge and spread another layer of chocolate onto each egg half. Add brigadeiro filling to fill the chocolate eggs almost up to the edges. Then seal the filling with another layer of melted chocolate and ensure that the filling is covered completely with the chocolate and nothing can leaks out. Refrigerate for about 20 minutes until set and firm.
- Onto a clean surface, unmold the chocolate eggs one by one by putting them upside down. On the outside, pour a thin layer of the melted chocolate and then cover with the chocolate sprinkles.

Nutrition Information

- Calories: 852 calories;
- Total Carbohydrate: 108.5 g
- Cholesterol: 78 mg
- Total Fat: 41.7 g
- Protein: 14.7 g
- Sodium: 191 mg

23. Brigadeiro

"That scrumptious sweet loved in Brazil called brigadeiro."
Serving: 20 | Prep: 10m | Ready in: 45m

Ingredients

- 3 tbsps. unsweetened cocoa
- 1 tbsp. butter
- 1 (14 oz.) can sweetened condensed milk

Direction

- Mix cocoa, condensed milk and butter in a medium saucepan, cook over medium heat. Stir in 10 minutes, until the mixture is thickened. Take away from heat and let stand to handle easily. Shape into small balls and eat immediately or let it chill until serving.

Nutrition Information

- Calories: 70 calories;
- Total Carbohydrate: 11.1 g
- Cholesterol: 8 mg
- Total Fat: 2.4 g
- Protein: 1.7 g
- Sodium: 29 mg

24. Buckeye Balls II

"These confectioners' sugar and peanut butter balls are covered with chocolate."
Serving: 30 | Prep: 45m | Ready in: 1h25m

Ingredients

- 1 1/2 cups creamy peanut butter
- 1/2 cup butter, softened
- 1 tsp. vanilla extract
- 4 cups sifted confectioners' sugar
- 6 oz. semi-sweet chocolate chips
- 2 tbsps. shortening

Direction

- Using waxed paper, line a baking sheet; put aside.

- Mix confectioners' sugar, vanilla, butter and peanut butter in a medium bowl, using hands to shape a smooth stiff dough. Form into balls with 2 tsps. of dough per ball. Transfer to the lined pan, keep in the fridge.
- In a metal bowl set over a pan of lightly simmering water, melt chocolate and shortening together. Stir occasionally until smooth; take out of the heat.
- Take balls out of the fridge. Insert a wooden toothpick into a ball, and dip into the melted chocolate. Transfer back to wax paper with chocolate side down; get rid of toothpick. Do the same with leftover balls. Keep in the fridge for half an hour to set.

Nutrition Information

- Calories: 204 calories;
- Total Carbohydrate: 22.8 g
- Cholesterol: 8 mg
- Total Fat: 12 g
- Protein: 3.7 g
- Sodium: 81 mg

25. Bugle Cones

"Creating these snacks is a breeze."
Serving: 2-1/2 dozen. | Prep: 20m | Ready in: 20m

Ingredients

- 2 tbsps. butter, softened
- 1-1/3 cups confectioners' sugar
- 1/4 tsp. salt
- 1/4 tsp. vanilla extract
- 2 tbsps. sweetened condensed milk
- 1 package (6 oz.) Bugles
- 1/2 cup semisweet chocolate chips, melted, optional
- Assorted sprinkles and/or ground nuts

Direction

- Beat the confectioners' sugar and butter in a small bowl until crumbly. Beat in the vanilla

and sugar. Put in milk and blend well (stiff blend).
- Form into 1/2-inch balls. Put a ball on each Bugle's top. If needed, dip some or all of the tops in the melted chocolate. Decorate with nuts and/or sprinkles.

Nutrition Information

- Calories: 107 calories
- Total Carbohydrate: 20 g
- Cholesterol: 5 mg
- Total Fat: 3 g
- Fiber: 0 g
- Protein: 1 g
- Sodium: 134 mg

26. Bunny Tails

"This is an easy recipe for a chocolate treat to serve at Easter."
Serving: 48 pieces | Prep: 20m | Ready in: 20m

Ingredients

- 1 cup white baking chips, melted
- 1 cup sweetened shredded coconut

Direction

- Melt chocolate and make teaspoonful drops of melted chocolate on parchment paper or waxed paper. Use sweetened flaked coconut to sprinkle each chocolate drop and allow to sit till they become dry.

Nutrition Information

- Calories: 29 calories
- Total Carbohydrate: 3 g
- Cholesterol: 1 mg
- Total Fat: 2 g
- Fiber: 0 g
- Protein: 0 g
- Sodium: 8 mg

27. Butter Cream Easter Egg Candies

"I used to have this every Easter."
Serving: 12 | Prep: 30m | Ready in: 5h

Ingredients

- 1/2 cup butter, softened
- 1 (8 oz.) package cream cheese, softened
- 1 tsp. vanilla extract
- 2 (16 oz.) packages confectioners' sugar
- 1 (12 oz.) bag semisweet chocolate chips
- 2 tbsps. pastel multi-colored candy sprinkles, or to taste

Direction

- In a bowl, with an electric mixer, beat butter until creamy and smooth. Mix vanilla and cream cheese into creamed butter until smooth; stir in confectioners' sugar until incorporated. Use plastic wrap to cover bowl; keep in the fridge for about 2 hours until firm.
- Form sugar mixture into small egg-shapes; place on a baking sheet. Keep in the fridge for 2 more hours until firm.
- Using waxed paper, line a baking sheet.
- In the top of a double boiler, over simmering water, melt chocolate chips; stir frequently; scrape down the sides, using a rubber spatula, to prevent scorching. Coat eggs with melted butter with a wooden skewer or fork until coated evenly.
- Place coated eggs on the lined baking sheet; decorate with sprinkles. Let chocolate harden, for half an hour. Put eggs in candy cups or paper muffin; keep in the fridge.

Nutrition Information

- Calories: 568 calories;
- Total Carbohydrate: 94.1 g
- Cholesterol: 41 mg
- Total Fat: 23.1 g
- Protein: 2.7 g
- Sodium: 114 mg

28. Butterscotch Fudge

"A quick dessert."
Serving: 24 | Ready in: 40m

Ingredients

- 1 (14 oz.) can sweetened condensed milk
- 1 (11 oz.) package butterscotch chips
- 1/2 (11 oz.) package white chocolate chips
- 1 tsp. butter flavored extract
- 1 tsp. rum flavored extract

Direction

- Constantly mix white chocolate chips, butterscotch chips and condensed milk in medium saucepan on medium heat till smooth and melted. Take off heat; mix rum flavorings and butter in. Put in 9x13-in. dish. Cover; refrigerate for 30 minutes till firm. Cut; serve.

Nutrition Information

- Calories: 161 calories;
- Total Carbohydrate: 20.7 g
- Cholesterol: 7 mg
- Total Fat: 7.3 g
- Protein: 1.7 g
- Sodium: 41 mg

29. Butterscotch Peanut Candy

"This simple to-make sweet is constantly a hit during the special seasons."
Serving: 2-1/4 lbs. (3-1/2 to 4 dozen). | Prep: 10m | Ready in: 10m

Ingredients

- 1 package (11-1/2 oz.) milk chocolate chips
- 1 package (10 oz.) butterscotch chips
- 1 tsp. butter-flavored shortening
- 3 cups salted peanuts

Direction

- Heat the shortening and chips in a microwave, uncovered, for 2 to 2-1/2 minutes on 50% power, until melted. Mix until smooth. Put in the peanuts. Drop onto the waxed paper-lined baking sheets by tablespoonfuls. Refrigerate for about 45 minutes, until firm.

Nutrition Information

- Calories: 240 calories
- Total Carbohydrate: 19 g
- Cholesterol: 4 mg
- Total Fat: 17 g
- Fiber: 2 g
- Protein: 6 g
- Sodium: 98 mg

30. Candied Lemon Peel

"You can add other spices, cloves and brandy to mixture if you use oranges; chop it up then add it into the cookies or eat it on its own."
Serving: 15 | Prep: 10m | Ready in: 1h40m

Ingredients

- 3 lemons
- 8 cups cold water, or as needed
- 2 cups white sugar, or as needed

Direction

- Cut lemon to 1/4-in. thick slices; remove fruit pulp. Halve rings so peels become long strips.
- Boil lemon peel and water in a small pan then drain water; with fresh cold water, repeat. Repeat boiling step thrice. Drain; put aside peels.
- Boil 2 cups sugar and 2 cups fresh water, mixing to dissolve sugar; lower heat to low. Mix in citrus peels; simmer till white pith is translucent. Keep peels in syrup to keep soft, refrigerated, or let them dry. In extra sugar, toss dry candied peels then keep at room temperature, airtight.

Nutrition Information

- Calories: 108 calories;
- Total Carbohydrate: 29 g
- Cholesterol: 0 mg
- Total Fat: 0.1 g
- Protein: 0.3 g
- Sodium: 4 mg

31. Candy Bar Fudge

"Creamy, chocolaty, and just heavenly. This holiday fudge recipe is a popular dessert for parties, reunions, and get-togethers. Be sure to prepare more than enough because kids and adults will ask for more."
Serving: 32 | Prep: 20m | Ready in: 2h30m

Ingredients

- 1/2 cup butter
- 1/3 cup unsweetened cocoa powder
- 1/4 cup packed brown sugar
- 1/4 cup milk
- 3 1/2 cups confectioners' sugar
- 1 tsp. vanilla extract
- 30 individually wrapped caramels, unwrapped
- 1 tbsp. water
- 2 cups salted peanuts
- 1/2 cup semisweet chocolate chips
- 1/2 cup milk chocolate chips

Direction

- Grease an 8 x 8-inch square baking pan.
- In a microwave-safe bowl, mix together cocoa powder, brown sugar, milk, and butter. Heat in the microwave until the mixture starts to boil. Add vanilla extract and confectioners' sugar, then stir. Pour mixture into the greased pan.
- In another microwave-safe bowl, combine caramels and water; heat in the microwave until the caramels start to melt. Add peanuts and stir. Pour mixture over the chocolate layer.

- In a small microwave-safe bowl, mix together milk chocolate chips and semisweet chocolate chips; heat in the microwave until melted. Pour into the caramel layer. Refrigerate for 2 hours or until firm before serving.

Nutrition Information

- Calories: 205 calories;
- Total Carbohydrate: 28.4 g
- Cholesterol: 9 mg
- Total Fat: 10 g
- Protein: 3.2 g
- Sodium: 124 mg

---

32. Candy Cane Reindeer

"Cute candy cane that can be a stocking stuffer. Red-hot candy noses, chocolate eyes and pretzel antlers!"
Serving: 1 dozen. | Prep: 30m | Ready in: 30m

Ingredients

- 8 oz. white candy coating, coarsely chopped
- 12 candy canes (6 inches)
- 12 to 20 pretzels
- 12 red-hot candies
- 24 black sugar pearls or miniature semisweet chocolate chips or black sprinkles

Direction

- Melt candy coating in a microwave; mix until smooth. Keep warm. Gripping the curved end of a candy cane, drizzle coating over the straight part of cane using a spoon. Shake off excess gently. Put on waxed paper to set. Keep coating the leftover candy canes. Crack pretzels into pieces to make them look like antlers; put 24 pieces aside.
- Dot a tiny amount of melted candy coating onto a red-hot for the reindeer's nose. Force onto the end of the curved part of the candy cane and hold for about 10 seconds. Put a tiny amount of coating on 2 sugar pearls to make the eyes and stick to candy cane above nose.

- Choose 2 pretzel pieces that look alike; on the candy cane where antlers will be stuck on, dot a tiny amount of coating. Force pretzel pieces into the coating and hold for about 30 seconds. Repeat with other reindeers. Put into mugs or drinking glasses; allow to dry for about 1 hour.

Nutrition Information

- Calories: 201 calories
- Total Carbohydrate: 37 g
- Cholesterol: 0 mg
- Total Fat: 6 g
- Fiber: 0 g
- Protein: 1 g
- Sodium: 124 mg

---

33. Caramel Peanut Fudge

"Bake sales, picnics, or family meal, this dessert will be a great hit"
Serving: 96 | Prep: 30m | Ready in: 2h20m

Ingredients

- BOTTOM LAYER
- 1 cup milk chocolate chips
- 1/4 cup butterscotch chips
- 1/4 cup creamy peanut butter
- FILLING
- 1/4 cup butter
- 1 cup white sugar
- 1/4 cup evaporated milk
- 1 1/2 cups marshmallow creme
- 1/4 cup creamy peanut butter
- 1 tsp. vanilla extract
- 1 1/2 cups chopped salted peanuts
- CARAMEL
- 1 (14 oz.) package individually wrapped caramels, unwrapped
- 1/4 cup heavy cream
- TOP LAYER
- 1 cup milk chocolate chips
- 1/4 cup butterscotch chips
- 1/4 cup creamy peanut butter

Direction

- Slightly grease a 9x13 inch dish.
- Make the bottom layer: In a small saucepan, combine 1/4 cup creamy peanut butter, 1/4 cup butterscotch chips and 1 cup milk chocolate chips over low heat. Cook while stirring until smooth and melted. Distribute evenly in greased pan. Refrigerate till set.
- For the filling: In a heavy saucepan, melt butter over medium-high heat. Mix in evaporated milk and sugar. Bring it to a boil and allow to boil 5 minutes. Take away from heat and whisk in vanilla, 1/4 cup peanut butter and marshmallow creme. Fold in peanut. Spoon over bottom layer, bring back to refrigerator until set.
- For the caramel: In a medium saucepan, combine cream and caramels over low heat. Cook while stirring until smooth and melted. Spread over filling. Chill till set.
- For the top layer: In a small saucepan, combine 1/4 cup peanut butter, 1/4 cup butterscotch chips, and 1 cup milk chocolate chips over low heat. Cook while stirring until smooth and melted. Pour over caramel layer. Chill for 1 hour before cutting into 1-inch squares.

Nutrition Information

- Calories: 85 calories;
- Total Carbohydrate: 10.1 g
- Cholesterol: 4 mg
- Total Fat: 4.6 g
- Protein: 1.5 g
- Sodium: 50 mg

---

34. Caramel Pretzel Bites

"This recipe is to make a pretzel log with nuts, chocolate and caramel."
Serving: 6 dozen. | Prep: 20m | Ready in: 45m

Ingredients

- 2 tsps. butter, softened
- 4 cups pretzel sticks
- 2-1/2 cups pecan halves, toasted
- 2-1/4 cups packed brown sugar
- 1 cup butter, cubed
- 1 cup corn syrup
- 1 can (14 oz.) sweetened condensed milk
- 1/8 tsp. salt
- 1 tsp. vanilla extract
- 1 package (11-1/2 oz.) milk chocolate chips
- 1 tbsp. plus 1 tsp. shortening, divided
- 1/3 cup white baking chips

Direction

- Use foil to line a 13x9 in. pan; use softened butter to grease foil. Spread pecans and pretzels on bottom of the prepared pan.
- Mix salt, milk, corn syrup, butter cubes, brown sugar in a large heavy saucepan; cook and stir on medium heat till a candy thermometer reaches 240 degrees (it's the soft ball stage). Get the pan off heat. Put in vanilla and stir. Transfer the mixture onto the pretzel mixture.
- Put a tbsp. of shortening and chocolate chips together and melt in a microwave; stir till the mixture becomes smooth. Spread over the caramel layer. Melt the rest of shortening and white baking chips in the microwave; stir till the mixture becomes smooth. Drizzle over top. Allow to sit till the mixture is set.
- Lift candy out of pan by foil; get rid of foil. Butter a knife and use the knife to chop candy to bite sized pieces.

Nutrition Information

- Calories: 146 calories
- Total Carbohydrate: 19 g
- Cholesterol: 10 mg
- Total Fat: 8 g
- Fiber: 1 g
- Protein: 1 g
- Sodium: 76 mg

35. Cashew Caramel Fudge

"A plate of this yummy confection makes a great present."
Serving: about 3 lbs.. | Prep: 25m | Ready in: 25m

Ingredients

- 2 tsps. plus 1/2 cup butter, softened, divided
- 1 can (5 oz.) evaporated milk
- 2-1/2 cups sugar
- 2 cups (12 oz.) semisweet chocolate chips
- 1 jar (7 oz.) marshmallow creme
- 24 caramels, quartered
- 3/4 cup salted cashew halves
- 1 tsp. vanilla extract

Direction

- Using foil, line a 9-inch square pan; spread 2 tsps. butter on the foil. Put aside.
- Mix the leftover butter, sugar and milk in a big heavy saucepan. Cook over medium heat and mix till sugar is melted. Bring to a rapid boil; allow to boil for 5 minutes, mixing continuously. Take off heat; mix in marshmallow creme and chocolate chips till melted. Fold the vanilla, cashews and caramels in.
- In prepped pan, pour the mixture. Cool down. Lift fudge out of pan using foil. Get rid of foil; into 1-inch squares, slice the fudge. Keep in an airtight container.

Nutrition Information

- Calories: 85 calories
- Total Carbohydrate: 14 g
- Cholesterol: 4 mg
- Total Fat: 4 g
- Fiber: 0 g
- Protein: 1 g
- Sodium: 33 mg

36. Chef John's Chocolate Bark

"This is a recipe for the beautiful chocolate bark which makes lovely edible gifts."
Serving: 18 | Prep: 15m | Ready in: 1h

Ingredients

- 6 (4 oz.) bars dark chocolate (65 to 70% cocao), chopped into small pieces
- 1 cup toasted walnuts, chopped
- 1 cup shelled, roasted, salted pistachios, chopped
- 1/2 cup dried goji berries
- 1/2 tsp. coarse sea salt (optional)

Direction

- Make small pieces of dark chocolate by chopping them down. Separate the chocolate pieces into 2 portions 2/3 of the mixture in 1 portion and the other 1/3 in 1 portion. Transfer the 2/3 of the dark chocolate into a heatproof bowl, a metal bowl is the best choice. Choose a bowl which is large enough so that it can sit on the rim of a pot but doesn't touch the water.
- Pour 2 inches of water in a pot and heat on medium high heat till the water just barely start to simmer. Turn heat to the lowest setting; put bowl over pot. Let chocolate melt without stirring till two thirds of the pieces have melted. Stir for about 2 minutes till all are melted and chocolate feels hot (not boiling hot) when you touch it (about 115 – 120°F).
- Put the one third of the dark chocolate pieces to the bowl. Stir till it is melted. Put bowl on the counter and stir sometimes, cool the chocolate for about 8 minutes till it's cool when you touch it and the chocolate liquid starts thickening up a bit. The chocolate should be shiny and smooth.
- Use parchment paper or waxed paper or a silicone mat to line a rimmed baking sheet. Pour the chocolate gradually into the prepared baking sheet, do not fill up all the way to the edges. Use goji berries, pistachios and

chopped walnuts to sprinkle over the chocolate. Sprinkle with a bit of coarse sea salt.
- Allow the chocolate mixture to stand at room temperature to cool down and harden. Crack into pieces.

Nutrition Information

- Calories: 291 calories;
- Total Carbohydrate: 27.3 g
- Cholesterol: 2 mg
- Total Fat: 19.5 g
- Protein: 5 g
- Sodium: 89 mg

37. Cherry Blossom Fudge

"Not only is this treat wonderful, it is also easy to make. This is so easy and it will disappear fast!"
Serving: 12 | Prep: 10m | Ready in: 2h15m

Ingredients

- 3/4 cup evaporated milk
- 1 cup white sugar
- 1 pinch salt
- 1 (3 oz.) package cherry flavored Jell-O®
- 1 cup butter
- 2 cups semisweet chocolate chips
- 1 tsp. vanilla extract
- 3/4 cup maraschino cherries, halved

Direction

- Use butter to grease an 8-inch square dish.
- Mix salt, sugar, milk in a medium saucepan on medium heat. Bring to a boil, mix in gelatin. Boil the mixture for 4 minutes. Get the saucepan off heat, mix in cherries, vanilla, chocolate chips, butter. Transfer the mixture into the prepared pan. Chill before serving, about 2 hours.

Nutrition Information

- Calories: 400 calories;
- Total Carbohydrate: 46.6 g

- Cholesterol: 45 mg
- Total Fat: 25 g
- Protein: 3.1 g
- Sodium: 161 mg

38. Cherry Chocolate Bark

"Peppermint bark recipe!"
Serving: 18 | Prep: 5m | Ready in: 40m

Ingredients

- 1 (12 oz.) bag semisweet chocolate chips
- 12 cherry-flavored candy canes, crushed
- 1/3 cup red confectioner's coating (optional)

Direction

- Line aluminum foil on 9x13-in. baking pan.
- Melt chocolate chips in microwave-safe ceramic/glass bowl for 1-3 minutes, varies on microwave, in 30-second intervals, mixing after every melting, till smooth. Don't overheat; chocolate will scorch. Spread melted chocolate quickly and evenly using a spatula in the prepared pan till its bottom is covered. Evenly drizzle the crushed candy on chocolate; lightly pat using clean spatula to help candy settle into chocolate.
- If using, melt red confectioners' coating in microwave-safe ceramic/glass bowl for 1-3 minutes, varies on microwave, in 30-second intervals, mixing after every melting. Put melted coating in resealable plastic bag; snip very small corner of bag off; use to drizzle bark with coating.
- Put pan in fridge/freezer for 30 minutes till hard. Remove from pan; peel foil off. Break to small pieces to serve.

Nutrition Information

- Calories: 180 calories;
- Total Carbohydrate: 31.9 g
- Cholesterol: < 1 mg
- Total Fat: 6.6 g
- Protein: 1 g

- Sodium: 12 mg

39. Cherry-pistachio Bark

"Occasion or no occasion, this sweet and tasty dessert is perfect to munch on. Both kids and adults will enjoy this chocolaty treat because it's easy to make."
Serving: 150 | Prep: 15m | Ready in: 1h22m

Ingredients

- 1 1/4 cups dried cherries
- 2 tbsps. water
- 2 (11 oz.) packages white chocolate chips
- 4 (3 oz.) bars vanilla-flavored candy coating
- 1 1/4 cups chopped pistachio nuts

Direction

- In a small glass bowl, place cherries and heat in the microwave for 2 minutes on high power; drain liquid, then set aside.
- In a separate microwave-safe bowl, place candy coating and chocolate chips together, then microwave until smooth and melted, occasionally. Add chopped pistachios and cherries, then stir; spread into a 15 x 10-inch pan lined with wax paper. Refrigerate for an hour or until firm.
- Once chilled, cut into 1-inch squares and serve. For unused chocolate pieces, store in an air-tight container.

Nutrition Information

- Calories: 45 calories;
- Total Carbohydrate: 4.8 g
- Cholesterol: 1 mg
- Total Fat: 2.6 g
- Protein: 0.7 g
- Sodium: 11 mg

40. Chestnut Truffles

"These classy truffles have chestnut puree that make a deceptively rich-tasting filling."
Serving: 48 | Ready in: 1h30m

Ingredients

- ½ cup nonfat dry milk
- ½ cup brandy
- 1 15-oz. can unsweetened chestnut puree
- ¾ cup sugar
- 1 tbsp. vanilla extract
- 6 oz. bittersweet (not unsweetened) chocolate, coarsely chopped, divided

Direction

- In a small bowl, dissolve dry milk in brandy and set it aside. In a heavy medium saucepan, mix vanilla, sugar, and chestnut puree. Then heat on medium-high heat while whisking until the resulting mixture is smooth. Cook the mixture while whisking continuously for 6 to 10 minutes until stiff and thickened. (Decrease the heat if the mixture starts to scorch.) Whisk in brandy-milk mixture and continue to cook for about 5 minutes more until mixture becomes thick enough to stand in peaks. Pour into a bowl and allow to cool to lukewarm for about 20 minutes.
- Line parchment or wax paper onto a baking sheet. Shape chestnut mixture into one-inch balls and put into the baking sheet prepared. Cover using plastic wrap and place in the refrigerator for about 20 minutes until chilled.
- Melt four oz. of chocolate in the top of the double boiler atop hot but not boiling water. Mix often until chocolate has melted and has reached a temperature of 120 degrees F. Take out the top of the double boiler from heat. Pour in the remaining two oz. of chocolate and mix until chocolate is shiny and smooth.
- Put chilled balls of chestnut filling onto a large sheet of plastic wrap, close together but not touching. Pour all the melted chocolate atop the balls (scrape the bowl thoroughly), and then roll each ball in the chocolate to coat

evenly. Place back the coated truffles into the baking sheet. (You will probably have about two oz. of chocolate left over. Save it for another use.) Leave the truffles to stand at room temperature for about 5 minutes until chocolate has set.

Nutrition Information

- Calories: 60 calories;
- Total Carbohydrate: 11 g
- Cholesterol: 0 mg
- Total Fat: 1 g
- Fiber: 1 g
- Protein: 1 g
- Sodium: 7 mg
- Sugar: 6 g
- Saturated Fat: 1 g

41. Chewy Chocolate Candies

"A delicious candy recipe."
Serving: 25 | Prep: 45m | Ready in: 45m

Ingredients

- 2 tbsps. butter, melted
- 2 (1 oz.) squares unsweetened chocolate, melted and cooled
- 1/2 cup light corn syrup
- 3 cups confectioners' sugar, divided
- 3/4 cup powdered milk
- 1 tsp. vanilla extract

Direction

- Stir the chocolate and butter together in a medium mixing bowl. Beat in the vanilla, powdered milk, 2 cups of confectioner's sugar and corn syrup. The dough will get stiff.
- Sprinkle the leftover 1 cup of confectioner's sugar on a work surface, then transfer the dough onto the work surface and knead it until the leftover sugar is combined. Form it into small logs and wrap it using waxed paper.

Nutrition Information

- Calories: 107 calories;
- Total Carbohydrate: 21.9 g
- Cholesterol: 3 mg
- Total Fat: 2.1 g
- Protein: 1.6 g
- Sodium: 31 mg

42. Chewy Chocolate Logs

"Everyone loves this recipe."
Serving: about 6 dozen. | Prep: 25m | Ready in: 25m

Ingredients

- 2 oz. unsweetened chocolate
- 2 tbsps. butter
- 1/2 cup light corn syrup
- 1 tsp. vanilla extract
- 3 cups confectioners' sugar, divided
- 3/4 cup instant nonfat dry milk powder

Direction

- Melt butter and chocolate over low heat in a saucepan. Pour into a bowl; add milk powder, 2 cups confectioners' sugar, vanilla and corn syrup. Combine well.
- Place the rest of the sugar on a clean surface; put dough on the surface; knead sugar into the dough until the dough has absorbed all of it. Form teaspoonfuls into 2-in. logs; use waxed paper to wrap; twist ends. Keep in the fridge until firm.

Nutrition Information

- Calories: 71 calories
- Total Carbohydrate: 15 g
- Cholesterol: 2 mg
- Total Fat: 1 g
- Fiber: 0 g
- Protein: 1 g
- Sodium: 26 mg

43. Chocolate Almond Bark

"If you are a chocolate lover, this one is totally for you!"
Serving: 16 | Prep: 5m | Ready in: 45m

Ingredients

- 1/2 cup chopped almonds
- 2 cups milk chocolate chips
- 1 tbsp. shortening

Direction

- Line parchment paper on a 9x13 in. baking pan. Put aside. In a skillet, put chopped almonds. Cook over medium high heat, until they turn golden brown, stirring often. Discard from the heat.
- Over the simmering water in a pan, melt shortening and chocolate chips in a metal bowl until they become smooth. Discard from the heat; stir in half of toasted almonds. Spread onto prepared baking pan. Top with the remaining almonds. Let chill until solid, about half an hour. To serve, break into bite-size pieces.

Nutrition Information

- Calories: 130 calories;
- Total Carbohydrate: 14.2 g
- Cholesterol: 5 mg
- Total Fat: 8.4 g
- Protein: 2.1 g
- Sodium: < 1 mg

44. Chocolate Almond Brittle

"After tons of experiments, I have successfully created this delicious candy recipe made with tasty almond orchards."
Serving: about 1 lb.. | Prep: 15m | Ready in: 15m

Ingredients

- 1 cup sugar
- 1/2 cup light corn syrup
- 1/8 tsp. salt
- 1 cup coarsely chopped almonds
- 1 tbsp. butter
- 1 tsp. vanilla extract
- 1-1/2 tsps. baking soda
- 3/4 lb. dark or milk chocolate candy coating

Direction

- Mix together salt, corn syrup and sugar in a 1 1/2-quart microwaveable bowl. Heat on high in the microwave without covering for 2 1/2 minutes. Mix in almonds; microwave on high for 2 1/2 minutes. Pour in vanilla and butter; microwave on high for a minute.
- Mix in baking soda. Once the mixture is frothy, immediately transfer to a greased metal baking sheet. Wait until fully cool. Break apart into 2-in pieces.
- Microwave chocolate until melted. Plunge one side of brittle in chocolate, then put onto waxed paper to harden. Keep in a tightly sealed container to store.

Nutrition Information

- Calories: 483 calories
- Total Carbohydrate: 73 g
- Cholesterol: 4 mg
- Total Fat: 22 g
- Fiber: 3 g
- Protein: 4 g
- Sodium: 313 mg

45. Chocolate Almond Popcorn

"Popcorn with almonds is the best for a movie watching on the holidays."
Serving: 25 | Prep: 10m | Ready in: 2h15m

Ingredients

- 1 cup white sugar
- 1 cup light corn syrup
- 1/2 cup butter
- 1/4 cup cocoa powder
- 2 tsps. salt

- 25 cups unsalted popped popcorn
- 3 cups roasted salted almonds

Direction

- Preheat the oven to 200°F (95°C).
- In a saucepan, combine salt, cocoa powder, butter, corn syrup and sugar together over medium-low heat until the mixture is smooth and starts to simmer. In a very large bowl, add the popcorn, stir with the almonds, and then pour the chocolate syrup over on top. Mix until all the almonds and popcorn are coated. On several large baking sheets, spread out the chocolate popcorn in a single layer.
- Bake in the preheated oven in about 1 hour until completely dry, stirring every 20 minutes or so to dry all the sides of popped corn. Cool down on the sheet, then add into sealed containers.

Nutrition Information

- Calories: 233 calories;
- Total Carbohydrate: 25.8 g
- Cholesterol: 10 mg
- Total Fat: 14.4 g
- Protein: 3.4 g
- Sodium: 337 mg

---

46. Chocolate Amaretto Fudge

"It's so satisfying."
Serving: 100 | Prep: 10m | Ready in: 2h

Ingredients

- 3/4 cup amaretto liqueur
- 1/2 cup sweetened condensed milk
- 3 cups white sugar
- 1/4 cup butter
- 1 1/2 cups semisweet chocolate chips
- 1 cup dark chocolate chips
- 1/2 cup white chocolate chips
- Top Layer:
- 3/4 cup white sugar

- 2 tbsps. sweetened condensed milk
- 2 tbsps. amaretto liqueur
- 1 1/2 cups white chocolate chips
- 3 tbsps. butter
- 2 drops red food coloring (optional)

Direction

- In a large saucepan, pour half a cup of the condensed milk and 3/4 cup of the amaretto liqueur over medium-low heat. Put in 3 cups of the sugar then stir until dissolved. Put in half a cup of white chocolate chips, dark chocolate chips, semisweet chocolate chips and a quarter cup of butter. Stir for 5 mins or until all the chocolate has melted and the mixture becomes smooth. Lower the heat to low; stir occasionally to avoid burning the mixture.
- In a small saucepan, heat 2 tbsps. of amaretto, 2 tbsps. of the condensed milk and 3/4 cup sugar over medium-low heat. Then cook while stirring for 5 mins or until sugar dissolves. Put in red food coloring, 3 tbsps. of the butter and 1 1/2 cups of the white chocolate chips. Stir for 3 mins or until they become smooth and the coloring is distributed evenly.
- Discard both saucepans from the heat. Add dark chocolate mixture to a square 10-in. aluminum foil pan. Allow to sit for 1-2 mins. Drop white chocolate mixture by spoonfuls on top; using a toothpick or butter knife, swirl into the dark chocolate layer. Lightly shake the pan to settle fudge. Place in the refrigerator for 90 mins or until firm. Cut into squares, about 1 inch.

Nutrition Information

- Calories: 92 calories;
- Total Carbohydrate: 14.2 g
- Cholesterol: 4 mg
- Total Fat: 3.5 g
- Protein: 0.7 g
- Sodium: 13 mg

47. Chocolate Angel Food Candy

"This candy is irresistible."
Serving: about 1-1/4 lbs.. | Prep: 20m | Ready in: 40m

Ingredients

- 1 tsp. butter
- 1 cup sugar
- 1 cup dark corn syrup
- 1 tbsp. white vinegar
- 1 tbsp. baking soda
- 1/2 lb. dark chocolate candy coating, coarsely chopped
- 1 tsp. shortening, divided
- 1/2 lb. milk chocolate candy coating, coarsely chopped

Direction

- Using foil, line a 9-in. square pan; grease foil with butter; put aside. Mix vinegar, corn syrup and sugar in a large heavy saucepan. Cook while stirring until sugar dissolves over medium heat. Boil. Cook without stirring until a candy thermometer registers 300° (hard-crack stage)
- Take out of the heat; stir in baking soda. Transfer to the lined pan immediately. Do not spread candy. Cool; lift candy out of pan with foil. Peel off foil gently; break candy into pieces.
- Melt half tsp. of shortening and dark chocolate coating in a microwave; stir until smooth. Coat 1/2 of the candies with the melted dark chocolate mixture; drip off excess. Transfer to waxed paper; rest until set. Do the same with milk chocolate coating and the rest of shortening with candies. Keep in an airtight container.

Nutrition Information

- Calories: 413 calories
- Total Carbohydrate: 76 g
- Cholesterol: 1 mg
- Total Fat: 14 g
- Fiber: 1 g
- Protein: 1 g
- Sodium: 431 mg

48. Chocolate Basket

"You can enjoy this treat anytime!"
Serving: 1-1/4 cups. | Prep: 60m | Ready in: 60m

Ingredients

- Materials needed:
- Thirteen 3-inch pretzel sticks
- Flexible plastic cover to a 16-oz. container (such as sour cream), about 4-1/2 inches diameter x 1/4 inch deep
- Paper towels
- Wire rack
- 1-quart bowl
- Waxed paper
- Chocolate clay:
- 10 oz. dark, milk or white chocolate candy coating, melted
- 1/3 cup light corn syrup

Direction

- Mix corn syrup and candy coating until just blended. Transfer to a sheet of waxed paper to 3/8-in. thickness (about an 8-in. square) and spread.
- Allow to stand without a cover for 2-3 hours at room temperature or until it becomes dry to the touch. Using plastic wrap, wrap tightly; allow to stand overnight. You can use it right away or store up to 2 weeks.
- To build the Base: 1, Coat pretzels completely with melted chocolate chips or chocolate candy coating. Arrange on a wire rack, refrigerate 10 minutes. Set the rest of the chocolate aside. (You can prepare pretzels one day ahead). Make sure that you use dry and clean plastic cover. Put 2 dampened paper towels in the bottom of the bowl; place cover on the towels (to hold it in place). Put ends of prepared pretzels around the cover's outer edge; placing the other ends against the bowl's

side to support the basket sides. Pour or scoop melted chocolate into cover until it reaches 1.8 in. from the top; set the rest of the chocolate aside. Make sure that all pretzel sticks are surrounded with chocolate. Chill for half an hour until chocolate is firm.

- Take out of the bowl. Loosen the edges of plastic carefully; cover; remove. Set base on waxed paper.
- Make 3 ropes about 20 in. long; braid and put aside. Melt the rest of the chocolate again; drop on top of each pretzel. Top with braided ropes; blend the ends to complete the edge. Use melted chocolate to glue pieces of broken pretzels; chill until set.
- Start to Weave, 2. Knead a 1-inch ball of Chocolate Clay until pliable but not soft; roll into 1/4-in.-thick ropes. Start on the pretzel's side, weave rope around pretzels loosely.
- Repeat; overlap with the next rope slightly; press ends together. Keep weaving between pretzels until you reach the top of pretzels; end the last rope on the pretzel's inside.
- Complete the basket, 3. Make 3 ropes about 20 in. long; braid; put aside. Melt the rest of the chocolate again and drop on top of pretzels. Top with braided ropes; finish the edge by blending the ends. Use melted chocolate to glue pieces of broken pretzels; chill until set.

---

49. Chocolate Billionaires

"Everyone loves these treats."
Serving: about 2 lbs.. | Prep: 45m | Ready in: 45m

Ingredients

- 1 package (14 oz.) caramels
- 3 tbsps. water
- 1-1/2 cups chopped pecans
- 1 cup crisp rice cereal
- 3 cups milk chocolate chips
- 1-1/2 tsps. shortening

Direction

- Using waxed paper, line 2 baking sheets; grease the paper; put aside. Mix water and caramels in a large heavy saucepan; cook while stirring until smooth over low heat. Stir in cereal and pecans until coated. Drop onto prepared pans by teaspoonfuls. Keep in the fridge until firm or for 10 minutes.
- In the meantime, melt shortening and chocolate chips in a microwave; stir until smooth. Coat candy with chocolates on all sides; drip off excess. Transfer on lined pans. Keep in the fridge until set. Keep in an airtight container.

Nutrition Information

- Calories: 172 calories
- Total Carbohydrate: 20 g
- Cholesterol: 4 mg
- Total Fat: 10 g
- Fiber: 1 g
- Protein: 2 g
- Sodium: 51 mg

---

50. Chocolate Candy Clusters

"I give these as blessings and carry them to parties — they're constantly a hit!"
Serving: about 3 dozen. | Prep: 20m | Ready in: 20m

Ingredients

- 8 oz. white baking chocolate, chopped
- 1 cup milk chocolate chips
- 1 cup (6 oz.) semisweet chocolate chips
- 1-1/2 cups chopped walnuts
- 1-1/2 cups miniature pretzels, broken

Direction

- Melt the chips and white chocolate for a minute at 70% power in a microwave-safe bowl; mix. Microwave at another 10 to 20-second intervals, mixing to smooth. Mix in pretzels and walnuts.

- Drop onto waxed paper-lined baking sheets with rounded tablespoonfuls. Refrigerate till firm. Keep in airtight container.

Nutrition Information

- Calories: 132 calories
- Total Carbohydrate: 12 g
- Cholesterol: 3 mg
- Total Fat: 9 g
- Fiber: 1 g
- Protein: 3 g
- Sodium: 41 mg

51. Chocolate Caramel Candy

"It may take a little more time to prepare but it's worth! A wonderful treat for Thanksgiving or Christmas."
Serving: 96

Ingredients

- 1 cup milk chocolate chips
- 1/4 cup butterscotch chips
- 1/4 cup creamy peanut butter
- 1/4 cup butter
- 1 cup white sugar
- 1/4 cup evaporated milk
- 1 1/2 cups marshmallow creme
- 1/4 cup creamy peanut butter
- 1 tsp. vanilla extract
- 1 1/2 cups chopped salted peanuts
- 1 (14 oz.) package caramels
- 1/4 cup heavy whipping cream
- 1 cup milk chocolate chips
- 1/4 cup butterscotch chips
- 1/4 cup creamy peanut butter

Direction

- Lightly coat a 13 x 9 inch pan with oil.
- For Base: In a small saucepan, mix 1/4 cup creamy peanut butter, 1/4 butterscotch chips and 1 cup milk chocolate chips together. Cook over low heat, stirring constantly, until smooth and melted. Spread into the prepared pan's bottom. Place in the fridge until set.
- For Filling: In a heavy saucepan, melt butter over medium-high heat. Mix in evaporated milk and sugar. Let the mixture come to a boil and stir for 5 minutes. Take away from heat and mix in vanilla, 1/4 cup of the peanut butter and marshmallow cream. Put in the peanuts, and spread the mixture over the base layer. Place in the fridge until set.
- For Caramel Layer: In a saucepan, mix cream and caramels, stir over low heat until smooth and melted. Spread over the filling top and put in the fridge until smooth.
- For Frosting Layer: In another saucepan, mix 1/4 cup peanut butter, 1/4 butterscotch chips and 1 cup milk chocolate chips together; stir over low heat until smooth and melted. Pour the mixture over the caramel layer. Place in the fridge for at least 1 hour. Cut into squares of 1 inch. Refrigerate for future use.

Nutrition Information

- Calories: 84 calories;
- Total Carbohydrate: 10.3 g
- Cholesterol: 3 mg
- Total Fat: 4.5 g
- Protein: 1.6 g
- Sodium: 44 mg

52. Chocolate Caramel Corn

"Tasty popcorn chocolate. You are going to love this one!"
Serving: 40 | Ready in: 1h

Ingredients

- 5 quarts popped popcorn
- 1 1/3 cups brown sugar
- 1 1/2 cups butter, divided
- 2 1/2 cups light corn syrup, divided
- 1 tsp. vanilla extract
- 4 cups milk chocolate chips

Direction

- Set the oven to 120°C (250°F) then begin preheating. Spread cooking spray on a large roasting pan. Transfer the popcorn to the roasting pan and keep warm in the oven.
- Mix together half a cup of corn syrup, a cup of butter and brown sugar in a heavy saucepan over medium heat. Heat up to 121°C to 129°C (250°F to 265°F) without blending, or until a tiny quantity of syrup dropped into cold water shapes a stiff ball. Expel from heat and mix in vanilla. Pour over popcorn with syrup and toss to coat. Put popcorn back to the oven.
- Mix together 2 cups corn syrup with the rest of half cup butter and chocolate chips in the same saucepan. Cook over medium heat, whisking, until chocolate melts. Remove from heat and immediately pour over popcorn, blending to coat.
- Put popcorn back to the oven, mixing occasionally, for 30 to 40 minutes. To cool entirely, remove and pour over waxed paper lined sheets.

Nutrition Information

- Calories: 269 calories;
- Total Carbohydrate: 35.5 g
- Cholesterol: 24 mg
- Total Fat: 14.9 g
- Protein: 1.6 g
- Sodium: 150 mg

53. Chocolate Caramel Turkey Legs

"These are turkey legs that contain chocolate and pretzels."
Serving: 20 servings. | Prep: 20m | Ready in: 20m

Ingredients

- 40 caramels
- 20 honey wheat braided pretzel twists
- 3 oz. milk chocolate, melted

Direction

- Melt caramels on high in the microwave for 10 to 15 seconds until softened. Make it look like turkey leg by molding 2 softened caramels around the lower half of each braided pretzel. Plunge in melted chocolate; let the excess drip off. Put on waxed paper; let sit until firm. Put in an airtight container 1-2 weeks to store.

Nutrition Information

- Calories: 112 calories
- Total Carbohydrate: 21 g
- Cholesterol: 2 mg
- Total Fat: 3 g
- Fiber: 0 g
- Protein: 1 g
- Sodium: 102 mg

54. Chocolate Cheese Candy

"This fudge is the easiest yet tastes the best."
Serving: 96 | Prep: 5m | Ready in: 20m

Ingredients

- 1/2 (1 lb.) loaf processed cheese food, cubed
- 2 (16 oz.) packages confectioners' sugar
- 1 cup margarine
- 1/2 cup unsweetened cocoa powder
- 1/2 cup semisweet chocolate chips
- 1 tsp. vanilla extract
- 1/2 cup chopped walnuts (optional)

Direction

- Mix margarine, chocolate chips, cocoa and processed cheese in a saucepan. Set over medium-low heat; cook while stirring frequently until melted and well blended.
- Take out of the heat; stir in walnuts, confectioners' sugar and vanilla. Transfer to a greased 9x13 inch baking dish. Cool; cut into small squares.

Nutrition Information

- Calories: 70 calories;
- Total Carbohydrate: 10.4 g
- Cholesterol: 2 mg
- Total Fat: 3.2 g
- Protein: 0.7 g
- Sodium: 52 mg

55. Chocolate Cherries

"It's sure to become one of your kids favorite food!"
Serving: 5 dozen. | Prep: 30m | Ready in: 30m

Ingredients

- 60 maraschino cherries with stems
- 2 cups confectioners' sugar
- 3 tbsps. butter, softened
- 3 tbsps. light corn syrup
- 1/4 tsp. salt
- 2 cups (12 oz.) semisweet chocolate chips
- 2 tbsps. shortening

Direction

- Using paper towels, pat the cherries dry. Put aside. Combine salt, corn syrup, butter and sugar in a small bowl, then mix well. Knead until they become smooth. Place in the refrigerator, covered, for about 60 mins.
- Shape into 1/2-in. balls, then flatten into 2-inch circle. Cover each circle around 1 cherry and roll lightly in hands. Arrange the cherries on waxed paper-lined baking sheets, stems up. Loosely cover, then place in the refrigerator for 60 mins.
- In a heavy saucepan or microwave, melt shortening and chocolate chips. Stir until they become smooth. Holding onto stem, submerge each cherry into the chocolate; let excess drip off. Place on the waxed paper; allow to stand until set. Place in the refrigerator until hardened. Preserve in a covered container. Place in the refrigerator for about 1 to 2 weeks. Then enjoy!

Nutrition Information

- Calories: 64 calories
- Total Carbohydrate: 11 g
- Cholesterol: 2 mg
- Total Fat: 3 g
- Fiber: 0 g
- Protein: 0 g
- Sodium: 18 mg

56. Chocolate Cherry Candies

"Special treat at Christmastime for family and friends."
Serving: about 4-1/2 dozen. | Prep: 40m | Ready in: 40m

Ingredients

- 2/3 cup creamy peanut butter
- 1/4 cup butter, softened
- 2 cups confectioners' sugar
- 1 cup finely chopped walnuts
- 1 cup flaked coconut
- 1/4 cup finely chopped maraschino cherries
- 1 tbsp. maraschino cherry juice
- 2 cups (12 oz.) semisweet chocolate chips
- 2 tbsps. shortening

Direction

- Beat confectioners' sugar, butter and peanut butter until crumbly. Mix in cherry juice, cherries, coconut and walnuts. Put in refrigerator with a cover for at least 1 hour. Form rounded teaspoonfuls of filling into balls. Put in a freezer for 10 minutes.
- Melt chocolate chips and shortening in a heavy saucepan or microwave; stir the mixture until smooth. Dunk balls in chocolate, let excess drip off; put on waxed paper. Put in refrigerator until chocolate is firm. Freeze option: Freeze candy in freezer containers, using waxed paper to separate layers. Before serving, serve frozen or thaw in refrigerator.

57. Chocolate Cherry Fudge

"This fudge stands out because of the cherries. It's ideal for the holidays."
Serving: 4-5 dozen. | Prep: 20m | Ready in: 20m

Ingredients

- 1 can (14 oz.) sweetened condensed milk
- 2 cups (12 oz.) semisweet chocolate chips
- 1/2 cup coarsely chopped almonds
- 1/2 cup chopped candied cherries
- 1 tsp. almond extract

Direction

- Mix chocolate chips and milk in a medium microwaveable bowl. Microwave for about 1 minute on high or until chips are melted and smooth when mixed. Mix in extract, cherries and almonds. Spread in a greased 8-in. square pan evenly. Put in the fridge, covered, until set. Slice into squares. Cover and store in the fridge.

Nutrition Information

- Calories: 59 calories
- Total Carbohydrate: 8 g
- Cholesterol: 2 mg
- Total Fat: 3 g
- Fiber: 0 g
- Protein: 1 g
- Sodium: 10 mg

58. Chocolate Cherry Truffles

"Amazing cherry truffles."
Serving: 4 dozen. | Prep: 01h30m | Ready in: 01h30m

Ingredients

- 1 cup finely chopped dried cherries
- 1/4 cup cherry brandy
- 11 oz. 53% cacao dark baking chocolate, chopped
- 1/2 cup heavy whipping cream
- 1 tsp. cherry extract
- COATING:
- 4 oz. milk chocolate, chopped
- 4 oz. dark chocolate, chopped
- Melted dark, milk and white chocolate and pearl dust

Direction

- Soak cherries in brandy, covered, in small bowl for 1 hour till cherries are soft.
- Put dark chocolate in small bowl. Put cream to just a boil in small saucepan. Put on chocolate; whisk till smooth. Mix soaked cherries with liquid and extract in; cool, occasionally mixing, to room temperature. Refrigerate till firm for 1 hour.
- Form to 1-in. balls; put on baking sheets and cover. Refrigerate for minimum 1 hour.
- Melt milk chocolate in microwave; mix till smooth. Dip 1/2 balls in milk chocolate; let excess drip off. Put on waxed paper and let stand till set.
- Melt dark chocolate; mix till smooth. Dip leftover balls in dark chocolate; let excess drip off. Put onto waxed paper; let stand till set. Drizzle melted chocolate over; decorate as desired with pearl dust. Keep in airtight container in the fridge.

Nutrition Information

- Calories: 80 calories
- Total Carbohydrate: 10 g
- Cholesterol: 3 mg
- Total Fat: 5 g
- Fiber: 1 g
- Protein: 1 g
- Sodium: 1 mg

59. Chocolate Chews

"These cookies are chocolaty and chewy."
Serving: 18

Ingredients

- 1 cup semisweet chocolate chips
- 1/2 cup butter, softened
- 1/2 cup white sugar
- 1/2 cup packed brown sugar
- 2 eggs
- 1/2 tsp. vanilla extract
- 2 cups all-purpose flour
- 1/2 tsp. baking powder
- 1/2 tsp. baking soda

Direction

- Over very low heat, melt the chocolate chips in a heavy saucepan. Stir to melt evenly.
- Cream sugars and butter together until light. Beat in one egg at a time. Stir in vanilla and melted chocolate.
- Whisk baking soda, baking powder and flour in a bowl. Slowly add to the butter mixture. Thoroughly blend. Form into 1-inch balls; arrange on greased cookie sheet.
- Bake for 12-14 minutes at 350°F (180°C). Let sit for 1-2 minutes on cookie sheet; transfer to a rack to cool.

Nutrition Information

- Calories: 194 calories;
- Total Carbohydrate: 28.1 g
- Cholesterol: 34 mg
- Total Fat: 8.6 g
- Protein: 2.6 g
- Sodium: 96 mg

60. Chocolate Chip Cookie Dough Fudge

"It's a delicious and flavorful cream cheese-based fudge."
Serving: 24 | Prep: 25m | Ready in: 1h25m

Ingredients

- 1/3 cup margarine, melted
- 2/3 cup light brown sugar, packed
- 1 pinch salt
- 3/4 cup all-purpose flour
- 1/4 cup semisweet mini chocolate chips
- 1 (8 oz.) package cream cheese, softened
- 1 (16 oz.) package confectioners' sugar
- 1 cup semisweet mini chocolate chips, melted
- 1 tsp. vanilla extract

Direction

- Use aluminum foil to line a 9"x9" baking dish then put aside.
- For cookie dough pieces: In a bowl, combine together salt, brown sugar and melted margarine. Stir in flour to form a dough and knead in 1/4 cup of chocolate chips. Shape the dough into a disk with the thickness of 1/2 inch to 3/4 inch, then put on a sheet of plastic wrap. Use your hands to form the disk into a square.
- Put into the freezer with square piece dough about 10 minutes, until stiff and cold, then cut into 1/2-in. square pieces. Chill the dough pieces while making the cream cheese fudge.
- In a bowl, combine confectioners' sugar and cream cheese together until smooth, then stir in vanilla extract and melted chocolate chips.
- Fold in the cookie dough pieces gently and spread candy out into prepped dish. Chill for a minimum of an hour, until firm, then take candy out of the dish lined with foil. Slice into squares and serve.

Nutrition Information

- Calories: 207 calories;
- Total Carbohydrate: 33.4 g
- Cholesterol: 10 mg

- Total Fat: 8.4 g
- Protein: 1.5 g
- Sodium: 60 mg

61. Chocolate Chip Cookie Dough Truffles

"An easy recipe for rich cookie truffles."
Serving: 24 | Prep: 10m | Ready in: 1h

Ingredients

- 1 (8 oz.) package cream cheese, softened
- 1 cup brown sugar
- 2 tsps. vanilla extract
- 2 1/4 cups all-purpose flour
- 1/4 tsp. salt
- 10 oz. semisweet chocolate chips
- 1 lb. confectioners' chocolate

Direction

- Mix vanilla extract, brown sugar and cream cheese till smooth in a bowl; add flour. Mix till incorporated. Sprinkle salt on dough; fold chocolate chips in. Shape dough to 1-2-in. balls; put on baking sheet. Freeze for about 30 minutes till set.
- In top of double boiler above simmering water, melt confectioners' chocolate, frequently mixing and scraping sides down using rubber spatula to prevent scorching. In chocolate, dip cookie balls; put on aluminum foil/waxed paper sheet for minimum of 20 minutes till hardened.

Nutrition Information

- Calories: 261 calories;
- Total Carbohydrate: 33.3 g
- Cholesterol: 11 mg
- Total Fat: 13.2 g
- Protein: 3.7 g
- Sodium: 56 mg

62. Chocolate Chow Mein Clusters

"It has the special flavor!"
Serving: 8 clusters. | Prep: 15m | Ready in: 15m

Ingredients

- 1/2 cup semisweet chocolate chips
- 1/2 cup butterscotch chips
- 1/2 cup chow mein noodles
- 1/2 cup salted peanuts

Direction

- Melt chocolate and butterscotch chips in a microwave. Stir until they become smooth. Mix in peanuts and chow mein noodles till well coated.
- Drop onto the waxed paper-lined baking sheet by rounded tablespoonfuls. Place in the refrigerator until set, about 120 mins.

Nutrition Information

- Calories: 199 calories
- Total Carbohydrate: 20 g
- Cholesterol: 1 mg
- Total Fat: 13 g
- Fiber: 2 g
- Protein: 4 g
- Sodium: 64 mg

63. Chocolate Cinnamon Mud Balls

"They are the best candies pie ever!"
Serving: 3 dozen. | Prep: 15m | Ready in: 25m

Ingredients

- 2 cups sugar
- 1/2 cup water
- 1/4 cup heavy whipping cream
- 1 tbsp. light corn syrup
- 1-1/2 oz. semisweet chocolate, chopped
- 1 to 2 tsps. ground cinnamon
- 1 tsp. vanilla extract
- Pinch salt

- 2-1/2 cups (15 oz.) semisweet chocolate chips
- 1 tbsp. shortening
- 1/2 cup ground nuts, optional

Direction

- Butter sides of the heavy saucepan. Put in first 5 ingredients. Over medium-high heat, cook while stirring until the sugar dissolves. Cook until a candy thermometer registers 238° (soft-ball stage), without stirring. Discard from heat. Let cool, until reaches 110°, without stirring.
- Place into a large bowl. Put in salt, vanilla and cinnamon. Beat for 2 mins or until stiff enough to knead and light-colored. Knead for 2 minutes in bowl, until they become smooth. Form into 1-inch balls. Freeze, covered, about 20 mins.
- Melt shortening and chips in a microwave. Stir until they become smooth. Submerge balls in the chocolate. Let the excess drip off. If desired, roll in nuts. Arrange on the waxed paper; allow to stand until set.

Nutrition Information

- Calories: 231 calories
- Total Carbohydrate: 39 g
- Cholesterol: 5 mg
- Total Fat: 10 g
- Fiber: 2 g
- Protein: 1 g
- Sodium: 14 mg

64. Chocolate Clusters

"This no-bake treat is so simple to make and is really worth it!"
Serving: 12

Ingredients

- 1 cup semisweet chocolate chips
- 1 cup butterscotch chips
- 1 cup peanuts
- 1 cup chow mein noodles

Direction

- Put the butterscotch chips and chocolate chips in a saucepan and let it melt over low heat setting. Remove the pan away from the heat and put in the chow mein noodles and peanuts right away. Mix everything together until well-coated. Drop the mixture onto a cookie sheet that is lined with wax paper; allow it to rest until the mixture has set then keep it in the fridge. Serve afterwards.

Nutrition Information

- Calories: 239 calories;
- Total Carbohydrate: 22.7 g
- Cholesterol: 0 mg
- Total Fat: 15.4 g
- Protein: 3.8 g
- Sodium: 34 mg

65. Chocolate Covered Cherries

"Tasty candies with a small red cherry inside are something you would wish for in a holiday party."
Serving: 50

Ingredients

- 8 tbsps. melted butter
- 6 tbsps. corn syrup
- 1 (14 oz.) can sweetened condensed milk
- 1 tsp. vanilla extract
- 3 lbs. confectioners' sugar
- 3 (10 oz.) jars maraschino cherries, drained
- 2 cups semisweet chocolate chips
- 1/2 tbsp. shortening

Direction

- In a large mixing bowl, mix together sugar, vanilla, sweetened condensed milk, corn syrup and butter. Knead the dough; then shape it into walnut–sized balls with a cherry in the centre. Chill in the freezer.
- In a double boiler, melt shortening and chocolate chips together. Dip the cooled balls

in the chocolate, allow to cool down on parchment paper.

Nutrition Information

- Calories: 209 calories;
- Total Carbohydrate: 42.4 g
- Cholesterol: 8 mg
- Total Fat: 4.7 g
- Protein: 1.2 g
- Sodium: 24 mg

---

66. Chocolate Covered Easter Eggs

"An amazing recipe that always receives rave reviews."
Serving: 48 | Prep: 30m | Ready in: 2h30m

Ingredients

- 1/2 cup butter, softened
- 1 tsp. vanilla extract
- 1 (8 oz.) package cream cheese, softened
- 2 1/2 lbs. confectioners' sugar
- 1 cup creamy peanut butter (optional)
- 1 cup flaked coconut (optional)
- 1 cup unsweetened cocoa powder (optional)
- 2 cups semisweet chocolate pieces
- 1 tbsp. shortening or vegetable oil (optional)

Direction

- Combine cream cheese, vanilla, and butter together in a large bowl. Add in confectioners' sugar to have a workable dough. Combine with your hands to achieve the best results.
- Divide the dough into fourths. Leave one portion plain. Combine the peanut butter into the second part. Combine coconut in the third part and cocoa powder in the last part. Roll each type of dough to form into egg shapes, then transfer onto a waxed paper-lined cookie sheet. Put in the fridge for at least 1 hour until hard.
- In a heat-proof bowl, melt the chocolate chips in a pan with simmering water. Stir from time

to time until they become smooth. Add in a tsp. of oil or shortening and stir until it thins to a desired degree of consistency if the chocolate becomes too thick to coat. Plunge the cooled candy eggs into the chocolate and place back onto the waxed paper-lined sheet until set. Put in the fridge for half an hour until hard.

Nutrition Information

- Calories: 204 calories;
- Total Carbohydrate: 30.9 g
- Cholesterol: 10 mg
- Total Fat: 9.3 g
- Protein: 2.4 g
- Sodium: 58 mg

---

67. Chocolate Covered Marshmallows

"Let's party! Have this quick and tasty recipe."
Serving: 10 | Prep: 10m | Ready in: 45m

Ingredients

- 2 cups semisweet chocolate chips
- 10 large marshmallows

Direction

- In a microwaveable glass or ceramic bowl, melt chocolate while stirring in 30-second intervals. Prevent overheating chocolate to avoid scorching.
- Using a toothpick or fork, pin marshmallow and soak in melted chocolate. Transfer coated marshmallow onto waxed paper or aluminum foil. Keep in freezer. For 5 minutes, set aside at room temperature. Serve.

Nutrition Information

- Calories: 184 calories;
- Total Carbohydrate: 27.1 g
- Cholesterol: 0 mg
- Total Fat: 10.1 g
- Protein: 1.5 g

- Sodium: 9 mg

68. Chocolate Covered Pecans

"Walnut parts are totally shrouded in chocolate."
Serving: 2 | Prep: 5m | Ready in: 10m

Ingredients

- 1/2 cup semi-sweet chocolate chips
- 3 tbsps. heavy cream
- 2 cups pecan halves

Direction

- In a medium metal bowl, mix the cream and chocolate chips and put the bowl on top of a pan of simmering water. Mix occasionally until smooth and melted. Take away from the heat. Mix the pecan halves into the chocolate until fully coated.
- Use a slotted spoon to remove a few pecans at a time. Separate the pecan halves then put onto a cookie sheet lined with waxed paper. Refrigerate about 10 minutes to set.

Nutrition Information

- Calories: 1024 calories;
- Total Carbohydrate: 42.1 g
- Cholesterol: 31 mg
- Total Fat: 98.6 g
- Protein: 12.1 g
- Sodium: 13 mg

69. Chocolate Covered Potato Chips

"You can use this for any nuts, popcorn and pretzels too!"
Serving: 16 | Prep: 30m | Ready in: 30m

Ingredients

- 1 lb. high quality milk chocolate, chopped
- 8 cups ridged potato chips

Direction

- Put 3/4 of the chocolate in heat safe bowl. Put above pan with simmering pan. Use a double broiler if you have one. Heat, occasionally mixing, till chocolate melts. Heat chocolate, occasionally mixing, to 43°C/110°F. If candy thermometer doesn't go that low, use a meat thermometer.
- When melted chocolate reaches temperature, take off heat; mix leftover chopped chocolate in till melted. Keep mixing till chocolate cools for 32°C/90°F. Touching a chocolate dab to lip will feel cool.
- One by one, dip potato chips into chocolate with tongs. Beginning at point farthest from you and working in to avoid dripping on finished chips, put on waxed paper. Cool till set. Refrigerate (optional).

Nutrition Information

- Calories: 363 calories;
- Total Carbohydrate: 35.4 g
- Cholesterol: 7 mg
- Total Fat: 21.6 g
- Protein: 4.8 g
- Sodium: 234 mg

70. Chocolate Cream Bonbons

"I have been loving this recipe since I was a girl."
Serving: about 6 dozen. | Prep: 20m | Ready in: 20m

Ingredients

- 4 cups confectioners' sugar
- 1 cup ground pecans or walnuts
- 1/2 cup plus 2 tbsps. sweetened condensed milk
- 1/4 cup butter, softened
- 3 cups (18 oz.) semisweet chocolate chips
- 2 tbsps. shortening

Direction

- Mix butter, milk, pecans and confectioners' sugar in large bowl. Form into 1-in. balls. Transfer to baking sheets lined with waxed paper. Keep in the fridge with a cover overnight.
- Melt shortening and chocolate chips in a microwave; stir until smooth. Coat balls in chocolate; let any excess drip off. Arrange on waxed paper; allow to rest until set. (If balls are not hard enough to dip, keep them in the freezer for a few minutes first.)

Nutrition Information

- Calories: 84 calories
- Total Carbohydrate: 13 g
- Cholesterol: 3 mg
- Total Fat: 4 g
- Fiber: 0 g
- Protein: 1 g
- Sodium: 11 mg

71. Chocolate Crunch Patties

"Potato chips are an interesting ingredient in this candy recipe."
Serving: about 4 dozen. | Prep: 15m | Ready in: 15m

Ingredients

- 2 cups (12 oz.) butterscotch chips
- 1 cup (6 oz.) milk chocolate chips
- 1-1/2 cups dry roasted peanuts
- 1 cup crushed thick ripple-cut potato chips

Direction

- Combine chocolate chips and butterscotch in a medium microwaveable bowl. Microwave for 1 to 3 minutes on 50% power, stirring every minute, until softened. Mix until smooth. Put in potato chips and peanuts; stir well. Drop mixture onto waxed paper-lined baking sheets by teaspoonfuls. Allow to firm.

Nutrition Information

- Calories: 209 calories
- Total Carbohydrate: 20 g
- Cholesterol: 3 mg
- Total Fat: 13 g
- Fiber: 1 g
- Protein: 4 g
- Sodium: 108 mg

72. Chocolate Crunchies

"My mom got this candy recipe from my grandmother, I got the recipe from my mum then I give the recipe to my daughter and we are all well known for delicious homemade candies."
Serving: 2-1/2 dozen. | Prep: 25m | Ready in: 25m

Ingredients

- 2 cups (12 oz.) semisweet chocolate chips
- 2 cups butterscotch chips
- 1/2 tsp. vanilla extract
- 3 cups chow mein noodles

Direction

- Place vanilla and chips in the top of a double boiler, put the double boiler over simmering water to melt vanilla and chips; stir till the mixture becomes smooth. Fold in noodles. Use the mixture to make teaspoonfuls drops on waxed paper. Chill it.

Nutrition Information

- Calories: 328 calories
- Total Carbohydrate: 40 g
- Cholesterol: 2 mg
- Total Fat: 19 g
- Fiber: 2 g
- Protein: 3 g
- Sodium: 67 mg

73. Chocolate Easter Eggs

"No locally acquired Easter treat can contrast with Mom's hand crafted chocolate-secured eggs."
Serving: 2 dozen. | Prep: 25m | Ready in: 25m

Ingredients

- 1/4 cup butter, softened
- 3/4 cup chunky peanut butter
- 1-1/2 to 2 cups confectioners' sugar, divided
- 1 cup sweetened shredded coconut
- 1/2 cup finely chopped walnuts
- 2 cups (12 oz.) semisweet chocolate chips
- 2 tbsps. shortening

Direction

- Cream peanut butter and butter in a big bowl until fluffy. Put in 1 cup confectioners' sugar slowly then blend well. Mix in nuts and coconut.
- Flip the peanut butter blend onto a lightly dusted surface with some of the leftover confectioners' sugar; knead in enough of the leftover confectioners' sugar until the blend remains the shape when formed. Form into small egg-shaped pieces. Cover then chill for an hour.
- Melt the shortening and chocolate chips in a microwave; mix until smooth. Dip the eggs into the mixture; let excess drip off. Put them onto waxed paper; allow to stand until set. Chill.

Nutrition Information

- Calories: 204 calories
- Total Carbohydrate: 20 g
- Cholesterol: 5 mg
- Total Fat: 14 g
- Fiber: 2 g
- Protein: 3 g
- Sodium: 70 mg

74. Chocolate Fish Lollipops

"The appealing-to-kids fish shape will make these chocolate lollipops even more delicious."
Serving: 6 servings. | Prep: 30m | Ready in: 30m

Ingredients

- 6 oz. milk chocolate candy coating, coarsely chopped
- 3/4 cup crisp rice cereal, lightly crushed
- Fish candy mold
- Lollipop sticks

Direction

- Microwave candy coating in a microwaveable bowl; mix in cereal. Pour into candy mold to 3/4 full. Insert a lollipop stick into the chocolate; add a little chocolate on top. Freeze for 15 minutes until the candy are firms. Take out of the mold.

Nutrition Information

- Calories: 160 calories
- Total Carbohydrate: 22 g
- Cholesterol: 0 mg
- Total Fat: 8 g
- Fiber: 1 g
- Protein: 1 g
- Sodium: 32 mg

75. Chocolate Fudge

"This easy basic fudge recipe is fun to follow."
Serving: 24

Ingredients

- 3 cups white sugar
- 1 cup evaporated milk
- 1/4 cup unsweetened cocoa powder
- 1/4 cup creamy peanut butter

Direction

- Mix cocoa, evaporated milk, white sugar in a 3 quart saucepan. Bring to a hard boil then lower to medium heat. Keep cooking till the mixture reaches 112°C (234°F). That is the soft ball stage.
- Put in peanut butter and stir till the mixture is blended well. Butter an 8x8-inch baking dish and transfer the mixture into the baking dish. Cool then divide into pieces.

Nutrition Information

- Calories: 129 calories;
- Total Carbohydrate: 27.1 g
- Cholesterol: 3 mg
- Total Fat: 2.3 g
- Protein: 1.6 g
- Sodium: 24 mg

76. Chocolate Haystacks

"Super Simple!"
Serving: Makes 3-1/2 doz. or 21 servings, 2 haystacks each. | Prep: 10m | Ready in: 1h10m

Ingredients

- 1 pkg. (4 oz.) BAKER'S Semi-Sweet Chocolate
- 1 cup butterscotch chips
- 2 cups chow mein noodles
- 2 cups JET-PUFFED Miniature Marshmallows
- 1/2 cup PLANTERS COCKTAIL Peanuts

Direction

- 1. In medium microwaveable bowl, microwave butterscotch chips and chocolate for 2-3 mins on HIGH, stirring after 1-1/2 mins, until almost melted. Mix until melted completely.
- 2. Put in the remaining ingredients, then stir until they are coated evenly.
- 3. Drop the chocolate mixture by tablespoonfuls onto the waxed paper-covered

baking sheet. Place in the refrigerator until firm, about 60 mins.

Nutrition Information

- Calories: 130
- Total Carbohydrate: 17 g
- Cholesterol: 0 mg
- Total Fat: 7 g
- Fiber: 0.9633 g
- Protein: 2 g
- Sodium: 55 mg
- Sugar: 11 g
- Saturated Fat: 4 g

77. Chocolate Hazelnut Truffles

Serving: Makes about 80 truffles

Ingredients

- Unsweetened cocoa powder for dusting
- 1 cup hazelnuts, toasted , loose skins rubbed off with a kitchen towel, and cooled
- 3/4 cup all-purpose flour
- 1/2 cup sugar
- 1/2 tsp. salt
- 1/2 stick (1/4 cup) unsalted butter
- 6 oz fine-quality bittersweet chocolate (not unsweetened), finely chopped
- 2 large whole eggs
- 2 large egg yolks
- 1 cup heavy cream
- 1/8 tsp. salt
- 12 oz fine-quality bittersweet chocolate (not unsweetened), finely chopped
- Special equipment: a small metal offset spatula

Direction

- Preparation: For hazelnut base: Prepare the oven by preheating to 350°F. Grease with butter the sides and bottom of an 8-inch square metal baking pan, then sprinkle with cocoa powder, getting rid of excess.

- Nicely grind nuts, flour, salt and sugar in a food processor
- In a 2-qt. saucepan, dissolve butter then separate from heat. Mix in chocolate until smooth. Stir in eggs, 1 at a time, stirring until smooth. Whisk in nut flour until just blended.
- Place batter in baking pan and equally spread and bake in the preheated oven for 15-20 minutes placing it at the center until top turns dry and firm and a tester poked into middle comes out with crumbs adhering. Let it fully cool for at least 2 hours in pan on rack.
- For ganache: In a bowl, lightly whisk egg yolks. Make cream with salt just to a boil in a small heavy saucepan, then mix half of it to yolks in a slow stream, stirring constantly. Stir yolk mixture into remaining cream and cook over low heat, stirring, until slightly thickened and an instant-read thermometer reads 170°F (keep from boiling).
- Separate from heat and stir in chocolate, stirring until smooth. Place ganache over hazelnut base in pan, using an offset spatula to smooth the top, and chill for at least 5 hours, covered, until solid.
- Use a warmed thin knife to slice into squares, cleaning off knife after every slice, and take from pan while still cold.
- Serve truffles at room temperature or cold.
- Cooks' notes: You can chill the truffles for up to 7 days.
- Froze in pan, tightly covered with foil, for 1 month.

78. Chocolate Islands

"This recipe is the winner."
Serving: 2 dozen. | Prep: 20m | Ready in: 20m

Ingredients

- 3 cups sweetened shredded coconut
- 2 cups confectioners' sugar
- 1/2 cup butter, melted
- 1 cup (6 oz.) semisweet chocolate chips, melted

Direction

- In a large bowl, place butter, sugar and coconut; stir well. Shape into balls; transfer to baking sheets. Create a thumbprint in the center of each; fill melted chocolate in thumbprint. Chill until firm.

Nutrition Information

- Calories: 164 calories
- Total Carbohydrate: 20 g
- Cholesterol: 10 mg
- Total Fat: 10 g
- Fiber: 1 g
- Protein: 1 g
- Sodium: 70 mg

79. Chocolate Krisps

"You can use any different types of nuts."
Serving: 12 | Prep: 15m | Ready in: 1h15m

Ingredients

- 2 cups semisweet chocolate chips
- 1 cup crispy rice cereal (such as Rice Krispies®)
- 1/2 cup chopped almonds

Direction

- Place 24 paper candy cups onto a tray.
- In a microwave-safe bowl, add chocolate chips and heat them in the microwave until melted, for about 2 minutes. Stir.
- Mix almonds and crispy rice cereal into the melted chocolate. Into each candy cup, drop a spoonful of the chocolate mixture. Chill in refrigerator until set, for about 1 to 2 hours.

Nutrition Information

- Calories: 165 calories;
- Total Carbohydrate: 20.5 g
- Cholesterol: 0 mg
- Total Fat: 10.4 g
- Protein: 2.2 g

- Sodium: 21 mg

80. Chocolate Marshmallow Candy Squares

"Children love these treats."
Serving: 4 dozen. | Prep: 15m | Ready in: 15m

Ingredients

- 1-1/2 tsps. butter
- 1 package (12 oz.) semisweet chocolate chips
- 1 package (10 to 11 oz.) butterscotch chips
- 1/2 cup peanut butter
- 1 package (16 oz.) miniature marshmallows
- 1 cup unsalted dry roasted peanuts

Direction

- Using foil, line a 13-in. x 9-in. pan; grease foil with 1-1/2 tsps. butter; put aside.
- Microwave peanut butter, butterscotch chips and chocolate chips for 2 minutes at 70% power; stir. Microwave until melted in 10-20 second intervals; stir until smooth. Let cool for a minute. Stir in peanuts and marshmallows.
- Place into lined pan and spread. Keep in the fridge until firm. Lift candy out of pan with foil. Get rid of foil; cut into 1-1/2-in. squares.

81. Chocolate Marshmallow Peanut Butter Squares

"This chocolate bar recipe is a combination of some other recipes."
Serving: 5 dozen | Prep: 15m | Ready in: 20m

Ingredients

- 1 can (14 oz.) sweetened condensed milk
- 1 package (11 oz.) peanut butter and milk chocolate chips
- 1/2 cup milk chocolate chips
- 1/2 cup creamy peanut butter
- 1 tsp. vanilla extract

- 1-1/2 cups miniature marshmallows
- 1 cup broken miniature pretzels
- 1 cup Rice Krispies

Direction

- Put the first 5 ingredients in a large heavy saucepan; cook, stirring, over low heat for about 5 minutes or until smooth, and blended. The mixture is expected to be very thick. Put off the heat; mix in remaining ingredients. Spread mixture all over the bottom of an oiled 13x9-inch pan.
- Cover and chill for about 4 hours until firm. Divide into squares. Keep in an airtight container in the fridge.

Nutrition Information

- Calories: 85 calories
- Total Carbohydrate: 12 g
- Cholesterol: 3 mg
- Total Fat: 4 g
- Fiber: 0 g
- Protein: 1 g
- Sodium: 50 mg

82. Chocolate Mascarpone Truffles

"Satiny truffles!"
Serving: about 4 dozen. | Prep: 45m | Ready in: 50m

Ingredients

- 12 oz. semisweet chocolate, chopped, divided
- 4 oz. dark chocolate, chopped
- 1/2 cup heavy whipping cream
- 1/2 cup Mascarpone cheese
- 1-3/4 cups pistachios, chopped

Direction

- Mix and cook cheese, cream, dark chocolate and 4-oz. semisweet chocolate in small heavy saucepan on low heat till smooth. Put in small bowl; cover. Refrigerate till firm enough to shape for 3 hours. Form to 1-in. balls; put onto waxed paper-lined baking sheets then chill till firm for 1-2 hours.

- Melt leftover semisweet chocolate in microwave; mix till smooth. Dip balls in chocolate; let excess drip off then roll into pistachios. Put on waxed paper; let it stand till set. Keep in the fridge.

Nutrition Information

- Calories: 103 calories
- Total Carbohydrate: 7 g
- Cholesterol: 9 mg
- Total Fat: 8 g
- Fiber: 1 g
- Protein: 2 g
- Sodium: 22 mg

83. Chocolate Mint Candy

"I make this yummy candy recipe every holiday."
Serving: about 2 lbs.. | Prep: 20m | Ready in: 20m

Ingredients

- 2 cups (12 oz.) semisweet chocolate chips
- 1 can (14 oz.) sweetened condensed milk, divided
- 2 tsps. vanilla extract
- 6 oz. white candy coating, coarsely chopped
- 2 to 3 tsps. peppermint extract
- 3 drops green food coloring

Direction

- Heat 1 cup milk and chocolate chips together in a heavy saucepan. Turn off the heat; mix in vanilla. Spread 1/2 the melted chocolate mixture over the bottom of an 8-inch square pan lined with waxed paper; refrigerate until set, for 10 minutes.
- In the meantime, cook while stirring candy coating and the rest of the milk over low heat in a heavy saucepan, until coating has melted and mixture becomes smooth. Mix in food coloring and peppermint extract. Spread

coating mixture over the bottom layer; refrigerate until set, for 10 minutes.

- Heat the rest of the chocolate mixture if needed; spoon over mint layer. Refrigerate until set, for 2 hours. Take candy out of the pan; divide into squares, about 1 inch.

Nutrition Information

- Calories: 60 calories
- Total Carbohydrate: 9 g
- Cholesterol: 2 mg
- Total Fat: 3 g
- Fiber: 0 g
- Protein: 1 g
- Sodium: 8 mg

84. Chocolate Molasses Taffy

"This old-style candy recipe is sure to please all of your guests."
Serving: 1 lb.. | Prep: 45m | Ready in: 01h15m

Ingredients

- 1 tsp. plus 3 tbsps. butter, divided
- 1 cup sugar
- 1 cup water
- 1 cup molasses
- 2 oz. unsweetened chocolate, chopped
- 1-1/2 tsps. vanilla extract

Direction

- Line aluminum foil over an 8x8-inch pan. Use 1 tsp. butter to grease the foil; put aside.
- Combine the rest of butter with molasses, water, and sugar in a large heavy saucepan. Heat to a boil, whisking constantly. Cook, undisturbed, until mixture reaches hard-ball stage or a candy thermometer registers 260°.
- Put off the heat; whisk in vanilla and chocolate. Transfer mixture to the prepared square pan. Allow to cool a bit. Score small square in the surface. Allow to cool entirely. Once cooled, cut along the scored lines. Use

waxed paper to wrap candy. Put candies into an airtight container to store.

Nutrition Information

- Calories: 23 calories
- Total Carbohydrate: 5 g
- Cholesterol: 1 mg
- Total Fat: 1 g
- Fiber: 0 g
- Protein: 0 g
- Sodium: 4 mg

85. Chocolate Mousse Balls

"This tasty recipe is so easy that you your children can get involved."
Serving: about 3 dozen. | Prep: 20m | Ready in: 20m

Ingredients

- 6 milk chocolate candy bars (1.55 oz. each)
- 1 container (12 oz.) frozen whipped topping, thawed
- 1 cup crushed vanilla wafers (about 30 wafers)

Direction

- Melt candy bars in a saucepan over low heat. Let cool for 10 minutes. Fold into the topping. Chill for 3 hours, covered.
- Roll into 1-inch balls and toss in wafer crumbs. Chill or freeze.

Nutrition Information

- Calories: 156 calories
- Total Carbohydrate: 18 g
- Cholesterol: 4 mg
- Total Fat: 9 g
- Fiber: 1 g
- Protein: 1 g
- Sodium: 32 mg

86. Chocolate Nut Balls

"My friends ask me for the recipe of this simple no-bake treat all the time."
Serving: about 5 dozen. | Prep: 20m | Ready in: 20m

Ingredients

- 2 cups graham cracker crumbs
- 2 cups chopped pecans
- 1 can (16 oz.) chocolate frosting
- 1 tsp. vanilla extract
- 1-1/2 cups confectioners' sugar

Direction

- Mix the first 4 ingredients together in a large bowl. Form mixture into balls, about 1 inch. Roll the balls in sugar. Chill for 60 minutes, then serve.

Nutrition Information

- Calories: 163 calories
- Total Carbohydrate: 20 g
- Cholesterol: 0 mg
- Total Fat: 9 g
- Fiber: 1 g
- Protein: 1 g
- Sodium: 69 mg

87. Chocolate Nut Candies

"One batch of this delicious candies is able to serve a crowd."
Serving: 12-1/2 dozen. | Prep: 15m | Ready in: 25m

Ingredients

- 3 cups (18 oz.) semisweet chocolate chips
- 2 cups creamy peanut butter
- 1 cup butter, cubed
- 1/2 cup evaporated milk
- 1/4 cup instant vanilla pudding mix
- 1 tsp. vanilla extract
- 2 lbs. confectioners' sugar
- 3 cups salted peanuts

Direction

- Melt peanut butter and chocolate chips over low heat in a heavy saucepan, whisking frequently. Transfer half of mixture to a buttered 15x10x1-inch pan, then chill. Put the rest of the chocolate mixture aside.
- Bring pudding mix, milk and butter in a separate saucepan to a boil; boil for 1 minute, whisking constantly. Put off the heat; transfer to a large mixing bowl; add vanilla. Slowly mix in sugar. Spread over the layer of chocolate in the pan; put into the fridge to chill.
- Put peanuts into the reserved chocolate mixture; spread over filling. Put into the fridge to chill. Divide into 1x1 1/2-inch bars.

88. Chocolate Nut Fudge

"You don't need to cook this treat that has the perfect balance of sweetness. It keeps well in the refrigerator when wrapped."
Serving: 36 | Prep: 15m | Ready in: 1h55m

Ingredients

- 1 (12 oz.) bag semisweet chocolate chips
- 1/2 cup sour cream
- 3/4 cup confectioners' sugar
- 1/4 tsp. salt
- 2 cups finely crushed vanilla wafer crumbs
- 1/2 cup broken walnuts

Direction

- Line aluminum foil in an 8-in by 8-in baking pan.
- On low heat, melt chocolate chips for 10 minutes in a big heavy pan until smooth and melted, constantly mix to prevent scorching. Mix salt, confectioners' sugar, and sour cream into the chocolate; stir in vanilla wafer crumbs and broken walnut pieces. Slather the fudge in the foil-lined pan. Chill until firm then slice into squares.

Nutrition Information

- Calories: 119 calories;
- Total Carbohydrate: 15.9 g
- Cholesterol: 1 mg
- Total Fat: 6.5 g
- Protein: 1.2 g
- Sodium: 50 mg

89. Chocolate Nut Fudge Rolls

"My mom gave me lots of recipes but these sweet and rich chocolate nut rolls are the one I make the most frequently."
Serving: about 2-1/4 lbs.. | Prep: 30m | Ready in: 55m

Ingredients

- 2 tbsps. butter
- 1 oz. unsweetened chocolate
- 3 cups sugar
- 1 cup whole milk
- 1/4 cup honey
- 1/8 tsp. salt
- 1 tsp. white vinegar
- 1 tsp. vanilla extract
- 2 cups (12 oz.) semisweet chocolate chips
- 1 tbsp. shortening
- 3 cups chopped walnuts

Direction

- Put chocolate and butter in a large heavy saucepan and melt on low heat. Put in salt, honey, milk and sugar. Bring to a boil on medium heat; remember to stir sometimes. To cover, put a lid on and keep boiling for 2 more minutes. Remove the lid and cook without stirring till a candy thermometer reaches 240 degrees (this is the soft ball stage). Get the saucepan off heat; add vinegar and stir.
- Allow the mixture to cool to 110 degrees. Put in vanilla; beat vigorously for 8 to 10 minutes till the mixture becomes thick there is no gloss remaining. Butter a baking sheet and transfer the thickened mixture on to the baking sheet. Allow the mixture to sit till it is cool enough to

handle. Knead for 2 to 3 minutes. Use the kneaded mixture to make 4x1-1/2 in. rolls. Use waxed paper to line baking sheets and lay rolls on the prepared baking sheets; chill the rolls for 3 to 4 hours.

- Put chocolate chips and shortening together and melt in the microwave; stir till the mixture becomes smooth. Dip rolls in chocolate; let the excess chocolate to drip off. Roll in nuts. Lay roll on the waxed paper-lined baking sheets and chill till they become firm. Divide into 1/4 in. slices.

Nutrition Information

- Calories: 394 calories
- Total Carbohydrate: 53 g
- Cholesterol: 5 mg
- Total Fat: 21 g
- Fiber: 2 g
- Protein: 6 g
- Sodium: 39 mg

90. Chocolate Orange Bites

"The perfect cookie with chocolate and orange!"
Serving: about 4 dozen. | Prep: 35m | Ready in: 35m

Ingredients

- 1 package (9 oz.) chocolate wafers, crushed
- Sugar substitute equivalent to 1/2 cup sugar
- 1/4 cup reduced-fat butter, melted
- 1/4 cup thawed orange juice concentrate
- 1 tsp. grated orange zest
- 1/2 cup confectioners' sugar
- Baking cocoa and/or additional confectioners' sugar

Direction

- In a small bowl, mix together the first five ingredients. Roll it into 3/4-in. balls; then roll the balls in confectioners' sugar. Refrigerate, covered, for at least 2 hours.

- Sprinkle them lightly with cocoa and/or confectioners' sugar before serving. Keep refrigerated in an airtight container.

Nutrition Information

- Calories: 35 calories
- Total Carbohydrate: 6 g
- Cholesterol: 2 mg
- Total Fat: 1 g
- Fiber: 0 g
- Protein: 0 g
- Sodium: 37 mg

91. Chocolate Orange Fudge

"A simple fudge recipe with the combination of semisweet chocolate chips, condensed milk, pecans and grated orange peel."
Serving: 20 | Prep: 5m | Ready in: 2h10m

Ingredients

- 2 1/2 cups semisweet chocolate chips
- 1 (14 oz.) can sweetened condensed milk
- 1/2 cup chopped pecans
- 2 tsps. grated orange peel

Direction

- Use parchment paper to line an 8"x8" square pan.
- In the top of a double boiler or in a bowl in the microwave, melt condensed milk and chocolate chips together. Stir the mixture until smooth and take away from the heat. Stir in grated orange peel and pecans.
- Transfer into prepped pan with the chocolate mixture. Refrigerate until firm, for 2 hours, then slice into squares. Store in the fridge with a cover.

Nutrition Information

- Calories: 183 calories;
- Total Carbohydrate: 24.3 g
- Cholesterol: 7 mg

- Total Fat: 10 g
- Protein: 2.7 g
- Sodium: 27 mg

92. Chocolate Peanut Brittle

"You only need a microwave to make this brittle."
Serving: about 1-1/4 lbs.. | Prep: 5m | Ready in: 20m

Ingredients

- 1 cup sugar
- 1/4 cup light corn syrup
- 2 cups salted peanuts
- 1 tsp. butter
- 1/4 cup baking cocoa
- 1 tsp. baking soda
- 1 tsp. vanilla extract

Direction

- Grease a metal spatula and a 15x10x1 in. pan. Set aside.
- Mix corn syrup and sugar in a microwave safe bowl (size 2 qt.). Microwave without a cover on high for 4 minutes; stir. Cook for 3 minutes more. Add butter, peanuts and stir. Microwave a half to a minute or till the mixture gets a light amber color (be careful as the mixture will be pretty hot).
- Mix in vanilla, baking soda, cocoa quickly till everything is combined. Transfer the mixture into the prepared pan immediately; use the prepared metal spatula to spread. Cool before cracking into pieces. Keep in an airtight container to store.

Nutrition Information

- Calories: 139 calories
- Total Carbohydrate: 16 g
- Cholesterol: 1 mg
- Total Fat: 7 g
- Fiber: 2 g
- Protein: 4 g
- Sodium: 132 mg

93. Chocolate Peanut Butter Balls

"Beautiful edible balls."
Serving: Makes abut 40 chocolate peanut butter balls

Ingredients

- 3/4 cup firmly packed light brown sugar
- 1/4 cup unsalted butter, melted and cooled, plus 6 tbsps. unsalted butter
- 3/4 cup graham cracker crumbs
- 1 cup creamy peanut butter
- a 12-oz. bag semisweet chocolate chips

Direction

- Mix together peanut butter, graham cracker crumbs, 1/2 stick of the butter, and brown sugar in a bowl until smooth. Cover and chill the mixture until firm enough to shape into balls, about 1 hour. Shape teaspoonfuls of chilled mixture into balls; deliberately place on a wax paper-lined baking sheet. Melt remaining 3/4 stick butter together with chocolate chips in a metal bowl placed over a pan of barely simmering water, mixing until smooth; allow chocolate mixture to cool. Use a fork to submerge the balls in chocolate mixture, coating nicely and allowing the excess to drip off; place coated balls on the baking sheet. Cover loosely and keep chilled for no less than 1 hour or all night. (If wanted, double-dip the balls.)

Nutrition Information

- Calories: 112
- Total Carbohydrate: 12 g
- Cholesterol: 3 mg
- Total Fat: 7 g
- Fiber: 1 g
- Protein: 2 g
- Sodium: 11 mg
- Saturated Fat: 3 g

94. Chocolate Peanut Butter Bars

"A healthy bar recipe without refined sugar and dairy."
| Prep: 15m

Ingredients

- 1 cup Rolled oats
- 1/2 cup Peanut butter
- 6 pieces Dates
- 2 tbsp. Coconut oil or cacao butter, melted
- 2 tbsp. Coconut nectar
- 1/2 tsp. Vanilla powder
- 1/2 cup Cacao butter, melted
- 1 tbsp. Coconut oil, melted
- 3 tbsp. Coconut nectar
- 1/2 cup Cacao powder
- 1/2 tsp. Vanilla powder
- 1 pinch Sea salt

Direction

- Blend initial 6 ingredients till well combined in a food processor, mixture should nicely hold together when pinched between fingers and slightly sticky.
- Put in lined square tin; use palm of your hand to flatten down well. Put in freezer to firm it.
- Meanwhile, blend all leftover ingredients till smooth and completely combined in blender/food processor. Put over base; put back in freezer for 1-2 hours or in the fridge for a few more hours.
- Remove slice from tin when set; leave to slightly soften so chocolate topping won't crack. Cut to thin bars. Bars are best from the fridge but you may freeze them and keep them for up to 3 months.

95. Chocolate Peanut Butter Candies

"This recipe is a winner."
Serving: 5-6 dozen. | Prep: 30m | Ready in: 30m

Ingredients

- 1-1/2 cups creamy peanut butter
- 1 cup butter, softened
- 1 lb. plus 1 cup confectioners' sugar
- 2 cups (12 oz.) milk chocolate chips

Direction

- Cream butter and peanut butter in a large bowl. Add sugar; combine well. Form into 1/2 in. balls. In a double boiler or microwave, melt chocolate chips. Coat balls in chocolate; place on waxed paper to cool.

Nutrition Information

- Calories: 218 calories
- Total Carbohydrate: 23 g
- Cholesterol: 16 mg
- Total Fat: 13 g
- Fiber: 1 g
- Protein: 3 g
- Sodium: 109 mg

96. Chocolate Peanut Butter Cups

"This is a simple but decadent confection which quells the urge to immerse chocolate bar in peanut butter."
Serving: 12 | Prep: 2h | Ready in: 2h

Ingredients

- 1 (11.5 oz.) package milk chocolate chips, divided
- 1 cup peanut butter
- 1/4 tsp. salt
- 1/2 cup confectioners' sugar

Direction

- Start by trimming twelve paper muffin cup liners to 1/2 of their own height.
- In a microwave safe container, put half chocolate chips and heat in microwave for two minutes and stir after every minute. Scoop the melted chocolate into the muffin cups and fill it halfway. Draw chocolate up the sides of cups using a spoon until coated evenly. Let it cool in a fridge until firm.
- Combine salt, confectioners' sugar and peanut butter together in a small bowl. Distribute into chocolate cups. Melt remaining chocolate and scoop atop peanut butter. Spread the chocolate to the edges of cups.

Nutrition Information

- Calories: 290 calories;
- Total Carbohydrate: 25.5 g
- Cholesterol: 9 mg
- Total Fat: 19.8 g
- Protein: 7.2 g
- Sodium: 192 mg

97. Chocolate Peanut Butter Fudge

"This is such a simple and fun formula to make."
Serving: 32

Ingredients

- 3 cups white sugar
- 1 cup evaporated milk
- 1/4 cup cocoa
- 1/2 cup peanut butter
- 1 tbsp. margarine
- 1 tbsp. butter

Direction

- Grease a 9x9-inch pan with butter.
- In a saucepan, mix cocoa, evaporated milk and sugar. Mix the blend over high heat to a rolling boil. Reduce to medium heat then keep cooking until reaching a soft ball shape.

- Take away from the heat, put in margarine and peanut butter. Beat until creamy using hand; pour into the prepared pan. Let cool then slice into squares.

Nutrition Information

- Calories: 114 calories;
- Total Carbohydrate: 20.7 g
- Cholesterol: 3 mg
- Total Fat: 3.4 g
- Protein: 1.7 g
- Sodium: 33 mg

98. Chocolate Peanut Clusters

"The best chocolate for Christmas!"
Serving: 10 dozen. | Prep: 10m | Ready in: 15m

Ingredients

- 2 lbs. white candy coating, coarsely chopped
- 1 package (12 oz.) semisweet chocolate chips
- 1 package (11-1/2 oz.) milk chocolate chips
- 5 cups salted dry roasted peanuts

Direction

- In a heavy saucepan, cook while stirring chips and candy coating over low heat until smooth and melted. Let cool for 10 mins. Then mix in peanuts.
- Drop on the waxed paper-lined baking sheets by rounded tablespoonfuls. Place in the refrigerator for 45 mins or until firm.

Nutrition Information

- Calories: 206 calories
- Total Carbohydrate: 20 g
- Cholesterol: 1 mg
- Total Fat: 14 g
- Fiber: 1 g
- Protein: 4 g
- Sodium: 103 mg

99. Chocolate Peanut Sweeties

"Propelled by my energy for nutty spread and chocolate, I consolidated a believed formula for nutty spread eggs with the salty mash of pretzels."
Serving: 5 dozen. | Prep: 30m | Ready in: 30m

Ingredients

- 1 cup peanut butter
- 1/2 cup butter, softened
- 3 cups confectioners' sugar
- 60 miniature pretzels (about 3 cups)
- 1-1/2 cups milk chocolate chips
- 1 tbsp. shortening

Direction

- Beat the butter and peanut butter in a small bowl until smooth. Beat in the confectioners' sugar until mixed. Form into balls of 1 inch; press one onto each pretzel. Put onto the baking sheets lined with waxed paper. Refrigerate for 1 hour until the peanut butter blend is set.
- Melt the oil and chocolate chips in a microwave; mix until smooth. Dip peanut butter ball into the chocolate; let excess drip off. Bring back to the baking sheet with pretzel side down. Refrigerate for minimum 30 minutes prior to serving. Keep in airtight container in the fridge.

Nutrition Information

- Calories: 182 calories
- Total Carbohydrate: 21 g
- Cholesterol: 10 mg
- Total Fat: 10 g
- Fiber: 1 g
- Protein: 3 g
- Sodium: 124 mg

100. Chocolate Pecan Bark

""Add a small touch of salt to the chocolate and you will have a much more elevated sweet treat.""
Serving: 16 | Prep: 15m | Ready in: 1h55m

Ingredients

- 1 cup coarsely chopped pecans
- 1/4 tsp. sea salt
- 1/4 tsp. blackening seasoning
- 2 1/2 cups bittersweet chocolate chips
- 1 (1 oz.) square unsweetened baking chocolate, roughly chopped
- 1/2 tsp. vanilla extract

Direction

- Set oven to 175°C (350°F) and start preheating. Use parchment paper to line a baking sheet.
- Scatter pecans over a baking sheet; sprinkle blackening seasoning and sea salt on top.
- Bake at 175°C (350°F) for 5-6 minutes until pecans are fragrant and toasted. Take out of the oven and let cool.
- Put a double boiler over simmering water and place chocolate chips in the top; pour in unsweetened baking chocolate little by little and whisk. Put in vanilla extract and heat for 5-10 minutes until chocolate melts and becomes smooth. Stir half of the pecans into chocolate mixture.
- Transfer pecan-chocolate mixture to the lined baking sheet and scatter remaining pecans over the top. Let cool for half an hour to room temperature. Use plastic wrap to cover and put in the refrigerator for no less than an hour until set. Break to divide into pieces.

Nutrition Information

- Calories: 184 calories;
- Total Carbohydrate: 20 g
- Cholesterol: < 1 mg
- Total Fat: 12.5 g
- Protein: 2.1 g
- Sodium: 42 mg

101. Chocolate Pecan Candies

"The homemade version of Turtles."
Serving: about 5 dozen. | Prep: 30m | Ready in: 30m

Ingredients

- 1/2 lb. pecan halves
- 75 caramels
- 3 tbsps. milk
- 1 lb. dark chocolate candy coating, melted

Direction

- Put pecan halves in pairs 2 in. apart on a waxed paper. In a heavy saucepan, cook and stir over medium-low heat the milk and caramels till melted. Pour approx. 2 tsps. caramel mixture on each pecan pair. Let sit till set.
- Butter your fingers and roll pecan clusters into balls. Dip them into the candy coating. Put onto baking sheets lined with waxed paper. Chill in refrigerator until set. Keep in an airtight container for storage.

Nutrition Information

- Calories: 114 calories
- Total Carbohydrate: 15 g
- Cholesterol: 1 mg
- Total Fat: 6 g
- Fiber: 1 g
- Protein: 1 g
- Sodium: 31 mg

102. Chocolate Pecan Caramels

"I have been making this recipe every year since 1964."
Serving: about 2-1/2 lbs. (about 6-3/4 dozen). | Prep: 20m | Ready in: 35m

Ingredients

- 1 tbsp. plus 1 cup butter, softened, divided
- 1-1/2 cups coarsely chopped pecans, toasted
- 1 cup (6 oz.) semisweet chocolate chips
- 2 cups packed brown sugar
- 1 cup light corn syrup
- 1/4 cup water
- 1 can (14 oz.) sweetened condensed milk
- 2 tsps. vanilla extract

Direction

- Use a foil to line a 13x9-in. pan; use 1 tbsp. of butter to grease the foil. Sprinkle chocolate chips and pecans on top; put aside.
- In a heavy saucepan that is set over medium heat, melt the rest of the butter. Add the water, corn syrup, and brown sugar. Cook and stir until the mixture boils. Stir in milk. Cook, stirring continuously until it reaches into a firm-ball stage (a candy thermometer reads 248°).
- Take off from the heat and add in the vanilla. Transfer into the prepared pan (without scraping the saucepan). Allow it to cool thoroughly before slicing.

Nutrition Information

- Calories: 190 calories
- Total Carbohydrate: 26 g
- Cholesterol: 16 mg
- Total Fat: 10 g
- Fiber: 1 g
- Protein: 1 g
- Sodium: 76 mg

103. Chocolate Peppermint Bark

"Chocolaty and peppermint-y."
Serving: 6 | Prep: 15m | Ready in: 1h21m

Ingredients

- 1 cup chocolate chips
- 1/2 cup white chocolate chips
- 1/2 tsp. vegetable oil
- 1/2 tsp. peppermint extract

Direction

- Line waxed paper on baking sheet.
- In top of double boiler above simmering water, melt chocolate chips for 3-5 minutes, frequently mixing and scraping sides down using a rubber spatula to prevent scorching.
- In top of another double boiler above simmering water, melt white chocolate chips for 3-5 minutes, frequently mixing and scraping sides down using a rubber spatula to prevent scorching. Mix peppermint extract and vegetable oil in.
- Put chocolate on lined baking sheet; use spatula to spread. Drizzle chocolate with white chocolate; use a fork to swirl.
- Refrigerate for 1 hour till bark is hardened.

Nutrition Information

- Calories: 223 calories;
- Total Carbohydrate: 26.1 g
- Cholesterol: 3 mg
- Total Fat: 14.1 g
- Protein: 2.2 g
- Sodium: 19 mg

---

104. Chocolate Peppermint Candies

"I always get requests to make these patties. The special filling made with cool mint is the tastiest part."
Serving: 3 dozen. | Prep: 20m | Ready in: 20m

Ingredients

- 3/4 cup sweetened condensed milk
- 1-1/2 tsps. peppermint extract
- 4 to 4-1/2 cups confectioners' sugar
- 3 cups (18 oz.) semisweet chocolate chips
- 2 tsps. shortening

Direction

- Mix together extract and milk in a bowl. Mix in 3 1/2-4 cups of confectioners' sugar until to make a stiff dough. Lightly dust a surface with

confectioners' sugar and place the dough. Add in enough remaining sugar and knead until the dough is very stiff and no longer sticky. Form into 1-in balls. Transfer to a baking sheet lined with waxed paper. Roll out into circles (1-1/2 inches in size). Allow to dry for an hour. Flip and allow to dry for another hour. In a double boiler or microwaveable bowl, heat shortening and chocolate chips until melted; wait until slightly cool. Plunge patties in chocolate mixture; put onto waxed paper to harden.

Nutrition Information

- Calories: 142 calories
- Total Carbohydrate: 26 g
- Cholesterol: 2 mg
- Total Fat: 5 g
- Fiber: 1 g
- Protein: 1 g
- Sodium: 10 mg

---

105. Chocolate Pizza Heart

"I discovered this formula in an old cookbook and changed a couple of fixings to suit my family's taste."
Serving: 1-3/4 lbs.. | Prep: 15m | Ready in: 15m

Ingredients

- 1-1/2 cups milk chocolate chips
- 1 cup butterscotch chips
- 3/4 cup miniature marshmallows
- 3/4 cup chopped salted peanuts
- 3/4 cup crushed potato chips
- 2 tbsps. sweetened shredded coconut
- 7 maraschino cherries, halved
- 1/4 cup milk chocolate M&M's
- 2 tbsps. vanilla or white chips
- 1/2 tsp. shortening

Direction

- Draw a 10-inch heart with a pencil on a waxed paper. Put the paper on a baking sheet, pencil mark down; put aside.

- Melt the butterscotch chips and chocolate in a big microwave-safe bowl; mix until smooth. Mix in potato chips, peanuts and marshmallows. Instantly distribute into the heart shape in the prepared pan. Dust with coconut; top with M&M's and cherries.
- Melt the shortening and vanilla chips in a microwave; mix until smooth. Pour on top. Refrigerate for 1-1/2 hours, until firm. Discard the waxed paper. Allow to stand at room temperature for 10 minutes prior to cutting.

Nutrition Information

- Calories: 291 calories
- Total Carbohydrate: 31 g
- Cholesterol: 5 mg
- Total Fat: 17 g
- Fiber: 1 g
- Protein: 5 g
- Sodium: 82 mg

---

106. Chocolate Pomegranate Candies

"In this chocolatey recipe, you get all the goodness from both dark and white chocolate."
Serving: about 1/2 lb.. | Prep: 10m | Ready in: 10m

Ingredients

- 6 oz. white baking chocolate, coarsely chopped
- 1/4 cup flaked coconut, toasted
- 1/4 cup pomegranate seeds
- 2 oz. dark chocolate, chopped

Direction

- Use foil to line an 8-inch square pan and butter the foil. Microwave white chocolate until melted and mix until smooth. Mix in pomegranate seeds and coconut.
- Transfer to the prepared pan. Microwave dark chocolate until melted. Drizzle melted dark chocolate on top of white chocolate mixture. Chill in the refrigerator for about an hour until

firm. Take the chocolate mixture out of the pan by lifting with foil. Discard foil and break apart into pieces. Keep in an airtight container to store.

Nutrition Information

- Calories: 155 calories
- Total Carbohydrate: 20 g
- Cholesterol: 1 mg
- Total Fat: 9 g
- Fiber: 1 g
- Protein: 2 g
- Sodium: 23 mg

---

107. Chocolate Pralines, Mexican Style

"These pralines are creamy thanks to its secret ingredients, marshmallows."
Serving: 36 | Prep: 20m | Ready in: 1h40m

Ingredients

- 1 1/2 cups white sugar
- 1/2 cup packed light brown sugar
- 1/2 cup evaporated whole milk
- 3 tbsps. light corn syrup
- 1 tbsp. unsweetened cocoa powder
- 4 large marshmallows
- 1/2 tsp. vanilla extract
- 2 tsps. butter
- 2 cups chopped pecans

Direction

- Using parchment paper, line a baking sheet.
- In a saucepan, stir cocoa powder, corn syrup, evaporated milk, light brown sugar and white sugar; over medium heat, bring the mixture to a full rolling boil. Lower the heat to medium low; cook while stirring constantly until the candy thermometer measures the syrup to be at 220°F (104°C). When you drop a small amount of syrup into cold water, it should form a soft ball that will become flat once you

take out of the water and place on a flat surface.

- Take pan out of the heat, stir in pecans, butter, vanilla extract and marshmallows; beat candy for about 10 minutes by hand until creamy and candy starts setting up slightly at the edges of the pan.
- Drop tsps. of warm candy onto the parchment paper; arrange space in between so that pralines can slightly spread. Cool candy thoroughly; serve.

Nutrition Information

- Calories: 100 calories;
- Total Carbohydrate: 14.6 g
- Cholesterol: 2 mg
- Total Fat: 4.9 g
- Protein: 0.8 g
- Sodium: 8 mg

108. Chocolate Pretzel Rings

"Everyone loves these chocolate-covered pretzels."
Serving: about 4 dozen. | Prep: 25m | Ready in: 30m

Ingredients

- 48 to 50 pretzel rings or squares
- 48 to 50 milk chocolate or striped chocolate kisses
- 1/4 cup milk chocolate M&M's

Direction

- Grease baking sheets and lay the pretzels on these greased sheets; put chocolate kiss in the center of each pretzel. Bake at 275 degrees till chocolate becomes soft, about 2-3 minutes. Get the pretzels out of oven.
- Put an M&M candy on each pretzel, press down lightly so that the pretzel holes are filled with chocolate. Chill in the fridge for 5-10 minutes till chocolate becomes firm. Keep in an airtight container at room temperature.

Nutrition Information

- Calories: 34 calories
- Total Carbohydrate: 5 g
- Cholesterol: 1 mg
- Total Fat: 2 g
- Fiber: 0 g
- Protein: 1 g
- Sodium: 31 mg

109. Chocolate Pretzel Treats

"You only need 3 ingredients to make this mouth-watering treat. Quick and easy treat using three easy to find ingredients: Hershey's® Kisses, pretzels, and M&M's®."
Serving: 40 | Prep: 10m | Ready in: 22m

Ingredients

- 1 (15 oz.) package small pretzel twists
- 1 (8 oz.) package milk chocolate candy kisses (such as Hershey's Kisses®), unwrapped
- 1 (1.69 oz.) package candy-coated milk chocolate pieces (such as M&M's®)

Direction

- To preheat: set oven to 80°C (175°F).
- Lay pretzels on a baking sheet. On the center of each pretzel put one candy kiss.
- Put the pretzels in the preheated oven to warm for 2 minutes till the candy kiss becomes slightly tender and shiny.
- Put a chocolate piece coated by candy on top of the candy kiss of each pretzel; press it down. Chill in the fridge for 10 minutes.

Nutrition Information

- Calories: 36 calories;
- Total Carbohydrate: 4.5 g
- Cholesterol: 1 mg
- Total Fat: 2 g
- Protein: 0.5 g
- Sodium: 12 mg

110. Chocolate Pretzels

"These chocolate pretzels are unique."
Serving: 24 | Prep: 10m | Ready in: 12m

Ingredients

- 24 circular pretzels
- 24 milk chocolate candy kisses
- 1 (1.69 oz.) package mini candy-coated chocolates

Direction

- Set the oven to 350°F (175°C) and start preheating.
- Arrange pretzels on baking sheets. Unwrap candy kisses; put one in each pretzel's center.
- Transfer to the prepared oven for 1-2 minutes until kisses melt. Take out of the oven; put a candy-coated chocolate in each pretzel's center. Chill in the fridge until set.

Nutrition Information

- Calories: 62 calories;
- Total Carbohydrate: 9.7 g
- Cholesterol: 1 mg
- Total Fat: 1.9 g
- Protein: 1.2 g
- Sodium: 70 mg

111. Chocolate Raisin Truffles

"Sweet and affordable!"
Serving: 2-1/2 dozen. | Prep: 15m | Ready in: 20m

Ingredients

- 1 cup milk chocolate chips
- 1/4 cup light corn syrup
- 2 tbsps. confectioners' sugar
- 1-1/2 tsps. vanilla extract
- 1-1/2 cups raisins
- Nonpareils, sprinkles and/or ground nuts

Direction

- Melt chips in microwave-safe bowl. Mix vanilla, confectioners' sugar and corn syrup in till smooth. Mix raisins in till coated evenly.
- By teaspoonfuls, drop on waxed paper-lined baking sheet then roll truffles in nuts/sprinkles/nonpareils.

Nutrition Information

- Calories: 61 calories
- Total Carbohydrate: 12 g
- Cholesterol: 1 mg
- Total Fat: 2 g
- Fiber: 0 g
- Protein: 1 g
- Sodium: 9 mg

112. Chocolate Rum Truffles

"Silky chocolatey candies."
Serving: 3 dozen. | Prep: 25m | Ready in: 25m

Ingredients

- 14 oz. semisweet chocolate, divided
- 1 cup heavy whipping cream
- 1/3 cup butter, softened
- 1 tsp. rum extract
- 1/2 cup finely chopped pecans or walnuts, toasted

Direction

- Chop 12-oz. chocolate coarsely; put aside. Heat cream on low heat in saucepan till bubbles appear around pan's sides. Take off heat; add chopped chocolate, mixing till smooth and melted.
- Cool it to room temperature; mix extract and butter in. Tightly cover; refrigerate till firm or for 6 hours.
- Grate leftover chocolate; put in shallow dish. Add nuts; put aside. Form tablespoonfuls chilled chocolate mixture to balls. Put onto waxed paper-lined baking sheets. Refrigerate

till easy to handle if truffles are soft. In chocolate-nut mixture, roll truffles. Keep in airtight container in the fridge.

Nutrition Information

- Calories: 54 calories
- Total Carbohydrate: 1 g
- Cholesterol: 14 mg
- Total Fat: 6 g
- Fiber: 0 g
- Protein: 0 g
- Sodium: 20 mg

113.Chocolate Salami

"This quick, easy and delicious dessert comes from Italy. It is great on its own but whip cream is also a terrific companion."
Serving: 6 | Prep: 10m | Ready in: 8h10m

Ingredients

- 1/2 cup white sugar
- 1/2 cup unsweetened cocoa powder (such as Hershey's®)
- 1/2 cup melted butter
- 1 (1 lb.) package sweetened chestnut puree
- 1/2 cup chopped almonds
- 1/2 cup chopped walnuts

Direction

- Mix chestnut puree, butter, cocoa powder, sugar together in a bowl. Fold in the walnuts and almonds till all blended evenly. Make a log by patting the mixture then use wax paper to wrap tightly. Chill in the fridge overnight then cut to serve the next day.

Nutrition Information

- Calories: 528 calories;
- Total Carbohydrate: 68.8 g
- Cholesterol: 41 mg
- Total Fat: 26.7 g
- Protein: 7.3 g

- Sodium: 111 mg

114. Chocolate Sour Cream Fudge

"This fudge is always sold out!"
Serving: 64 | Prep: 10m | Ready in: 40m

Ingredients

- 2 cups white sugar
- 1/2 cup sour cream
- 1/3 cup light corn syrup
- 2 tbsps. butter
- 1 tsp. vanilla extract
- 2 (1 oz.) squares unsweetened chocolate
- 1/2 cup chopped walnuts

Direction

- Brush an 8 inch square baking dish with butter, and put aside. Mix butter, corn syrup, sour cream and sugar in a heavy saucepan. Boil; cook with a cover for a minute. Stir until blended well. Take the lid out; without stirring, heat to between 234 and 240°F (112 to 116°C), or until when you drop a small amount of syrup into cold water, it becomes a soft balls that becomes flat when you take it out of water and transfer to a flat surface.
- Take out of the heat; add vanilla and chocolate. Do not stir. Place the pan on a wire rack until the mixture cools to about 175°F (80°C). This may take about 15 minutes.
- Using wooden spoon, beat the fudge until it become thicken and no longer glossy. Stir in walnuts; transfer to the buttered dish. Evenly spread; put aside to cool. Cut into small squares.

Nutrition Information

- Calories: 47 calories;
- Total Carbohydrate: 8 g
- Cholesterol: 2 mg
- Total Fat: 1.8 g
- Protein: 0.3 g
- Sodium: 5 mg

115. Chocolate Spiders

"It's fast, simple and very tasty!"
Serving: 20 | Prep: 5m | Ready in: 30m

Ingredients

- 1 lb. chocolate confectioners' coating
- 1 (8.5 oz.) package chow mein noodles

Direction

- Chop chocolate confectioners' coating. Then put into heatproof bowl over the simmering water. Cook until smooth and melted, stirring occasionally. Discard from the heat. Mix in chow mein noodles until they are distributed evenly. Spoon out to the preferred size onto the waxed paper. Allow to cool thoroughly. Then serve or preserve.

Nutrition Information

- Calories: 172 calories;
- Total Carbohydrate: 17.6 g
- Cholesterol: 0 mg
- Total Fat: 12.7 g
- Protein: 2.8 g
- Sodium: 54 mg

116. Chocolate Spoons

"For this recipe, you will need 20 to 24 plastic spoons."
Serving: 24

Ingredients

- 1 cup semisweet chocolate chips
- 3/4 cup milk chocolate chips

Direction

- In a microwave-safe bowl, microwave semisweet chocolate pieces for 2 to 3 minutes until melted and mix until smooth. Dip the spoons into chocolate. Place the spoons onto the wax paper and chill in the refrigerator until the chocolate is hard.
- In a microwave, melt the milk chocolate pieces for 2 to 3 minutes and mix until smooth. Add the chocolate to the plastic bag and cut its corner off. Drizzle melted chocolate onto the spoons. Chill in the refrigerator until the chocolate hardens.
- Wrap each spoon individually and keep in a dry, cool place.

Nutrition Information

- Calories: 84 calories;
- Total Carbohydrate: 10.6 g
- Cholesterol: 1 mg
- Total Fat: 4.4 g
- Protein: 1.1 g
- Sodium: 0 mg

117. Chocolate Truffle

"Coffee flavored and velvety candies."
Serving: 1 dozen. | Prep: 25m | Ready in: 25m

Ingredients

- 3/4 cup semisweet chocolate chips
- 3 tbsps. plus 1 tsp. cream cheese, softened
- 1-3/4 tsps. instant coffee granules
- 1/2 tsp. water
- 4 oz. dark chocolate candy coating, chopped
- 3 tbsps. vanilla or white chips
- 1 tsp. shortening

Direction

- Melt chocolate chips in a small microwave-safe bowl. Add water, coffee granules and cream cheese; stir well. Chill till firm enough to handle.
- Form to 1-inch balls; put onto a waxed paper-lined baking sheet and chill till firm for 1-2 hours.
- Melt candy coating in a microwave-safe bowl. In coating, dip balls; put on a baking sheet. Let stand till set.

- Melt shortening and vanilla chips in another microwave-safe bowl; mix till smooth. Put in a plastic/pastry bag; cut hole in corner of bag. Drizzle on truffles. Keep in the fridge.

Nutrition Information

- Calories: 125 calories
- Total Carbohydrate: 14 g
- Cholesterol: 5 mg
- Total Fat: 8 g
- Fiber: 1 g
- Protein: 1 g
- Sodium: 15 mg

118.Chocolate Truffles

"A super easy recipe."
Serving: Makes 30 to 36 truffles

Ingredients

- 12 oz. good-quality semi-sweet or bittersweet chocolate
- 2/3 cup heavy cream or nondairy whipping cream
- 2 tbsps. Dutch processed cocoa powder
- 2 tbsps. confectioner's sugar
- 3 tbsps. finely chopped unsalted pistachios, almonds, or hazelnuts

Direction

- By hand/food processor fitted with metal blade, chop chocolate finely; put into medium bowl. Put cream into small heavy saucepan; put on rolling boil on medium heat. Put cream on chocolate; mix gently to melt chocolate with a wooden spoon. Don't stir/whisk too strongly or you'll put air in. Cover; chill for 2 hours till firm.
- Line waxed/parchment paper on baking sheet. Drop mixture by rounded teaspoonfuls with small melon baller/ice-cream scoop on prepped sheet. Freeze for 20 minutes till firm.
- Put chopped nuts, confectioner's sugar and cocoa into 3 different shallow bowls.

- Roll 1/3 balls into cocoa mixture, 1/3 in confectioner's sugar and 1/3 in chopped nuts. Roll between your palms quickly to shape them to perfect round shape. Reroll in sugar/nuts if too much falls off. In 1 layer, put back onto parchment-lined baking sheet/other parchment-lined container. Use plastic to cover; chill till serving time. You can make this 10 days in advance; remain refrigerated.

Nutrition Information

- Calories: 73
- Total Carbohydrate: 8 g
- Cholesterol: 5 mg
- Total Fat: 5 g
- Fiber: 1 g
- Protein: 1 g
- Sodium: 3 mg
- Saturated Fat: 3 g

119. Chocolate Turtles

"We can never have enough of these lovely candies. This is also a perfect sweet gift for your friends."
Serving: 3 dozen. | Prep: 30m | Ready in: 30m

Ingredients

- 1 package (14 oz.) caramels
- 1-1/2 tbsps. milk
- 1 package (6 oz.) pecan halves
- 1 cup (6 oz.) semisweet chocolate chips
- 1 tbsp. shortening

Direction

- Microwave or heat milk and caramels in a double boiler to melt. Mix until the mixture is smooth. Arrange pecan halves in groups of 3 on a greased baking sheet. Scoop 1 tbsp. melted caramel over each pecan cluster.
- Put in the refrigerator. Melt shortening and chocolate chips, then spread over clusters. Chill in the refrigerator.

Nutrition Information

- Calories: 101 calories
- Total Carbohydrate: 12 g
- Cholesterol: 1 mg
- Total Fat: 6 g
- Fiber: 1 g
- Protein: 1 g
- Sodium: 28 mg

120. Chocolate Turtles® (the Candy)

"Homemade chocolate turtles."
Serving: 40 | Prep: 15m | Ready in: 1h25m

Ingredients

- 2 cups pecan halves
- 2 (12 oz.) bags chocolate chips
- 25 individually wrapped caramels, unwrapped
- 2 tbsps. water
- 1/2 cup butter, softened

Direction

- Set the oven to 350°F (175°C) and start preheating.
- Place pecans on a baking sheet.
- Bake pecans in the prepared oven until lightly browned and fragrant, about 7 minutes.
- In the top of a double boiler, over simmering water, melt chocolate chips; stir frequently and scrape down the sides, using a rubber spatula, to prevent it from scorching.
- Using aluminum foil, line a baking sheet; grease with butter.
- In a saucepan, over low heat, mix butter, water and caramels; cook while stirring occasionally until smooth and melted. Fold in pecans.
- Drop caramel mixture onto the lined baking sheet by spoonful. Let cool to harden.
- Drizzle chocolate over caramel nut clusters. Keep in the fridge for about an hour to set.

Nutrition Information

- Calories: 162 calories;
- Total Carbohydrate: 16.2 g
- Cholesterol: 7 mg
- Total Fat: 11.7 g
- Protein: 1.5 g
- Sodium: 34 mg

121. Chocolate Walnut Fudge

"The best fudge recipe I've ever made!"
Serving: 36 | Prep: 10m | Ready in: 2h

Ingredients

- 1/2 cup butter
- 1 cup semisweet chocolate chips
- 1 tsp. vanilla extract
- 2 cups white sugar
- 1 (5 oz.) can evaporated milk
- 10 large marshmallows
- 1 cup chopped walnuts

Direction

- Grease an 8x8 inch dish with butter.
- Put vanilla, chocolate chips and butter in a mixing bowl. Put aside.
- Mix marshmallows, milk and sugar together in a medium saucepan over medium heat. Heat up to a boil, mixing constantly. Lower the heat to low and cook 6 minutes longer, mixing frequently. Take off from heat.
- Add marshmallow mixture over the mixture in the mixing bowl. Beat the whole mixture until it loses its gloss and thickens. Fold in nuts quickly and add to greased pan. Chill a few hours until set.

Nutrition Information

- Calories: 121 calories;
- Total Carbohydrate: 16.5 g
- Cholesterol: 8 mg
- Total Fat: 6.4 g
- Protein: 1 g

- Sodium: 24 mg

122. Chocolate Zebra Clusters

"These beautiful treats are very easy to make."
Serving: 2-1/2 dozen. | Prep: 30m | Ready in: 30m

Ingredients

- 2 cups (12 oz.) semisweet chocolate chips
- 12 oz. white candy coating, coarsely chopped, divided
- 1-1/4 cups salted peanuts
- 1-1/4 cups crisp rice cereal
- 2-1/4 cups miniature marshmallows
- 1 tsp. shortening

Direction

- Using waxed paper, line 2 baking sheets; put aside. Melt 7 oz. white candy coating and chips at 70% power in a microwave; stir until smooth. Stir in cereal and peanuts. Slightly cool; fold in marshmallows. Drop onto lined baking sheets by rounded tablespoonfuls.
- Melt the rest of the candy coating and shortening in microwave; stir until smooth. Place in a plastic bag or pastry; create a small hole in the corner of the bag. Drizzle over clusters. Keep in the fridge for 5 minutes or until set. Keep in an airtight container.

Nutrition Information

- Calories: 166 calories
- Total Carbohydrate: 20 g
- Cholesterol: 0 mg
- Total Fat: 10 g
- Fiber: 1 g
- Protein: 2 g
- Sodium: 40 mg

123. Chocolate, Peanut & Pretzel Toffee Crisps

"It's a yummy treat!"
Serving: 2-1/2 lbs.. | Prep: 25m | Ready in: 35m

Ingredients

- 40 saltines
- 3/4 cup butter, cubed
- 3/4 cup packed brown sugar
- 1 tsp. vanilla extract
- 2 cups (12 oz.) semisweet chocolate chips
- 1 cup cocktail peanuts
- 1 cup broken pretzel sticks
- 3/4 cup M&M's minis

Direction

- Start preheating the oven to 350°. Line foil on a 15x10x1-inch baking pan. Lightly coat foil with oil. Place on the foil with the saltines in a single layer.
- Melt butter in a large heavy saucepan over medium heat. Mix in the brown sugar. Boil; cook while stirring until the sugar dissolves, or about 2-3 mins. Discard from the heat; then stir in the vanilla. Evenly spread over crackers.
- Bake until bubbly, or about 8 to 10 mins. Sprinkle with the chocolate chips immediately. Let the chips soften for 2 mins, spread over the top. Scatter on top with M&M's minis, pretzels and peanuts; settle the toppings into chocolate by shaking the pan. Let it cool.
- Place in the refrigerator, uncovered, until set, or about 60 mins. Break it into pieces. Keep in an airtight container.

124. Chocolate-coated Pretzels

"Pretty pretzels at any occasion for all year round."
Serving: 5-6 dozen. | Prep: 15m | Ready in: 15m

Ingredients

- 1 to 1-1/4 lbs. white and/or milk chocolate candy coating, coarsely chopped

- 1 package (8 oz.) miniature pretzels
- Nonpariels, colored jimmies and colored sugar, optional

Direction

- Melt half of the candy coating at a time in a microwave; mix until smooth. Dip the pretzels into the candy coating; let excess coating drip off. Put the pretzels onto a waxed paper; let them sit until almost set. Garnish as you want; let them sit until set.

Nutrition Information

- Calories: 134 calories
- Total Carbohydrate: 21 g
- Cholesterol: 0 mg
- Total Fat: 5 g
- Fiber: 0 g
- Protein: 1 g
- Sodium: 140 mg

125. Chocolate-covered Apricot-pecan Pretzels

"Really delicious treat for holidays with these salty pretzel rods dipped in a caramel, apricot and pecan mixture and covered with dark chocolate."
Serving: 3-1/2 dozen. | Prep: 01h15m | Ready in: 01h15m

Ingredients

- 1 package (6 oz.) dried apricots, finely chopped
- 1-1/3 cups chopped pecans, divided
- 2 packages (11 oz. each) Kraft caramel bits
- 1/4 cup water
- 42 pretzel rods
- 3 cups dark chocolate chips
- 1 tbsp. shortening

Direction

- Mix together 2/3 cup of pecans and apricots in a small bowl, then put bowl aside.

- Melt caramel bits in a big heavy saucepan filled with water on medium low heat, while stirring continuously. Scoop over 2/3 of each pretzel with caramel, then rotate rod to coat all sides and let excess caramel drip off.
- Use apricot mixture to sprinkle over caramel. On a baking sheet lined with waxed paper, position pretzel and chill in the refrigerator until set, about half an hour.
- Melt chips in another heavy saucepan along with shortening on low heat, while stirring continuously. Scoop over coated ends of pretzels with chocolate and let the excess chocolate drip off. Move pretzels back to the baking sheet and use leftover pecans to sprinkle on top. Keep in airtight containers.

Nutrition Information

- Calories: 228 calories
- Total Carbohydrate: 33 g
- Cholesterol: 0 mg
- Total Fat: 11 g
- Fiber: 1 g
- Protein: 3 g
- Sodium: 165 mg

126. Chocolate-covered Chips

"These candies are wonderful as they are not only sweet but also savory. People always ask for more!"
Serving: about 4 lbs.. | Prep: 25m | Ready in: 25m

Ingredients

- 1-1/2 lbs. white candy coating, coarsely chopped
- 1 package (14 oz.) ridged potato chips
- 1-1/2 lbs. milk chocolate or dark chocolate candy coating, coarsely chopped

Direction

- Put white coating in a microwave to melt and stir till becomes smooth. Dip chips halfway in coating; let the excess coating drip off. Use waxed paper to line baking sheets and lay chips on the prepared baking sheets to set.

- Melt dark chocolate or milk chocolate. Dip the other half of chips in melted milk/ dark chocolate, let the excess drip off. Lay chips on waxed paper to set. Keep in an airtight container.

Nutrition Information

- Calories: 196 calories
- Total Carbohydrate: 24 g
- Cholesterol: 0 mg
- Total Fat: 11 g
- Fiber: 1 g
- Protein: 1 g
- Sodium: 61 mg

127. Chocolate-covered Coffee Beans

"This recipe has both chocolate and coffee flavors."
Serving: 1 cup. | Prep: 30m | Ready in: 30m

Ingredients

- 2/3 cup semisweet chocolate chips
- 1-1/2 tsps. shortening
- 1/2 cup coffee beans
- Baking cocoa, optional

Direction

- Melt shortening and chocolate chips in a microwave; stir until smooth. Coat coffee beans with chocolate; let any excess drip off. Transfer to waxed paper; allow to rest for 10-15 minutes.
- Roll in cocoa if preferred; allow to rest until set. Keep in an airtight container.

Nutrition Information

- Calories: 39 calories
- Total Carbohydrate: 5 g
- Cholesterol: 0 mg
- Total Fat: 2 g

- Fiber: 0 g
- Protein: 0 g
- Sodium: 2 mg

128. Chocolate-covered Pomegranate Seeds

"Chocolate covered pomegranate seeds."
Serving: about 1 lb. (2 dozen) | Prep: 5m | Ready in: 10m

Ingredients

- 1 package (12 oz.) dark chocolate chips
- 1 cup pomegranate seeds, patted dry

Direction

- Melt chocolate chips in a microwave; mix until smooth. Mix in pomegranate seeds.
- Drop the mixture onto the baking sheets that are lined with a waxed paper by tablespoonfuls. Chill in the refrigerator until firm, about 1 hour. Keep in between layers of waxed paper that are placed in an airtight container and store inside the fridge.

Nutrition Information

- Calories: 70 calories
- Total Carbohydrate: 10 g
- Cholesterol: 0 mg
- Total Fat: 4 g
- Fiber: 1 g
- Protein: 1 g
- Sodium: 5 mg

129. Chocolate-covered Praline Chews

"Beautiful and tasty treats."
Serving: about 3 dozen. | Prep: 40m | Ready in: 01h25m

Ingredients

- 1 cup sugar

- 1 cup light corn syrup
- Dash salt
- 1/4 cup butter, cubed
- 2 tsps. milk
- 2 cups pecan halves
- 1/2 tsp. vanilla extract
- 6 oz. white candy coating, coarsely chopped
- 6 oz. milk chocolate candy coating, coarsely chopped

Direction

- Combine the sugar, corn syrup and salt in a large heavy saucepan. Heat until boiling over medium heat; cook till it reads 245° on a candy thermometer (firm-ball stage), stir sometimes. Mix in the butter, milk and pecans slowly. Keep on cooking until the temperature turns back to 245°. Take off the heat; mix in the vanilla. On greased baking sheets, immediately drop tablespoonfuls of the mixture. Let cool.
- Melt white candy coating in a microwave at 70% power for 1 minute; stir. Microwave at more 10- to 20-second intervals, stir till smooth.
- Into the coating, dip candies halfway and let the excess drip off. Put them onto baking sheets lined with waxed paper; chill in refrigerator until set, for 15 minutes.
- Melt milk chocolate coating in a microwave at 70% power for 1 minute; stir. Microwave at more 10- to 20-second intervals, mix till smooth.
- Dip the other half of each candy and let the excess drip off. Put them back onto baking sheets; chill in refrigerator until set.

130. Chocolate-dipped Apricots

"This is a healthy dessert recipe for chocolate-dipped dried apricots and can satisfy your sweet tooth. Experiment this chocolate-dipped fruit with your favorite dried fruit slices."
Serving: 36 | Ready in: 45m

Ingredients

- ½ cup bittersweet chocolate chips
- 36 dried apricots
- 2 tbsps. chopped pistachios

Direction

- Line parchment or wax paper onto a baking sheet.
- In a small glass bowl, put chocolate chips. Heat for 1 minute in microwave on Medium. Mix and then continue heating in microwave in 20-second intervals while stirring after each interval until melted. (Alternatively, melt in the top of a double boiler atop hot but not boiling water.)
- Submerge half of each apricot into melted chocolate. Allow the excess to fall back into the bowl. Put the dipped fruit onto the prepared baking sheet. Sprinkle pistachios on top of the chocolate. Chill for about 30 minutes until the chocolate is set.

Nutrition Information

- Calories: 21 calories;
- Total Carbohydrate: 4 g
- Cholesterol: 0 mg
- Total Fat: 1 g
- Fiber: 1 g
- Protein: 0 g
- Sodium: 0 mg
- Sugar: 3 g
- Saturated Fat: 0 g

131. Chocolate-dipped Candy Canes

"A great and easy combination of chocolate and peppermint."
Serving: 1 dozen. | Prep: 20m | Ready in: 25m

Ingredients

- 1 cup semisweet chocolate chips
- 12 candy canes (6 inches each)
- 3 oz. white baking chocolate, chopped
- Optional toppings: assorted colored sugars or sprinkles and crushed candies

Direction

- Melt chocolate chips in a microwave; stir until smooth. Dip candy canes' curved ends into chocolate; let the excess drip off. Put onto a waxed paper.
- Melt white baking chocolate in a microwave; mix until smooth. Drizzle over the chocolate. If desired, garnish with toppings. Let it sit until set.
- Use to stir servings of hot cocoa.

132. Chocolate-dipped Peanut Nougat

"If you need a delicious gifts or a special holiday dessert, this peanut and marshmallow crème sweet treat is really for you."
Serving: about 4-1/2 lbs. (about 150 pieces). | Prep: 40m | Ready in: 60m

Ingredients

- 1 tbsp. butter
- 1 jar (16 oz.) dry roasted peanuts
- 3 jars (7 oz. each) marshmallow creme
- 2-1/4 cups sugar
- 2-1/4 cups corn syrup
- 6 tbsps. butter, cubed
- 1-1/2 tsps. vanilla extract
- 1/4 tsp. salt
- 1 to 1-1/2 lbs. dark or milk chocolate candy coating, melted

Direction

- Use foil to line a 15x10x1 in. pan, let the ends of foil extend over sides of pan by an inch; use a tbsp. of butter to grease foil. Use peanuts to sprinkle evenly into pan.
- Put marshmallow crème in a large heatproof bowl. Mix corn syrup and sugar in a large heavy saucepan. Bring to a boil on medium heat and stir constantly to dissolve sugar. Dip a pastry brush in water then use the brush to wash down sides of pan to remove sugar crystals. Cook without stirring for 10 minutes till a candy thermometer reaches 280 degrees (this is the soft crack stage).
- Get the saucepan off heat; allow it to cool for 2 minutes. Transfer the sugar mixture over marshmallow crème (remember not to scrape the saucepan). Mix in salt, vanilla, cubes of butter. Pour the mixture over peanuts in pan immediately, remember to spread evenly. Let sit for 3 hours in minimum or till set.
- Lift candy out of pan by foil. Remove foil gently. Grease a knife and use the knife to cut candy into 1x1 in. squares.
- Dip candy into melted candy coating; let the excess coating to drip off. Line baking sheets by waxed paper then place candy on baking sheets; chill in the fridge till candy is set. Place between waxed paper layers and store in airtight containers.

133. Chocolate-dipped Pretzel Rods

"These beautiful pretzels can be a lovely gift."
Serving: about 4-1/2 dozen. | Prep: 25m | Ready in: 35m

Ingredients

- 3 cups chopped toasted almonds
- 2 packages (14 oz. each) caramels, unwrapped
- 2 tbsps. water
- 2 packages (10 oz. each) pretzel rods
- 2 packages (10 to 12 oz. each) white baking chips

- 2 packages (10 to 12 oz. each) dark chocolate chips
- Assorted sprinkles, optional

Direction

- Arrange almonds in a shallow dish. Microwave water and caramels in a large measuring cups on high power, stirring after each 60 seconds, until caramels are melted.
- Immerse 3/4 of each pretzel into melted caramel, dripping off excess. (Rewarm caramel in the microwave if the mixture looks too thick for dipping). Roll coated pretzels in almonds. Arrange on waxed paper until firm.
- Melt white baking chips in a microwave; whisk until no lumps remain. Immerse 1/2 of the caramel-coated pretzels in the melted white baking chips, dripping off the excess. Garnish with sprinkles if desired; place back onto the waxed paper until firm. Repeat the steps with the rest of pretzels and chocolate chips.
- Wrap pretzels in cellophane gift bags and tie with ribbon; or store in airtight container

Nutrition Information

- Calories: 245 calories
- Total Carbohydrate: 34 g
- Cholesterol: 3 mg
- Total Fat: 12 g
- Fiber: 2 g
- Protein: 5 g
- Sodium: 278 mg

134. Chocolate-dipped Pretzels

"This chocolate-dipped pretzel recipe will comfort your sweet tooth immediately."
Serving: 24 | Ready in: 45m

Ingredients

- ½ cup bittersweet chocolate chips
- 24 pretzel twists, preferably whole-wheat, or 12 pretzel rods, broken in half

- 2 tbsps. cocoa nibs (see Tip)

Direction

- Use wax or parchment paper to line a baking sheet.
- In a small glass bowl, add chocolate chips. Microwave on medium setting for about one minute. Stir and keep on microwaving on in 20-second intervals until melted while stirring after every interval. (Another way: melt chocolate chips in the top of a double boiler over hot water but not boiling.)
- Dip half of each pretzel piece into the melted chocolate. Allow the excess to drip back into bowl. Put dipped pretzels on prepared baking sheet. Sprinkle the chocolate with cocoa nibs. Chill for a half hour until chocolate is set.

Nutrition Information

- Calories: 35 calories;
- Total Carbohydrate: 6 g
- Cholesterol: 0 mg
- Total Fat: 2 g
- Fiber: 1 g
- Protein: 1 g
- Sodium: 8 mg
- Sugar: 2 g
- Saturated Fat: 1 g

135. Chocolate-dipped Treats

"These chocolate marshmallow treats are perfect for Christmas."
Serving: about 4 dozen. | Prep: 15m | Ready in: 15m

Ingredients

- 1 cup (6 oz.) semisweet chocolate chips
- 1 tbsp. shortening
- 1/4 tsp. ground cinnamon
- Large marshmallows, miniature pretzels and/or whole fresh strawberries

Direction

- Melt shortening and chocolate chips in a microwave. Stir in cinnamon. Coat 3/4 of each pretzel, marshmallow and/or strawberry in chocolate. Arrange on a baking sheet lined with waxed paper. Keep in the fridge for about half an hour until set.

Nutrition Information

- Calories: 19 calories
- Total Carbohydrate: 2 g
- Cholesterol: 0 mg
- Total Fat: 1 g
- Fiber: 0 g
- Protein: 0 g
- Sodium: 0 mg

136. Chocolate-peanut Butter Keto Cups

"You can keep it either in the freezer or fridge."
Serving: 12 | Prep: 15m | Ready in: 1h18m

Ingredients

- 1 cup coconut oil
- 1/2 cup natural peanut butter
- 2 tbsps. heavy cream
- 1 tbsp. cocoa powder
- 1 tsp. liquid stevia
- 1/4 tsp. vanilla extract
- 1/4 tsp. kosher salt
- 1 oz. chopped roasted salted peanuts

Direction

- In a saucepan, melt coconut oil over low heat, for 3 to 5 minutes. Mix in peanut butter till smooth. Whisk in salt, vanilla extract, liquid stevia, cocoa powder, and heavy cream.
- Add the mixture of chocolate and peanut butter into the 12 silicone muffin molds. Sprinkle the top with peanuts evenly. Put the molds onto a baking sheet.

- Place the chocolate-peanut butter mixture in the freezer until firm, for at least 1 hour. Take off from the molds and place them into an airtight container or resealable plastic bag.

Nutrition Information

- Calories: 246 calories;
- Total Carbohydrate: 3.3 g
- Cholesterol: 3 mg
- Total Fat: 26 g
- Protein: 3.4 g
- Sodium: 89 mg

137. Chocolaty Peanut Clusters

"It's so easy to make candy!"
Serving: 6-1/2 lbs.. | Prep: 25m | Ready in: 02h25m

Ingredients

- 1 jar (16 oz.) salted dry roasted peanuts
- 1 jar (16 oz.) unsalted dry roasted peanuts
- 1 package (11-1/2 oz.) milk chocolate chips
- 1 package (10 oz.) peanut butter chips
- 3 packages (10 to 12 oz. each) white baking chips
- 2 packages (10 oz. each) 60% cacao bittersweet chocolate baking chips

Direction

- Combine peanuts in a 6-quart slow cooker. Layer with remaining ingredients in order given (but don't stir). Cook, covered, on low, stirring halfway through cooking until the chips are melted, about 120-150 mins.
- Combine by stirring. Drop onto waxed paper by tablespoonfuls. Place in the refrigerator until set. Keep at the room temperature in an airtight container.

Nutrition Information

- Calories: 205 calories
- Total Carbohydrate: 18 g
- Cholesterol: 3 mg

- Total Fat: 14 g
- Fiber: 2 g
- Protein: 5 g
- Sodium: 68 mg

138. Christmas Bark Candy

""When M&M candies are used, this recipe is very attractive despite the absence of peppermint.""
Serving: 16 | Prep: 5m | Ready in: 15m

Ingredients

- 1 (10 oz.) package vanilla baking chips
- 2 tsps. vegetable oil
- 1 1/2 cups mini candy-coated chocolate pieces

Direction

- Use a foil or wax paper to line the baking pan. Combine vegetable oil and vanilla chips in a microwave-safe bowl, heat in a microwave on high until the chips liquefy. Stir until smooth, chill for 2 minutes. Add candy-coated chocolate pieces and stir. Pour the mixture into the baking pan, let it cool for 10 minutes and split into fragments.

Nutrition Information

- Calories: 177 calories;
- Total Carbohydrate: 21.3 g
- Cholesterol: 2 mg
- Total Fat: 8.9 g
- Protein: 1.9 g
- Sodium: 46 mg

139. Christmas Chocolate Bark 3 Ways: Pistachio, Pink Peppercorn, And Currant Bark

"A stunning chocolate bark with a festive Christmas feel."
Serving: 8 | Prep: 10m | Ready in: 57m

Ingredients

- 3 (4 oz.) bars dark chocolate, chopped, divided
- 4 tbsps. pink peppercorns
- 2 tbsps. chopped pistachio nuts
- 2 tbsps. dried currants

Direction

- In a microwave-safe bowl, heat 2/3 of dark chocolate in 15-second intervals for 1 to 2 minutes, mixing after every interval, till chocolate is nearly melted but some pieces remain. Take out of the microwave and mix till fully smooth. Put in the leftover 1/3 of dark chocolate. Mix thoroughly till the entire chocolate has melted.
- On a flat work area, lay out a big parchment paper sheet. Onto parchment paper, transfer the melted chocolate and with a spatula, spread into an even, thin layer. Quickly sprinkle currants, pistachios and pink peppercorns on top of chocolate before it firms.
- Let the chocolate sit for approximately 45 minutes to firm completely. Break apart into randomly sized portions and keep in an airtight container.

Nutrition Information

- Calories: 250 calories;
- Total Carbohydrate: 28.9 g
- Cholesterol: 2 mg
- Total Fat: 14.7 g
- Protein: 3 g
- Sodium: 14 mg

140. Coconut Almond Candy

"The mystery fixing in this handcrafted sweet is a genuine amazement."
Serving: 2 dozen. | Prep: 45m | Ready in: 45m

Ingredients

- 2 cups sweetened shredded coconut
- 1/2 cup mashed potatoes (with added milk and butter)
- 1/4 tsp. vanilla extract
- 1/8 tsp. salt, optional
- 2 cups confectioners' sugar
- 24 unblanched almonds, toasted
- 1 package (11-1/2 oz.) milk chocolate chips
- 1 tbsp. butter

Direction

- Mix salt (if needed), vanilla, potatoes and coconut in a big bowl. Beat in the confectioners' sugar gradually. Refrigerate with the cover for 1 hour, until firm enough to form.
- Form a blend into twenty-four 1-inch ovals using hands dusted with confectioners' sugar. Slightly flatten, and wrap each around 1 almond. Put onto baking sheets lined with waxed paper; freeze for minimum 30 minutes, until firm.
- Melt the butter and chips in a microwave; mix until smooth. Dip the candies in the chocolate blend with a fork; let excess drip off. Bring back to the baking sheets; refrigerate until set. Keep in an airtight container in the refrigerator between layers of waxed paper.

Nutrition Information

- Calories: 167 calories
- Total Carbohydrate: 23 g
- Cholesterol: 5 mg
- Total Fat: 8 g
- Fiber: 1 g
- Protein: 2 g
- Sodium: 61 mg

141. Coconut Chocolate Delights

"This deliciousness of this recipe was confirmed by my husband and friends."
Serving: about 6-1/2 dozen. | Prep: 01h15m | Ready in: 01h15m

Ingredients

- 1 package (8 oz.) cream cheese, softened
- 1 package (15-1/2 oz.) Oreo cookies, crushed
- 1 package (14 oz.) sweetened shredded coconut
- 2 cups sliced almonds
- 2 tsps. vanilla extract
- 3-1/2 cups semisweet chocolate chips
- 2 tbsps. plus 1-1/2 tsps. shortening

Direction

- Beat cream cheese in a large mixing bowl until no lumps remain. Add cookie crumbs and beat well. Put in vanilla, almonds and coconut; stir well. Form mixture into balls, about 1 inch in diameter. Arrange the balls on baking sheets; chill, covered, for a minimum of 1 hour.
- Combine shortening and chocolate chips in a microwaveable bowl. Microwave until melted, on high, stirring after each 15 seconds; whisk until no lumps remain. Immerse balls into melted chocolate, dripping off excess. Arrange on waxed paper until firm. Keep candies chilled in an airtight container in the fridge.

Nutrition Information

- Calories: 224 calories
- Total Carbohydrate: 23 g
- Cholesterol: 6 mg
- Total Fat: 15 g
- Fiber: 2 g
- Protein: 3 g
- Sodium: 104 mg

142. Coconut Chocolate-covered Cherries

"This recipe is divine."
Serving: about 5 dozen. | Prep: 25m | Ready in: 25m

Ingredients

- 1/2 cup butter, softened
- 3-3/4 cups confectioners' sugar
- 1/2 cup sweetened condensed milk
- 1 tsp. vanilla extract
- 2 cups sweetened shredded coconut
- 2 cups finely chopped walnuts
- 2 jars (16 oz. each) maraschino cherries with stems, well drained and patted dry
- 2 packages (11-1/2 oz. each) milk chocolate chips
- 1 tbsp. shortening

Direction

- Beat confectioners' sugar and butter until smooth in a large bowl. Whisk in vanilla and milk until well mixed and mixture resembles softened butter. Fold in walnuts and coconut.
- Form 2 teaspoonfuls of coconut mixture around each cherry with moist hands, shaping a ball. Transfer to a baking sheet lined with waxed paper. Keep in the fridge with a cover until chilled or for an hour.
- Melt shortening and chocolate chips in a microwave; stir until smooth. Dunk coated cherries in chocolate. Transfer to waxed paper; allow to rest until set. Keep in an airtight container at room temperature for up to 1 month.

Nutrition Information

- Calories: 131 calories
- Total Carbohydrate: 17 g
- Cholesterol: 6 mg
- Total Fat: 7 g
- Fiber: 1 g
- Protein: 2 g
- Sodium: 31 mg

143. Coconut Cream Eggs

"The filling of these natively constructed chocolate Easter eggs is great smooth and not very sweet."
Serving: 3 dozen. | Prep: 20m | Ready in: 20m

Ingredients

- 1 package (8 oz.) cream cheese, softened
- 1 tbsp. butter, softened
- 4 cups confectioners' sugar
- 1 cup sweetened shredded coconut
- 2 cups (12 oz.) semisweet chocolate chips
- 1 tbsp. shortening

Direction

- Beat the butter and cream cheese in a bowl until smooth. Put in coconut and sugar. Refrigerate until easy to manage, about 1-1/2 hours. Mold rounded tablespoonfuls of coconut blend into egg shapes with hands sprinkled with confectioners' sugar. Put onto a baking sheet lined with waxed paper. Freeze until slightly firm, about 2 hours.
- Melt the shortening and chocolate chips. Take a few eggs at a time out of the freezer; dip into chocolate blend until fully coated. Bring back to waxed paper; refrigerate until hardened. Keep in the fridge.

Nutrition Information

- Calories: 137 calories
- Total Carbohydrate: 21 g
- Cholesterol: 8 mg
- Total Fat: 7 g
- Fiber: 1 g
- Protein: 1 g
- Sodium: 30 mg

144. Coconut Joys

"This no-bake treat recipe is for those who are fans of coconut."
Serving: 1-1/2 dozen. | Prep: 20m | Ready in: 20m

Ingredients

- 1-1/2 cups sweetened shredded coconut
- 1 cup confectioners' sugar
- 1/4 cup butter, melted
- 1 oz. milk chocolate, melted
- 2 tbsps. chopped pecans

Direction

- Combine butter with confectioners' sugar and coconut in a large bowl. Shape mixture into balls about 1 inch.
- Create an indentation in the middle of each ball using the end of a wooden spoon handle. Fill the indentation with chocolate. Scatter top with pecans. Arrange on a baking sheet lined with waxed paper. Refrigerate until chocolate is hardened. Keep chilled in the fridge.

Nutrition Information

- Calories: 101 calories
- Total Carbohydrate: 11 g
- Cholesterol: 7 mg
- Total Fat: 6 g
- Fiber: 0 g
- Protein: 0 g
- Sodium: 38 mg

145. Coconut Snacks

"It is so simple that even your children can make."
Serving: 4 dozen. | Prep: 10m | Ready in: 10m

Ingredients

- 1 cup creamy peanut butter
- 1 cup confectioners' sugar
- 1/2 cup nonfat dry milk powder
- 4 tbsps. water

- 1 cup (6 oz.) semisweet chocolate chips
- 1-1/2 cups sweetened shredded coconut

Direction

- Beat water, milk, sugar and peanut butter in a bowl until they become smooth. Then fold in the chocolate chips. Shape into 1-inch balls, then roll in the coconut. Let chill until firm.

Nutrition Information

- Calories: 154 calories
- Total Carbohydrate: 16 g
- Cholesterol: 1 mg
- Total Fat: 10 g
- Fiber: 1 g
- Protein: 4 g
- Sodium: 79 mg

146. Coconut Yule Trees

"Everyone loves this macaroon recipe."
Serving: 2 dozen. | Prep: 15m | Ready in: 15m

Ingredients

- 3 cups sweetened shredded coconut
- 2 cups confectioners' sugar
- 1/4 cup butter, softened
- 1/4 cup half-and-half cream
- 1 tsp. almond extract
- 2 to 4 oz. dark chocolate candy coating
- Vanilla frosting, green sugar and assorted sprinkles

Direction

- Mix the first 5 ingredients in a large bowl. Drop by tablespoonfuls onto a baking sheet lined with waxed paper; keep in the fridge for an hour with a cover. Form into trees; transfer back to baking sheet.
- Melt chocolate coating in a microwave; stir until smooth. Scoop over or dip trunks of trees; let any excess drip off. Arrange on waxed paper; allow to rest until set. Garnish

trees as preferred with sprinkles, green sugar and frosting.

Nutrition Information

- Calories: 130 calories
- Total Carbohydrate: 17 g
- Cholesterol: 6 mg
- Total Fat: 7 g
- Fiber: 1 g
- Protein: 0 g
- Sodium: 51 mg

147. Coffee Shop Fudge

"This recipe is a winner."
Serving: 2 lbs.. | Prep: 15m | Ready in: 15m

Ingredients

- 1 cup chopped pecans
- 3 cups (18 oz.) semisweet chocolate chips
- 1 can (14 oz.) sweetened condensed milk
- 2 tbsps. strong brewed coffee, room temperature
- 1 tsp. ground cinnamon
- 1/8 tsp. salt
- 1 tsp. vanilla extract

Direction

- Using foil, line an 8-in. square pan; butter the foil; put aside. Arrange pecans in a microwave-safe pie plate. Microwave without a cover for 3 minutes on high; after each minute, stir; put aside.
- Mix salt, cinnamon, coffee, milk and chocolate chips in a 2-qt. microwave-safe bowl. Microwave without a cover for a minute on high. Stir until smooth. Mix in pecans and vanilla. Spread immediately into the prepared pan.
- Keep in the fridge with a cover for about 2 hours until firm. Take out of the pan; cut into 1-in. squares. Keep at room temperature (70°-80°), covered.

Nutrition Information

- Calories: 311 calories
- Total Carbohydrate: 39 g
- Cholesterol: 11 mg
- Total Fat: 18 g
- Fiber: 3 g
- Protein: 5 g
- Sodium: 64 mg

148. Cookie Balls

"Immediately after dipping, you can decorate with colored sprinkles/chocolate jimmies. "
Serving: 36 | Prep: 50m | Ready in: 1h

Ingredients

- 1 lb. chocolate sandwich cookies, crushed
- 1 (8 oz.) package cream cheese, softened
- 1 lb. vanilla-flavored candy coating, melted

Direction

- Mix cream cheese and crushed cookies to make stiff dough in big mixing bowl; roll to balls. Use fork to dip in melted candy coating; rest on waxed paper till set.

Nutrition Information

- Calories: 148 calories;
- Total Carbohydrate: 16.7 g
- Cholesterol: 9 mg
- Total Fat: 8.6 g
- Protein: 1.9 g
- Sodium: 91 mg

149. Cookie Dough Truffles

"Easy truffles with yummy filling."
Serving: 5-1/2 dozen. | Prep: 60m | Ready in: 60m

Ingredients

- 1/2 cup butter, softened

- 3/4 cup packed brown sugar
- 1 tsp. vanilla extract
- 2 cups all-purpose flour
- 1 can (14 oz.) sweetened condensed milk
- 1/2 cup miniature semisweet chocolate chips
- 1/2 cup chopped walnuts
- 1-1/2 lbs. dark chocolate candy coating, coarsely chopped

Direction

- Cream brown sugar and butter till fluffy and light in big bowl; beat vanilla in. Alternately with milk, add flour slowly, beating well after every addition. Mix walnuts and chocolate chips in.
- Form to 1-in. balls; put onto waxed paper-lined baking sheets. Cover loosely; refrigerate till firm for 1-2 hours.
- Melt candy coating in microwave; mix till smooth. In coating, dip balls; let excess drip off. Put onto waxed paper-lined baking sheets and refrigerate for 15 minutes till firm. Remelt leftover candy coating if desired and drizzle on candies. Keep in the fridge.

Nutrition Information

- Calories: 121 calories
- Total Carbohydrate: 17 g
- Cholesterol: 6 mg
- Total Fat: 6 g
- Fiber: 0 g
- Protein: 1 g
- Sodium: 20 mg

150. Cookies & Cream Truffle Balls

"For simple truffles, I fold treats and cream cheddar into balls and dunk them in white chocolate."
Serving: about 3 dozen. | Prep: 30m | Ready in: 30m

Ingredients

- 1 package (14.3 oz.) Oreo cookies
- 1 package (8 oz.) cream cheese, softened

- 1 package (10 to 12 oz.) white baking chips, melted
- Green jimmies and sprinkles, optional

Direction

- In a food processor, pulse the cookies until fine crumbs shape. Put in the cream cheese; pulse until just mixed. Refrigerate with the cover until firm enough to form.
- Form the blend into 1-inch balls; put onto the waxed paper-lined baking sheets. Freeze with the cover for several hours to overnight.
- Dip the balls into the melted chips; let the excess drip off. Bring back to the pans. Dust instantly with sprinkles and jimmies if desired; allow to stand until set. Store in the covered containers in the fridge.

Nutrition Information

- Calories: 117 calories
- Total Carbohydrate: 13 g
- Cholesterol: 8 mg
- Total Fat: 7 g
- Fiber: 0 g
- Protein: 1 g
- Sodium: 73 mg

151. Cookies 'n' Cream Fudge

"Your kids will very like this!"
Serving: 3 dozen. | Prep: 25m | Ready in: 25m

Ingredients

- 16 Oreo cookies, broken into chunks, divided
- 1 can (14 oz.) sweetened condensed milk
- 2 tbsps. butter
- 2-2/3 cups white baking chips
- 1 tsp. vanilla extract
- Crushed peppermint candies, optional

Direction

- Line aluminum foil on an 8-inch square dish and spray with the cooking spray. Place 1/2 of broken cookies in the pan.
- Combine chips, butter and milk in a heavy saucepan. Over low heat, cook while stirring until the chips melt. Discard from the heat, then mix in vanilla.
- Transfer over the cookies in pan. If desired, add peppermint candies and remaining cookies on top. Place in the refrigerator, covered, at least 60 mins. Cut into squares.

Nutrition Information

- Calories: 133 calories
- Total Carbohydrate: 17 g
- Cholesterol: 8 mg
- Total Fat: 7 g
- Fiber: 0 g
- Protein: 2 g
- Sodium: 64 mg

152. Cookies 'n' Creme Fudge

"A great cookie recipe."
Serving: 40

Ingredients

- 3 (6 oz.) packages white chocolate baking squares
- 1 (14 oz.) can EAGLE BRAND® Sweetened Condensed Milk
- 1/8 tsp. salt
- 3 cups coarsely crushed chocolate creme-filled sandwich cookies

Direction

- Melt salt, sweetened condensed milk and white chocolate squares in heavy saucepan on low heat. Take off heat; mix crushed cookies in.
- Evenly spread in 8-in. wax paper-lined square pan; chill till firm or for 2 hours.

- Turn fudge on cutting board. Peel paper off; cut to squares. Keep leftovers in the fridge, covered.

Nutrition Information

- Calories: 143 calories;
- Total Carbohydrate: 15 g
- Cholesterol: 6 mg
- Total Fat: 6.3 g
- Protein: 1.5 g
- Sodium: 62 mg

153. Cookies-and-cream Truffles

"Put truffles to mini muffin liners/individual paper cups in airtight container in the fridge for 2 weeks."
Serving: 42 | Prep: 20m | Ready in: 1h25m

Ingredients

- 1 (14 oz.) package chocolate sandwich cookies (such as Oreo®)
- 1 (8 oz.) package cream cheese, cubed and softened
- 1 lb. semisweet chocolate, chopped
- 1 tbsp. shortening

Direction

- Line waxed paper on a baking sheet.
- In a food processor, pulse chocolate sandwich cookies till they're fine crumbs. Put 1/2 cup of crumbs in a small bowl then set aside. Put cream cheese in leftover crumbs in the food processor; pulse till combined well.
- Use dampened hands to form cream cheese mixture to walnut-sized balls.
- In a microwave-safe glass/ceramic bowl, melt shortening and chocolate in 30-second intervals, mixing after every melting, for 1-3 minutes.
- In chocolate mixture, dip balls; use a fork to turn to coat completely. Use 2 forks to lift truffles from chocolate mixture; let excess chocolate drip into bowl. Put truffles on the

prepared baking sheet; sprinkle leftover cookie crumbs immediately on truffles.

- Chill truffles for 1 hour till firm in the fridge.

Nutrition Information

- Calories: 119 calories;
- Total Carbohydrate: 13 g
- Cholesterol: 6 mg
- Total Fat: 7.4 g
- Protein: 1.7 g
- Sodium: 61 mg

154. Cow Pies Candy

"Children in my family really enjoy these cow pies."
Serving: 2 dozen. | Prep: 20m | Ready in: 20m

Ingredients

- 2 cups (12 oz.) milk chocolate chips
- 1 tbsp. shortening
- 1/2 cup raisins
- 1/2 cup chopped slivered almonds

Direction

- Melt shortening and chocolate chips over low heat in a heavy saucepan or microwave, stir until no lumps remain. Turn off the heat; mix in almonds and raisins. Drop by tablespoonfuls onto a sheet of waxed paper. Refrigerate until ready to serve.

Nutrition Information

- Calories: 199 calories
- Total Carbohydrate: 22 g
- Cholesterol: 6 mg
- Total Fat: 12 g
- Fiber: 2 g
- Protein: 3 g
- Sodium: 24 mg

155. Cranberry Almond Bark

"Special almond bark using dried cranberries. It's so simple and quick to make yet so impressive."
Serving: 1 lb.. | Prep: 15m | Ready in: 15m

Ingredients

- 8 oz. white baking chocolate, chopped
- 3 oz. semisweet chocolate, chopped
- 3/4 cup whole blanched almonds, toasted
- 3/4 cup dried cranberries

Direction

- Melt white chocolate in a microwave 70% power for a minute; mix. Microwave 10 to 20 seconds intervals, mixing until smooth. Keep melting semi-sweet chocolate. Mix cranberries and almonds into white chocolate. Spread it onto a waxed paper-lined baking tray thinly.
- Sprinkle semi-sweet chocolate on top of the white chocolate with a spoon. Using a knife, cut through to swirl. Refrigerate until firm. Crush into pieces. Chill in an airtight container.

Nutrition Information

- Calories: 75 calories
- Total Carbohydrate: 8 g
- Cholesterol: 0 mg
- Total Fat: 5 g
- Fiber: 1 g
- Protein: 2 g
- Sodium: 4 mg

156. Cranberry Fudge

"The combination of cranberries and chocolate wins every time."
Serving: 16

Ingredients

- 1 (12 oz.) package fresh or frozen cranberries
- 1/2 cup light corn syrup

- 2 cups semisweet chocolate chips
- 1/2 cup confectioners' sugar
- 1/4 cup evaporated milk
- 1 tsp. vanilla extract

Direction

- Line plastic wrap on the bottom and sides of an 8x8-inch pan. Put aside.
- Bring corn syrup and cranberries in a medium saucepan to a boil. Boil on high until liquid is reduced to three tbsps., stirring occasionally, about 5-7 minutes. Take away from the heat.
- Add the chocolate chips immediately, stirring until they are completely melted. Put in the vanilla extract, evaporated milk, and confectioner's sugar, vigorously stirring until the mixture is glossy and thick. Transfer into the pan. Chill, covered, until firm.

Nutrition Information

- Calories: 229 calories;
- Total Carbohydrate: 35.8 g
- Cholesterol: 1 mg
- Total Fat: 8.8 g
- Protein: 2.5 g
- Sodium: 11 mg

157. Creamy Orange Fudge

"This simple fudge with orange flavor is a combination of cream cheese, white chocolate, orange extract, and powdered sugar.""
Serving: 12 | Prep: 10m | Ready in: 20m

Ingredients

- 2 lbs. white chocolate, melted
- 2 (8 oz.) packages cream cheese
- 6 cups confectioners' sugar
- 1 tbsp. orange extract

Direction

- Beat cream cheese with melted chocolate until incorporated. Beat in confectioner's sugar until

no lumps remain. Whisk in orange extract. Pour mixture into an 8-inch square dish and spread; allow to set before dividing into squares. Store candies in the fridge.

Nutrition Information

- Calories: 785 calories;
- Total Carbohydrate: 108.3 g
- Cholesterol: 57 mg
- Total Fat: 37.4 g
- Protein: 7.3 g
- Sodium: 179 mg

158. Create-a-bark

"This recipe can be customized to your interest."
Serving: about 2 lbs.. | Prep: 15m | Ready in: 15m

Ingredients

- 1 package (24 oz.) white candy coating, coarsely chopped
- 2 cups of one or more of the following: dessert mints, jelly beans, M&M's, sugar-coated cereal, miniature sandwich cookies, etc.

Direction

- Melt candy coating in a microwave. Mix in the candy, cereal and/or cookies. Spread on a baking sheet lined with foil. Let cool. Crush into pieces.

Nutrition Information

- Calories: 339 calories
- Total Carbohydrate: 58 g
- Cholesterol: 0 mg
- Total Fat: 12 g
- Fiber: 0 g
- Protein: 0 g
- Sodium: 15 mg

159. Crunchy Chocolate Cups

"These easy-made chocolates is delicious."
Serving: about 5 dozen. | Prep: 25m | Ready in: 25m

Ingredients

- 1 package (12 oz.) semisweet chocolate chips
- 1 package (11 oz.) butterscotch chips
- 1 package (10 oz.) peanut butter chips
- 1 cup coarsely crushed cornflakes
- 1/2 cup chopped peanuts, optional

Direction

- Melt peanut butter chips, butterscotch chips and chocolate chips over low heat in a microwave-safe bowl; stir until smooth. Stir in cornflakes. If preferred, add peanuts. Allow to rest until slightly cooled or for 10-15 minutes.
- Drop into miniature foil cups, by teaspoonful, arranged on a 15x10x1-in. baking sheet. Keep in the fridge until set.

Nutrition Information

- Calories: 84 calories
- Total Carbohydrate: 10 g
- Cholesterol: 0 mg
- Total Fat: 5 g
- Fiber: 1 g
- Protein: 1 g
- Sodium: 27 mg

160. Crunchy Chocolate Eggs

"These chocolate candies is requested often."
Serving: about 4-1/2 dozen. | Prep: 40m | Ready in: 40m

Ingredients

- 1 cup packed brown sugar
- 1 cup light corn syrup
- 1 cup peanut butter
- 2 cups cornflakes
- 2 cups crisp rice cereal
- 1/2 cup finely chopped peanuts
- 3-3/4 cups semisweet chocolate chips
- 1-1/2 tsps. shortening
- Candy sprinkles

Direction

- Combine peanut butter, corn syrup and brown sugar in a heavy saucepan. Cook while stirring over medium heat until they become smooth. Discard from heat; mix in peanuts and cereals.
- Drop onto waxed paper-lined baking sheets by tablespoonfuls when cool enough to handle. Shape into the egg shapes. Place in the refrigerator until firm.
- Melt shortening and chocolate chips in a microwave, then stir until they become smooth. Submerge eggs in the chocolate; let the excess drip off. Arrange on the waxed paper-lined baking sheets. Garnish with the sprinkles. Allow to stand until set.

161. Dairy State Fudge

"This delicious fudge features hickory nuts. These candies are best enjoyed during the holidays."
Serving: 64 pieces (about 1 inch). | Prep: 20m | Ready in: 20m

Ingredients

- 1 package (8 oz.) cream cheese, softened
- 2 tbsps. butter
- 2 lbs. white candy coating, coarsely chopped
- 1 to 1-1/2 cups chopped pecans, walnuts or hickory nuts

Direction

- Whisk cream cheese in a bowl until fluffy; set aside. Melt butter over a double broiler; put in almond bark. Heat and mix until smooth and melted.
- Pour over and beat the cream cheese for 7-10 minutes until glossy and smooth; fold in nuts. Transfer to a greased nine-inch square pan. Refrigerate.

Nutrition Information

- Calories: 108 calories
- Total Carbohydrate: 8 g
- Cholesterol: 8 mg
- Total Fat: 8 g
- Fiber: 0 g
- Protein: 1 g
- Sodium: 29 mg

---

162. Dandy Caramel Candies

"The chewy treats will please anyone."
Serving: about 9 dozen. | Prep: 30m | Ready in: 30m

Ingredients

- 1-1/2 tsps. plus 1 cup butter, divided
- 1 cup sugar
- 1 cup packed brown sugar
- 1 cup dark corn syrup
- 2 cups heavy whipping cream
- 3-3/4 cups chopped pecans (about 1 lb.)
- 1 tsp. vanilla extract
- Dark or milk chocolate candy coating, melted

Direction

- Butter 1-1/2 tsps. of butter over a pan, about 13 inches x 9 inches. Put aside. Combine cream, butter, corn syrup and sugars in a heavy saucepan.
- Boil, stirring constantly, over medium-high heat. Over medium heat, cook until a candy thermometer registers 248° (firm-ball stage). Discard from heat; mix in vanilla and pecans. Spread into the prepared pan quickly. Let cool.
- Cut into 1-inch squares. Transfer the squares on the waxed paper-lined baking sheets; let chill thoroughly. Submerge each candy into the melted candy coating. Place in the refrigerator until firm.

Nutrition Information

- Calories: 93 calories
- Total Carbohydrate: 8 g

- Cholesterol: 12 mg
- Total Fat: 7 g
- Fiber: 0 g
- Protein: 1 g
- Sodium: 28 mg

---

163. Dark Chocolate Almond Rocks

"Sweet and nutty dark chocolate almond rocks!"
Serving: 20 | Prep: 10m | Ready in: 28m

Ingredients

- 1/2 cup almonds, crushed into chunks
- 7 oz. dark chocolate chips (50% cacao)

Direction

- In big skillet, spread almonds; toast for 3-5 minutes till starting to brown on medium heat. Put almonds in bowl.
- In top of double boiler above simmering water, melt chocolate, frequently mixing and scraping side down to avoid scorching for 5 minutes; take off heat. Put almonds in; mix till coated evenly.
- On waxed paper-lined plate, drop spoonfuls of chocolate-almond mixture.
- Chill for 10 minutes till set.

Nutrition Information

- Calories: 60 calories;
- Total Carbohydrate: 7.1 g
- Cholesterol: 0 mg
- Total Fat: 3.8 g
- Protein: 1 g
- Sodium: 3 mg

164. Dark Chocolate Orange Truffles

"Wonderful and decadent truffles."
Serving: 2-1/2 dozen. | Prep: 10m | Ready in: 15m

Ingredients

- 1 package (12 oz.) dark chocolate chips
- 3/4 cup heavy whipping cream
- 1 tsp. orange extract
- 1/3 cup sugar

Direction

- Melt chocolate in microwave; mix till smooth. Mix cream in slowly till blended. Mix extract in; cool to room temperature, occasionally mixing. Refrigerate till firm. Form to 3/4-in. balls then roll in sugar.

Nutrition Information

- Calories: 82 calories
- Total Carbohydrate: 8 g
- Cholesterol: 7 mg
- Total Fat: 5 g
- Fiber: 0 g
- Protein: 1 g
- Sodium: 2 mg

165. Dark Chocolate Popcorn

"This tasty snack can be enjoyed at any time of the day."
Serving: 16 | Prep: 10m | Ready in: 42m

Ingredients

- 3/4 cup white sugar
- 1/2 cup butter
- 1/4 cup unsweetened cocoa powder
- 1/4 cup corn syrup
- 1 tsp. vanilla extract
- 8 cups popped popcorn

Direction

- Start preheating the oven to 250°F (120°C). Oil a 9x13-in. baking plate.
- In a saucepan, gently boil corn syrup, cocoa powder, butter, and sugar; cook for 1-2 minutes until thickened. Mix in vanilla extract. Put the popcorn in a big bowl, add cocoa mixture and toss until the mixture has fully coated the popcorn. Spread evenly in the prepared baking plate.
- Put in the preheated oven and bake for 30 minutes, tossing sometimes, until the mixture sets.
- Take out of the oven and let cool to room temperature; crumble into clusters.

Nutrition Information

- Calories: 138 calories;
- Total Carbohydrate: 16.6 g
- Cholesterol: 15 mg
- Total Fat: 8.3 g
- Protein: 0.7 g
- Sodium: 103 mg

166. Dark Chocolate Pumpkin Truffles

"Delicious and pretty truffles!"
Serving: 2-1/2 dozen. | Prep: 30m | Ready in: 30m

Ingredients

- 2/3 cup reduced-fat cream cheese
- 1/2 cup confectioners' sugar
- 2/3 cup canned pumpkin
- 1 tsp. pumpkin pie spice
- 1 tsp. vanilla extract
- 2-1/4 cups crushed reduced-fat graham crackers
- 1 package (10 oz.) dark chocolate chips

Direction

- Beat confectioners' sugar and cream cheese till blended in small bowl. Beat vanilla, pie spice and pumpkin in; mix cracker crumbs in. Freeze till firm enough to shape for 20 minutes, covered.

- Form pumpkin mixture to 1-in. balls; put onto waxed paper-lined baking sheets; freeze till firm for 20 minutes.
- Melt chocolate in microwave; mix till smooth. In chocolate, dip truffles; let excess drip off. Put on baking sheets; refrigerate till set. Keep in airtight containers in the fridge.

Nutrition Information

- Calories: 97 calories
- Total Carbohydrate: 13 g
- Cholesterol: 4 mg
- Total Fat: 5 g
- Fiber: 1 g
- Protein: 2 g
- Sodium: 60 mg

---

on high without covering for 2 minutes and stir. Microwave in intervals of 30 seconds while whisking until smooth. Mix in salt and liqueur. Put in white baking chips; whisk until partly melted. Pour mixture into prepped pan. Put in the refrigerator till firm, about an hour.

- Take the fudge out of the pan by lifting with foil. Peel off the foil and slice into square pieces of an inch. Keep refrigerated in a tightly sealed container to store.

Nutrition Information

- Calories: 85 calories
- Total Carbohydrate: 10 g
- Cholesterol: 2 mg
- Total Fat: 5 g
- Fiber: 0 g
- Protein: 1 g
- Sodium: 13 mg

---

167. Dark Chocolate Raspberry Fudge

"You know raspberry and dark chocolate blends together very perfectly. This fudge recipe takes advantage of the iconic combination."
Serving: 3 lbs. (81 pieces). | Prep: 15m | Ready in: 20m

Ingredients

- 1 package (10 to 12 oz.) white baking chips
- 1 tsp. butter, softened
- 3 cups dark chocolate chips
- 1 can (14 oz.) sweetened condensed milk
- 1/4 cup raspberry liqueur
- 1/8 tsp. salt

Direction

- Scatter a single layer of baking chips over a small baking sheet. Put in the freezer for half an hour. Use foil to line a pan of 9 inches square; butter the foil.
- Mix milk and dark chocolate chips in a microwaveable bowl. Heat in the microwave

---

168. Dark Chocolate-covered Berries, Almonds, And Pretzel Crisps®

""This super quick snack to make is a combination of dark chocolate, crunchy almonds, sweet berries and pretzels.""
Serving: 12 | Prep: 10m | Ready in: 40m

Ingredients

- 4 (4 oz.) bars 70% dark chocolate, chopped
- 1 tbsp. coconut oil
- 1 tsp. vanilla extract
- 1 (6 oz.) container blueberries, stemmed
- 1/2 cup lightly roasted whole almonds
- 12 thin pretzel crackers (such as Snack Factory® Pretzel Crisps®)

Direction

- Use waxed paper or silicone baking liner to line a baking sheet.
- Put a double boiler on simmering water; mix in vanilla extract, coconut oil and dark chocolate. Stir constantly for 5 minutes until

melted (make sure to scrape down the sides with a rubber spatula). Put off the heat and allow to cool for 15 minutes until it is at room temperature.

- Place 2 tbsps. of the chocolate mixture in a small bowl.
- Mix almonds and blueberries into the remaining chocolate mixture. Evenly spread a layer onto the lined baking sheet. Lightly press in pretzel crackers. Drizzle with saved 2 tbsps. chocolate.
- Put in the freezer for 15-20 minutes to firm up. Gently beak into pieces to serve.

Nutrition Information

- Calories: 381 calories;
- Total Carbohydrate: 49.4 g
- Cholesterol: 2 mg
- Total Fat: 19.3 g
- Protein: 6.4 g
- Sodium: 762 mg

169. Delectable Maple Nut Chocolates

"My dad cherished anything with maple enhancing, so my mom changed a brownie formula to suit his preferences."
Serving: about 13 dozen. | Prep: 55m | Ready in: 60m

Ingredients

- 1 can (14 oz.) sweetened condensed milk
- 1/2 cup butter, cubed
- 7-1/2 cups confectioners' sugar
- 2 cups chopped walnuts
- 2 tsps. maple flavoring
- 1 tsp. vanilla extract
- 4 cups (24 oz.) semisweet chocolate chips
- 2 oz. bittersweet chocolate, chopped
- 2 tsps. shortening

Direction

- Mix butter and milk in a small saucepan. Cook and mix until butter is melted over low heat.

Put confectioners' sugar in a big bowl; put in the milk blend then beat till smooth. Mix in vanilla, maple flavoring and walnuts. Roll into balls of 3/4-inch; put onto baking sheets lined with waxed paper. Refrigerate for 1 hour, until firm.

- Melt the shortening, bittersweet chocolate and chips in a microwave; mix until smooth. Dip the balls into the chocolate; let the excess drip off. Put them onto waxed paper; allow to stand until set. Keep in airtight container.

Nutrition Information

- Calories: 67 calories
- Total Carbohydrate: 10 g
- Cholesterol: 2 mg
- Total Fat: 3 g
- Fiber: 0 g
- Protein: 1 g
- Sodium: 8 mg

170. Double Chocolate Fudge

"This recipe is what chocolate lovers crave for."
Serving: 5 lbs. (150 pieces). | Prep: 25m | Ready in: 25m

Ingredients

- 1-1/2 tsps. plus 2 tbsps. butter, divided
- 4-1/2 cups sugar
- 1 can (12 oz.) evaporated milk
- Pinch salt
- 1 jar (7 oz.) marshmallow creme
- 12 oz. German sweet chocolate, chopped
- 2 cups (12 oz.) semisweet chocolate chips
- 2 cups chopped walnuts, optional

Direction

- Line foil over a 15x10x1-inch pan; use 1 1/2 tsps. butter to grease the foil.
- Combine the rest of butter, salt, milk, and sugar in a heavy large saucepan. Heat over medium heat, stirring constantly, until mixture comes to a rapid boil. Cook, stirring constantly, for 5 minutes. Turn off the heat.

- Whisk in marshmallow creme until melted. Add both chocolates and stir until melted. Mix in walnuts, if desired. Instantly pour mixture into the prepared pan, spreading evenly. Chill in the fridge until solid.
- Lift fudge out of the pan using foil. Discard the foil; divide fudge into squares about 1 inch. Place candies between layers of waxed paper in airtight container, and chill in the fridge.

Nutrition Information

- Calories: 47 calories
- Total Carbohydrate: 9 g
- Cholesterol: 1 mg
- Total Fat: 1 g
- Fiber: 0 g
- Protein: 0 g
- Sodium: 7 mg

---

171. Double Chocolate Walnut Fudge

"Try this and you will love it!"
Serving: about 2-1/2 lbs.. | Prep: 10m | Ready in: 30m

Ingredients

- 1 tsp. butter
- 1 package (12 oz.) semisweet chocolate chips
- 1 can (14 oz.) sweetened condensed milk, divided
- 1 cup chopped walnuts, divided
- 2 tsps. vanilla extract, divided
- 1 package (11-1/2 oz.) milk chocolate chips

Direction

- Line foil on a 9-inch square pan. Coat the foil with butter.
- Combine 3/4 cup of milk and semisweet chocolate chips in a large heavy saucepan over low heat. Discard from the heat. Then stir in one tsp. of vanilla and half a cup of walnuts. Spread into the prepared pan.

- Combine the remaining milk and milk chocolate chips in another saucepan. Discard from the heat. Then stir in the remaining walnuts and vanilla. Spread the mixture over the first layer. Cover and place in refrigerator until firm, about 120 mins. Lift fudge out of the pan with foil. Discard the foil; slice the fudge into 1-inch squares. Preserve in airtight container between layers of the waxed paper.

Nutrition Information

- Calories: 69 calories
- Total Carbohydrate: 8 g
- Cholesterol: 3 mg
- Total Fat: 4 g
- Fiber: 0 g
- Protein: 1 g
- Sodium: 10 mg

---

172. Duo-chocolate Fudge

"This delectable fudge formula is for each one of those milk chocolate sweethearts out there!"
Serving: 48

Ingredients

- 1 lb. milk chocolate
- 1 lb. semi-sweet chocolate chips
- 2 1/2 tbsps. butter
- 2 cups marshmallow creme
- 2 cups chopped walnuts (optional)
- 1 (12 fluid oz.) can evaporated milk
- 4 cups white sugar

Direction

- Lightly grease a 9x13-inch pan with butter.
- Mix the nuts, marshmallow cream, butter, semi-sweet chocolate and milk chocolate in a big bowl.
- Mix the sugar and evaporated milk in a big saucepan over medium heat. Mix continuously and boil for 4 minutes.
- Pour the hot sugar blend on chocolate blend and mix using large spoon until well

combined (do this quickly before fudge starts hardening). When well mixed, pour the fudge into a 9x13-inch buttered baking pan. Spread out then smooth in a pan.

- Put aside for 6 hours for cooling and hardening. When ready to serve, slice into squares.

Nutrition Information

- Calories: 222 calories;
- Total Carbohydrate: 33.1 g
- Cholesterol: 6 mg
- Total Fat: 10 g
- Protein: 2.4 g
- Sodium: 25 mg

---

173. Easter Creme Egg® Rocky Road

"You can use your creativity to make the treat of your own."
Serving: 12 | Prep: 25m | Ready in: 1h30m

Ingredients

- 3 1/2 oz. miniature marshmallows
- 8 fondant-filled chocolate eggs (such as Cadbury Creme Eggs®)
- 6 digestive biscuits, broken into pieces
- 1 (14 oz.) can sweetened condensed milk
- 3 (4 oz.) bars dark chocolate, chopped
- 2 tbsps. unsalted butter
- 10 colored mini chocolate eggs

Direction

- Set out all the ingredients first. Crush the biscuits, unwrap the chocolate eggs and measure the marshmallows.
- In a kettle or pot, boil some water; transfer to a mug. Dip a sharp knife for a minute into the hot water. Take the knife out; wipe dry using paper towel. Cut along the seam of 2 chocolate eggs with the hot knife, splitting them in half lengthwise. Leave 6 eggs whole.

- Grease a 9-inch square baking pan. Using parchment paper to line the sides and bottom, leaving an overhang on 2 sides. Place 3 whole eggs randomly on the bottom. Put aside.
- In top of a double boiler over simmering water, place butter, chocolate and condensed milk. Stir frequently, scraping down sides using a rubber spatula to prevent scorching, for about 5 minutes until melted and smooth.
- Take the bowl out of the heat; stir in biscuits and marshmallows until well mixed. Place on greased pan; cover 3 eggs on the bottom. Quickly add 3 leftover whole eggs on top, along with 4 egg halves. Scatter mini eggs on top. Keep in the fridge for 1-2 hours until chocolate is set.
- Lift the rocky road out of the pan gently with edges of the parchment paper. Transfer to a cutting board; use the hot knife method applied in step 2 to cut into squares. To get gooey centers oozing out of each slice, cut through some of the whole eggs.

Nutrition Information

- Calories: 429 calories;
- Total Carbohydrate: 61 g
- Cholesterol: 21 mg
- Total Fat: 19.1 g
- Protein: 5.9 g
- Sodium: 105 mg

---

174. Easter Eggs

"This recipe is a perfect choice if you want to surprise your family.""
Serving: 60 | Prep: 3h | Ready in: 3h10m

Ingredients

- 2 lbs. confectioners' sugar
- 1/4 lb. margarine, softened
- 1 (8 oz.) package cream cheese
- 2 tsps. vanilla extract
- 12 oz. peanut butter
- 1 lb. flaked coconut

- 4 cups semisweet chocolate chips
- 2 tbsps. shortening

Direction

- Mix vanilla extract, cream cheese, margarine, and sugar together in a mixing bowl. Separate batter into 2 equal portions; place the 2 portions in 2 individual bowls. Mix coconut into 1 bowl and peanut butter into the other.
- Shape the dough into egg-forms with your hands; place them on cookie sheets. Freeze the eggs until frozen.
- Once the eggs have frozen, melt shortening and chocolate in the top of a double-boiler. Immerse eggs into chocolate until well coated. Arrange the coated eggs on cookie sheets lined with waxed paper, and put them back into the freezer to harden. Once chocolate has hardened, remove eggs to the fridge.

Nutrition Information

- Calories: 226 calories;
- Total Carbohydrate: 25.2 g
- Cholesterol: 4 mg
- Total Fat: 14.3 g
- Protein: 2.7 g
- Sodium: 59 mg

175. Easy Chocolate Clusters

"You can utilize this basic formula to make a major clump of chocolate treat without a ton of object."
Serving: 3-1/2 dozen. | Prep: 10m | Ready in: 02h10m

Ingredients

- 2 lbs. white candy coating, broken into small pieces
- 2 cups (12 oz.) semisweet chocolate chips
- 4 oz. German sweet chocolate, chopped
- 1 jar (24 oz.) dry roasted peanuts

Direction

- Mix the German chocolate, chocolate chips and candy coating in a 3-quarts slow cooker. Cover and cook for an hour on high. Lower heat to low; cover and cook until melted, for another hour and mix every 15 minutes.
- Mix in the peanuts. Drop by teaspoonfuls onto waxed paper. Allow to stand until set. Store at room temperature.

Nutrition Information

- Calories: 521 calories
- Total Carbohydrate: 51 g
- Cholesterol: 0 mg
- Total Fat: 35 g
- Fiber: 4 g
- Protein: 9 g
- Sodium: 265 mg

176. Easy Chocolate Drops

"This chocolate cookie needs no baking but still awesome."
Serving: 18

Ingredients

- 3 tbsps. margarine
- 3 tbsps. peanut butter
- 1 cup semisweet chocolate chips
- 3 cups whole wheat flake cereal

Direction

- Mix chocolate chips, peanut butter and margarine in a medium-sized saucepan. Cook on low heat, while mixing often till becomes melted. Take out of the heat and mix in cereal. Drop by spoonfuls onto wax paper or the greased cookie sheets, and keep chilled in the refrigerator till becomes set.

Nutrition Information

- Calories: 95 calories;
- Total Carbohydrate: 10.5 g
- Cholesterol: 0 mg

- Total Fat: 6.1 g
- Protein: 1.6 g
- Sodium: 69 mg

177. Easy Chocolate Truffles

"A basic yet versatile recipe."
Serving: 48

Ingredients

- 8 oz. good-quality semi- or bittersweet chocolate, coarsely chopped
- 4 oz. unsweetened chocolate
- 8 tbsps. unsalted butter
- 1 (14 oz.) can sweetened condensed milk
- Your choice of flavoring (see below)
- Your choice of coating (see below)

Direction

- Heat milk, butter and chocolates in pan till butter and chocolates melt partially. Take off heat; mix till melted completely. Whisk desired flavoring in till smooth and creamy.
- Put in bowl; let stand for about 2 hours till firm enough to hold its own shape.
- 1 level tbsp. at a time, use tbsp. (spring action 1 tbsp. scoop is preferred) to mold chocolate to balls. Put onto greased parchment paper-lined cookie sheet.
- Put preferred coating into small bowl. One by one, drop truffles in bowl using greased fingertips. Shake the bowl back and forth to completely coat truffles. By hand, roll truffles to make round if needed. Put back on parchment. Can be refrigerated for up to 5 days in airtight container/frozen for up to 1 month. Let stand to slightly soften at room temperature before serving.

Nutrition Information

- Calories: 78 calories;
- Total Carbohydrate: 7.8 g
- Cholesterol: 8 mg
- Total Fat: 5.4 g

- Protein: 1.3 g
- Sodium: 11 mg

178. Easy Mint Chocolate Truffles

"One of my favorite candy recipes."
Serving: 70 truffles. | Prep: 20m | Ready in: 30m

Ingredients

- 1 tbsp. plus 3/4 cup butter, divided
- 3 cups sugar
- 1 can (5 oz.) evaporated milk
- 2 cups (12 oz.) semisweet chocolate chips
- 1/2 tsp. peppermint extract
- 1 jar (7 oz.) marshmallow creme
- 1 tsp. vanilla extract
- baking cocoa, finely chopped nuts or chocolate sprinkles

Direction

- Line foil on 15x10x1-in. pan; use 1 tbsp. butter to grease foil. Put aside.
- Boil leftover butter, milk and sugar in heavy saucepan on medium heat. Cook, constantly mixing, till it's soft-ball stage/candy thermometer reads 234°. Take off heat; mix peppermint extract and chips in till chocolate melts. Mix vanilla and marshmallow crème till smooth. Spread in prepped pan.
- Refrigerate for 3 hours or till firm, uncovered. Lift from pan; slice to 1 1/2-in. squares then roll each to a ball. In cocoa/sprinkles/nuts, roll truffles. Refrigerate in airtight container.

Nutrition Information

- Calories: 174 calories
- Total Carbohydrate: 28 g
- Cholesterol: 13 mg
- Total Fat: 7 g
- Fiber: 1 g
- Protein: 1 g
- Sodium: 53 mg

179. Easy Oreo Truffles

"Yummy and easy truffles."
Serving: 42 | Ready in: 1h30m

Ingredients

- 1 (16 oz.) package OREO Chocolate Sandwich Cookies, divided
- 1 (8 oz.) package PHILADELPHIA Cream Cheese, softened
- 2 (8 oz.) packages BAKER'S Semi-Sweet Baking Chocolate, melted

Direction

- In food processor, crush 9 cookies to fine crumbs; keep for later. You can also finely crush cookies using a rolling pin in resealable plastic bag. Crush leftover 36 cookies into fine crumbs; put in medium bowl then add cream cheese. Mix till blended well. Roll cookie mixture to 42 balls, 1-in. in diameter.
- In chocolate, dip balls; put onto wax paper-covered baking sheet. You can store leftover chocolate at room temperature for another time. Sprinkle reserved cookie crumbs on top.
- Refrigerate for 1 hour till firm; store leftover truffles in the fridge, covered.

180. Easy Rocky Road Fudge

"Try this and you will love it!"
Serving: about 3-1/4 lbs.. | Prep: 20m | Ready in: 20m

Ingredients

- 2 cups (12 oz.) semisweet chocolate chips
- 1 can (14 oz.) sweetened condensed milk
- 2 tbsps. butter
- 3 cups salted dry roasted peanuts
- 1 package (10-1/2 oz.) miniature marshmallows

Direction

- Combine butter, milk and chocolate chips in a saucepan. Over medium heat, cook while stirring until mixture becomes smooth and chips have melted. Discard from heat; stir in marshmallows and peanuts. Spread into an oiled 13-inch x 9-inch pan. Place in the refrigerator until firm. Cut into squares.

Nutrition Information

- Calories: 60 calories
- Total Carbohydrate: 7 g
- Cholesterol: 2 mg
- Total Fat: 3 g
- Fiber: 0 g
- Protein: 1 g
- Sodium: 39 mg

181.English Toffee Bars

"What's sweeter than gathering with your family around holiday and make fragrant batches of yummy toffee? This recipe calls for chocolate coating that will satisfy any sweet tooth."
Serving: 2-1/4 lbs.. | Prep: 35m | Ready in: 35m

Ingredients

- 1 tbsp. plus 1-3/4 cups butter, softened, divided
- 2 cups sugar
- 1 tbsp. light corn syrup
- 1 cup chopped pecans
- 1/4 tsp. salt
- 1 lb. milk chocolate candy coating, coarsely chopped

Direction

- Use 1 tbsp. butter to grease a 15x10x1-inch pan and put aside. Heat the rest of butter in a heavy 3-quart saucepan until melted. Pour in corn syrup and sugar; put over medium heat and stir while cooking until the mixture reaches 295 degrees on a candy thermometer (soft-crack stage). Take away from the heat; mix in salt and pecans.

- Immediately transfer to the greased pan. Wait for 5 minutes. Score the bar into lines with a sharp knife. Cool at room temperature.
- Use a knife to slice into square pieces if needed. Microwave candy coating until melted, stirring frequently. Coat each square with the melted candy coating. Let sit until set on waxed paper.

Nutrition Information

- Calories: 214 calories
- Total Carbohydrate: 21 g
- Cholesterol: 25 mg
- Total Fat: 15 g
- Fiber: 1 g
- Protein: 1 g
- Sodium: 110 mg

182. Erika's "frango" Mints

"I have used different flavors of extracts."
Serving: 24 | Prep: 15m | Ready in: 4h15m

Ingredients

- 1 (12 oz.) bag chocolate chips
- 1 1/2 cups confectioners' sugar
- 1/2 cup egg substitute
- 1/4 cup butter, softened
- 1 tsp. mint extract
- 1 tsp. vanilla extract

Direction

- Use a waxed paper to line a baking sheet or plate.
- In a double boiler's top that is set over simmering water, melt the chocolate, stirring regularly and scraping down the sides using a rubber spatula.
- Beat butter, egg substitute, and confectioners' sugar in a bowl using an electric mixer until creamy and smooth. Add in the melted chocolate and beat until well combined. Beat vanilla extract and mint extract into the mixture of chocolate until fluffy and light.

- Drop chocolate mixture onto the prepared baking sheet by a heaping teaspoonful. Refrigerate for at least 4 hours until firm.

Nutrition Information

- Calories: 120 calories;
- Total Carbohydrate: 16.7 g
- Cholesterol: 5 mg
- Total Fat: 6.3 g
- Protein: 1.2 g
- Sodium: 25 mg

183. Extra Easy Fudge

"This fudge is easy to make yet tasty."
Serving: 48

Ingredients

- 2 cups milk chocolate chips
- 2 1/2 cups prepared chocolate frosting
- 1 cup chopped walnuts

Direction

- Using foil, line an 8x8 inch square pan. Butter the foil lightly.
- Melt chocolate chips while stirring constantly over low heat in a small saucepan. Take the melted chocolate out of the heat; stir in nuts and frosting; mix until smooth. Transfer into the lined pan; keep in the fridge until firm. When firm, slice into small squares.

Nutrition Information

- Calories: 124 calories;
- Total Carbohydrate: 13 g
- Cholesterol: 2 mg
- Total Fat: 7.7 g
- Protein: 0.8 g
- Sodium: 56 mg

184. Famous Coconut-almond Balls

"A great chocolate dish with almonds and coconut inside."
Serving: 13 | Prep: 15m | Ready in: 30m

Ingredients

- 4 cups flaked coconut
- 1/4 cup light corn syrup
- 1 (12 oz.) package semisweet chocolate chips
- 1/4 cup shortening
- 26 whole almonds

Direction

- Use waxed paper to line a big flat surface or 2 cookie sheets, then put on top with a big cooling rack. In a big bowl, add coconut. In the microwave, heat corn syrup for a minute, until syrups is boiled. Drizzle over coconut instantly and stir until well-blended.
- Form coconut into 26 balls using a tbsp. measure and your hands, then arrange on wire racks. Allow to rest for 10 minutes, then re-roll each ball to prevent loose ends from sticking out.
- In a big glass bowl, melt chocolate and shortening in the microwave or in saucepan on stovetop while stirring for 1-2 times. Working rapidly, put over each ball with 1 tbsp. of chocolate then press on top of each ball gently with an almond. Allow balls to stand until set.

Nutrition Information

- Calories: 379 calories;
- Total Carbohydrate: 28.4 g
- Cholesterol: 0 mg
- Total Fat: 31.4 g
- Protein: 3.6 g
- Sodium: 17 mg

185. Festive Holiday Bark

"The perfect, sweet and salty candy-coated pretzels."
Serving: 42

Ingredients

- 16 oz. vanilla flavored confectioners' coating
- 2 cups small pretzel twists
- 1/2 cup red and green candy-coated chocolate

Direction

- Use waxed paper or parchment paper to line a cookie sheet.
- In a microwave safe bowl, add the candy coating. Microwave for 2 1/2 minutes. Microwave and stir in 30 second intervals till smooth and thoroughly melted.
- Add candy coated chocolate pieces and pretzels in a large bowl. Pour melted coating on top and well mix to coat. Spread out on to baking sheet lined with waxed paper. Let sit until firm or refrigerate to set up quicker. Keep at room temperature in a container.

Nutrition Information

- Calories: 77 calories;
- Total Carbohydrate: 9.6 g
- Cholesterol: 3 mg
- Total Fat: 4 g
- Protein: 0.9 g
- Sodium: 43 mg

186. Fondant-filled Candies

"A simple method to make two happy and one of a kind confections from one essential formula!"
Serving: 4-1/2 dozen. | Prep: 30m | Ready in: 30m

Ingredients

- 2/3 cup sweetened condensed milk
- 1 tbsp. light corn syrup
- 4-1/2 to 5 cups confectioners' sugar
- 2 to 4 drops peppermint oil

- 2-1/2 lbs. dark chocolate candy coating, coarsely chopped, divided
- 1 jar (16 oz.) maraschino cherries

Direction

- Mix the corn syrup and milk in a big bowl. Beat in the confectioners' sugar gradually (the blend is going to be stiff). Split into 2 parts.
- To create peppermint patties: Put the peppermint oil into 1 portion. Form into balls with 1/2 teaspoonfuls then flatten. Melt 1 lb. of candy coating in a microwave, mix until smooth. Dip the peppermint disks in the coating using a slotted spoon; let excess drip off. Put onto waxed paper for hardening. Refrigerate in airtight container.
- To make chocolate-covered cherries: Drain the cherries, save 3 tbsps. juice; put aside the cherries. Mix the leftover fondant and the juice. If required, put in more confectioners' sugar to shape a stiff blend.
- Roll into balls of 1-inch; flatten to circles of 2-inch. Wrap each circle around a cherry then form it carefully into a ball. Put onto baking sheets lined with waxed paper. Loosely cover. Melt the leftover candy coating; dip the cherries in the coating; let excess drip off. Put on waxed paper until hardened. Refrigerate for 1 to 2 weeks in an airtight container for candy to ripen and middle to soften.

Nutrition Information

- Calories: 343 calories
- Total Carbohydrate: 59 g
- Cholesterol: 3 mg
- Total Fat: 13 g
- Fiber: 1 g
- Protein: 1 g
- Sodium: 11 mg

187. Fried Egg Candy

"Every kid I know loves these sweet treats and also enjoys helping when I am making them."
Serving: about 3-1/2 dozen. | Prep: 30m | Ready in: 30m

Ingredients

- 1 package (15 oz.) pretzel sticks
- 1 package (12 oz.) vanilla or white chips
- 48 yellow M&M's

Direction

- Arrange groups of 2 pretzel sticks on waxed paper, keep a small gap between each group. Put vanilla chips into a microwave safe bowl, heat the bowl at 70% power till the chips are melted; stir till the mixture becomes smooth. Use the vanilla chip liquid to make tablespoonful drops on each pair of pretzel sticks. To make "yolks", lay 1 or 2 M&M in the center of each "egg".

Nutrition Information

- Calories: 176 calories
- Total Carbohydrate: 27 g
- Cholesterol: 4 mg
- Total Fat: 6 g
- Fiber: 1 g
- Protein: 3 g
- Sodium: 327 mg

188. Fudge-topped Brownies

"This recipe is a combination of fudge and brownies. It's great to serve at any gatherings."
Serving: about 10 dozen. | Prep: 25m | Ready in: 50m

Ingredients

- 1 cup butter
- 4 oz. unsweetened chocolate, chopped
- 2 cups sugar
- 2 tsps. vanilla extract
- 4 large eggs

- 1-1/2 cups all-purpose flour
- 1 tsp. baking powder
- 1/2 tsp. salt
- 1 cup chopped walnuts
- TOPPING:
- 4-1/2 cups sugar
- 1 can (12 oz.) evaporated milk
- 1/2 cup butter, cubed
- 1 package (12 oz.) semisweet chocolate chips
- 1 package (11-1/2 oz.) milk chocolate chips
- 1 jar (7 oz.) marshmallow creme
- 2 tsps. vanilla extract
- 2 cups chopped walnuts

Direction

- Melt chocolate and butter in a microwave or a heavy saucepan; whisk until smooth. Take away from the heat, mix in vanilla and sugar. Add eggs, stir thoroughly. Mix together salt, baking powder, and flour; add to the chocolate mixture. Mix in walnuts. Add to an oil-coated 13x9-inch baking pan. Bake at 350° until the top springs back when you gently touch it, or about 25-30 minutes. Put on a wire rack to cool as you make the topping.
- In a big heavy saucepan, mix together butter, milk, and sugar; boil over medium heat. Lower the heat, simmer without a cover, whisking continually, about 5 minutes. Take away from the heat. Mix in vanilla, marshmallow crème, and chocolate chips until smooth. Add walnuts. Spread onto the warm brownies. Freeze until firm, or about 3 hours. Slice into squares, about 1 inch each. Put in the fridge to store.

Nutrition Information

- Calories: 128 calories
- Total Carbohydrate: 18 g
- Cholesterol: 15 mg
- Total Fat: 6 g
- Fiber: 0 g
- Protein: 2 g
- Sodium: 46 mg

189. Fudgy Buttons

"This Grandma's fudge is quick to prepare."
Serving: about 1-1/2 dozen. | Prep: 20m | Ready in: 20m

Ingredients

- 2 tbsps. butter
- 1-1/2 tsps. baking cocoa
- 1/2 cup confectioners' sugar
- 1/2 tsp. milk
- 2 tbsps. creamy peanut butter

Direction

- Melt butter in a small saucepan; take out of the heat. Add cocoa; combine well. Stir in sugar. Add milk; stir until smooth. Add peanut butter; combine well. Drop by teaspoonfuls onto waxed paper; make tops flat and form into 1-in. patties. Keep in the fridge until serving.

Nutrition Information

- Calories: 70 calories
- Total Carbohydrate: 8 g
- Cholesterol: 7 mg
- Total Fat: 4 g
- Fiber: 0 g
- Protein: 1 g
- Sodium: 43 mg

190. Fudgy Christmas Wreath

"These candies are sure to be a big hit in your next Christmas party."
Serving: about 24 servings. | Prep: 30m | Ready in: 30m

Ingredients

- 1 can (14 oz.) sweetened condensed milk
- 2 cups (12 oz.) semisweet chocolate chips
- 1 cup chopped walnuts
- 1/2 tsp. vanilla extract
- Red and green maraschino cherries

Direction

- Cook chocolate chips and milk over low heat in a saucepan for about 6 minutes, stirring, until chocolate is melted and mixture thickens lightly. Put off the heat; whisk in vanilla and nuts. Allow mixture to cool for about 15 minutes, until it begins to firm. Line waxed paper on a baking sheet. Place chocolate mixture into small mounds by 2 tablespoonfuls to shape a wreath. Garnish with cherries. Refrigerate until solid; serve cold.

Nutrition Information

- Calories: 152 calories
- Total Carbohydrate: 18 g
- Cholesterol: 6 mg
- Total Fat: 9 g
- Fiber: 1 g
- Protein: 3 g
- Sodium: 23 mg

191. Fudgy Coconut Squares

""*Every time I try these yummy, rich layered bars, it reminds me of my childhood. My parents were missionaries in Thailand, and mom was clever enough to have these popular ingredients there- the squares reminded us of the candy bars back home.*""
Serving: about 4 dozen. | Prep: 20m | Ready in: 01h10m

Ingredients

- 1 cup butter, softened
- 1-1/2 cups sugar
- 3 eggs
- 1 tsp. vanilla extract
- 1 cup all-purpose flour
- 1/4 cup baking cocoa
- 1/2 cup chopped walnuts
- 1 can (14 oz.) sweetened condensed milk
- 1 cup sweetened shredded coconut
- ICING:
- 2 cups confectioners' sugar

- 1/4 cup baking cocoa
- 5 tbsps. evaporated milk
- 2 tbsps. butter, melted
- 1/2 tsp. vanilla extract

Direction

- Cream sugar and butter in a bowl. Mix in vanilla and eggs; blend well. Mix the walnuts, cocoa and flour; then put to the creamed mixture. Place into a greased 13x9-inch baking pan then spread. Put in the oven and bake for 30 minutes at 350°F or until a toothpick pricked in the middle comes out clean.
- Mix coconut and condensed milk; gently spread over the hot chocolate layer. Then bake for 20 minutes at 350°F or until coconut is lightly browned.
- Mix icing ingredients until it turns smooth; spread over warm bars. Keep in the refrigerator for at least 1-hour prior to slicing.

Nutrition Information

- Calories: 289 calories
- Total Carbohydrate: 39 g
- Cholesterol: 56 mg
- Total Fat: 14 g
- Fiber: 1 g
- Protein: 4 g
- Sodium: 129 mg

192. Gaye's Microwave Fudge

"*This recipe is perfect for chocolate lovers. Create a luscious chocolate dessert that everyone cannot resist. Add chopped nuts, and it becomes extra exciting.*"
Serving: 12 | Prep: 3m | Ready in: 15m

Ingredients

- 4 cups confectioners' sugar
- 1/2 cup unsweetened cocoa powder
- 1/4 cup milk
- 1/2 cup butter
- 2 tsps. vanilla extract

Direction

- Slightly oil or grease a 9 x 9 baking dish.
- Using a microwave-safe bowl, mix cocoa and confectioners' sugar, and stir together. Add milk into the mixture, as well as the butter. Do not mix the butter yet. Instead, heat the mixture in the microwave for 2 minutes until the butter melts. Add vanilla and stir thoroughly until the mixture becomes smooth. Use the chocolate as sauce or dip for your favorite desserts.
- Alternatively, you can chill the mixture in the freezer for at least 10 minutes and create a chocolate bar.

Nutrition Information

- Calories: 243 calories;
- Total Carbohydrate: 43.9 g
- Cholesterol: 21 mg
- Total Fat: 8.3 g
- Protein: 1 g
- Sodium: 58 mg

---

193. German Chocolate Fudge

"A very simple recipe for tasty chocolate fudge to try."
Serving: 80 | Prep: 15m | Ready in: 2h21m

Ingredients

- 2 cups semisweet chocolate chips
- 12 (1 oz.) squares German sweet chocolate
- 1 (7 oz.) jar marshmallow creme
- 4 1/2 cups white sugar
- 2 tbsps. butter
- 1 (12 fluid oz.) can evaporated milk
- 1/8 tsp. salt
- 2 cups chopped pecans

Direction

- In a large bowl, mix marshmallow crème, German sweet chocolate, and chocolate chips.

- In a heavy skillet, mix salt, evaporated milk, butter, and sugar. Boil on medium heat. Then cook and constantly stir for 6 minutes.
- Add hot syrup to the chocolate mixture. Use a wooden spoon to stir until it becomes smooth. Add in pecans and stir.
- Place over a buttered 10x15-inch pan. Allow to stand until firm; then slice into squares.

Nutrition Information

- Calories: 134 calories;
- Total Carbohydrate: 20.8 g
- Cholesterol: 2 mg
- Total Fat: 5.8 g
- Protein: 1.2 g
- Sodium: 13 mg

---

194. German Christmas Nougatkugeln (nougat Balls)

"Use high quality ingredients for this recipe."
Serving: 15 | Prep: 45m | Ready in: 1h30m

Ingredients

- 4 oz. semi-sweet chocolate chunks
- 1 cup confectioners' sugar
- 1 1/2 tbsps. unsweetened cocoa powder
- 2 tsps. vanilla extract
- 2 tbsps. strong brewed coffee, or as needed
- 1 cup ground hazelnuts

Direction

- In top of double boiler, melt chocolate above just-barely simmering water, frequently mixing and scraping sides down using a rubber spatula to avoid scorching. Take bowl off heat.
- Mix cocoa powder and confectioner's sugar in another bowl. Use wire whisk to break lumps up. Mix coffee and vanilla in; mix nuts in and extra coffee if needed to create a smooth mixture. You should get the mixture fairly thick.

- Let mixture cool enough to handle; form mixture to balls, 1/2 - 3/4-in. diameter balls. In melted chocolate, dip balls; chill till firm.

Nutrition Information

- Calories: 101 calories;
- Total Carbohydrate: 13.9 g
- Cholesterol: 0 mg
- Total Fat: 5.4 g
- Protein: 1.2 g
- Sodium: 1 mg

195. Gianduja

"I love how I blend hazelnuts and chocolate in this recipe. This recipe of mine became more popular and known as a sophisticated Christmas candy."
Serving: about 3 lbs.. | Prep: 20m | Ready in: 20m

Ingredients

- 1-1/2 lbs. shelled hazelnuts, skins removed
- 3/4 cup canola oil
- 1-1/2 lbs. bittersweet chocolate, chopped
- 3 milk chocolate Toblerone candy bars (3.52 oz. each), chopped

Direction

- Use a foil to line an 8-inch square dish. Blend the oil and hazelnuts in a food processor until the mixture forms a paste, covered.
- Melt the bittersweet chocolate in a large saucepan. Add 2 1/4 cups of hazelnut mixture into the saucepan. Pour half of the mixture in a prepared dish. Store the dish inside the refrigerator until the mixture is firm.
- Melt the candy bars and add the remaining hazelnut mixture. Spread the mixture over the bittersweet layer and store inside the refrigerator until firm.
- Reheat remaining bittersweet mixture if necessary and pour it over the candy bar layer. Place it again inside the refrigerator and store until firm. Slice candy bars into 1-inch squares

and place it in an airtight container. Keep refrigerated.

Nutrition Information

- Calories: 168 calories
- Total Carbohydrate: 10 g
- Cholesterol: 1 mg
- Total Fat: 15 g
- Fiber: 2 g
- Protein: 2 g
- Sodium: 2 mg

196. Giant Homemade Almond Butter Cups

"This candy recipe has a nice balance of sweetness and bitterness. It's very healthy also.""
Serving: 10 | Prep: 10m | Ready in: 21m

Ingredients

- 10 oz. dark chocolate chips
- 10 paper muffin cup liners
- 1 1/2 cups almond butter
- 1 cup confectioners' sugar

Direction

- Melt chocolate in 15-second periods in a ceramic or microwaveable glass bowl, for 1 to 3 minutes, stirring after each melting.
- Line muffin cup liners with approximate 2 tsps. of chocolate.
- In another bowl, combine almond butter with confectioners' sugar until well incorporated. Shape mixture into 10 balls. Press ball onto the chocolate layer, leaving a rim at edges, about 1/8 inch.
- Pour the rest of chocolate over almond butter to cover evenly. Allow to sit for 10 to 15 minutes at room temperature until set.

Nutrition Information

- Calories: 419 calories;
- Total Carbohydrate: 39.4 g

- Cholesterol: 0 mg
- Total Fat: 29.5 g
- Protein: 7.1 g
- Sodium: 176 mg

197. Gingerbread Truffles

"These truffles have seasonal charm."
Serving: Makes about 2 dozen

Ingredients

- 3/4 cup whipping cream
- 10 whole allspice
- 10 whole cloves
- 1 tbsp. mild-flavored (light) molasses
- 1 1/2 tsps. grated peeled fresh ginger
- 1/2 tsp. ground cinnamon
- Pinch of salt
- 7 oz. plus 12 oz. bittersweet (not unsweetened) or semisweet chocolate, chopped
- 7 oz. plus 12 oz. high-quality white chocolate (such as Lindt or Perugina), chopped
- 1/2 cup chopped crystallized ginger plus additional for garnish

Direction

- In heavy medium saucepan, bring the first 7 ingredients just to boiling; take out of the heat; allow to steep for an hour.
- In a large metal bowl set over a saucepan of simmering water, mix 7 oz. of each white chocolate and bittersweet chocolate; stir until melted and smooth. Take the bowl out of the water. Strain cream mixture into chocolate; stir to blend. Stir in half cup chopped crystallized ginger. Chill filling for at least 3 hours until firm.
- Use parchment to line a baking sheet. With 1-inch melon baller, spoon filling and roll between palms to shape into balls. Arrange on parchment. Place truffles in the fridge to chill for a minimum of 2 hours.
- Using parchment, line another sheet. In a medium metal bowl placed over a saucepan of

simmering water, arrange 12 oz. bittersweet chocolate; stir until smooth and melted. Take the bowl out of the water. Cool until the inserted thermometer into chocolate reads 115°F. Submerge 1 truffle in chocolate quickly. Lift the truffle out with fork; tap fork against the bowl's side to drip off excess coating. Slide truffle off fork and onto the lined sheet with a knife. Do the same with the rest of the truffles. Chill until set.
- Using parchment, line another baking sheet. In a separate medium metal bowl placed over a saucepan of simmering water, arrange 12 oz. white chocolate; stir until smooth and melted. Take the bowl out of the water. Cool until the inserted thermometer into chocolate reads 100°F. Hold a truffle between your index finger and thumb; coat halfway with white chocolate. Transfer to the lined sheet. Do the same with leftover truffles. If preferred, press small pieces of crystallized ginger atop truffles. Chill for about half an hour until firm. (You can prepare this a week ahead. Keep chilled with a cover.)

Nutrition Information

- Calories: 306
- Total Carbohydrate: 35 g
- Cholesterol: 16 mg
- Total Fat: 20 g
- Fiber: 2 g
- Protein: 3 g
- Sodium: 46 mg
- Saturated Fat: 12 g

198. Gobbler Goodies

"Make your Thanksgiving turkey more awesome and interesting with this recipe."
Serving: 28 servings. | Prep: 30m | Ready in: 35m

Ingredients

- 1/4 cup butter, cubed
- 4 cups miniature marshmallows

- 6 cups crisp rice cereal
- 28 Oreo cookies
- 1-1/2 cups chocolate frosting
- 1 package (11 oz.) candy corn

Direction

- Melt butter in a large saucepan. Stir in marshmallows, over low heat, until melted. Mix in cereal. Allow mixture to cool for 10 minutes. Shape cereal mixture into 1 1/2-inch balls using your buttered hands. Twist apart the sandwich cookies; distribute frosting on the inside of the cookies.
- Arrange 28 cookie halves under cereal balls to shape the base for each turkey. Lay 3 pieces of candy corn on the rest of cookie halves in a fan pattern. Press each cookie half onto cereal ball to make the tail. Use frosting to attach the remaining candy corn to make turkey's head.

Nutrition Information

- Calories: 220 calories
- Total Carbohydrate: 39 g
- Cholesterol: 4 mg
- Total Fat: 7 g
- Fiber: 0 g
- Protein: 1 g
- Sodium: 184 mg

199. Golf Balls

"I have made these candies for my family and friends for years and they always melt our hearts."
Serving: 18 | Prep: 20m | Ready in: 1h40m

Ingredients

- 1 lb. confectioners' sugar
- 1 1/2 cups chunky peanut butter
- 1 cup butter
- 2 cups flaked coconut
- 1 cup chopped walnuts
- 1 cup graham cracker crumbs
- 1 1/2 lbs. semisweet chocolate chips

Direction

- Put graham cracker crumbs, walnuts, coconut, butter, peanut butter and sugar in a large bowl and use hands to mix till everything thoroughly is blended. Roll to make 1 inch balls and lay them on a baking sheet. Chill in the fridge for an hour.
- Put the chocolate in a microwave-safe ceramic or glass bowl and melt chocolate in the microwave in half a minute intervals for 1-3 minutes, remember to stir after each melting (the time to melt chocolate depends on the power of your microwave). Remember not to overheat to prevent chocolate from scorching. Dip peanut butter balls into the chocolate till all are properly coated. Let the chocolate balls to become harden then serve.

Nutrition Information

- Calories: 597 calories;
- Total Carbohydrate: 62.4 g
- Cholesterol: 27 mg
- Total Fat: 39.5 g
- Protein: 8.5 g
- Sodium: 233 mg

200. Gooey Peanut Treats

"Adolescents need just four simple fixings to prepare a major panful of these chocolaty, shelled nut stuffed squares."
Serving: 2 to 2-1/2 dozen. | Prep: 5m | Ready in: 5m

Ingredients

- 2 cups (12 oz.) semisweet chocolate chips
- 1 can (14 oz.) sweetened condensed milk
- 1 jar (16 oz.) salted dry roasted peanuts
- 1 package (10-1/2 oz.) miniature marshmallows

Direction

- Melt the milk and chocolate chips in a microwave; mix until combined. Mix in the marshmallows and peanuts. Tap into a 13x9-inch greased pan. Prior to slicing, cool entirely.

Nutrition Information

- Calories: 231 calories
- Total Carbohydrate: 27 g
- Cholesterol: 5 mg
- Total Fat: 13 g
- Fiber: 2 g
- Protein: 6 g
- Sodium: 94 mg

201. Graham Cracker Fudge

"The sweetness in this fudge recipe is perfect.""
Serving: 30 | Prep: 5m | Ready in: 2h20m

Ingredients

- 1 (12 oz.) bag milk chocolate chips
- 2 (14 oz.) cans sweetened condensed milk
- 1 (14.4 oz.) package graham cracker, crushed into fine crumbs

Direction

- Combine condensed milk and chocolate chips over low heat in a saucepan; cook while stirring until chocolate is melted and no lumps remain in the mixture. Whisk in crushed graham crackers. Transfer mixture to a well-greased 13x9-inch glass baking dish; evenly smooth the surface. Let mixture cool for about 2 hours until set. Enjoy!

Nutrition Information

- Calories: 202 calories;
- Total Carbohydrate: 31.5 g
- Cholesterol: 13 mg
- Total Fat: 7.4 g
- Protein: 3.8 g
- Sodium: 134 mg

202. Halloween Chocolate Spiders

"With this spooky candy idea, you will have the perfect treat for this Halloween."
Serving: 2 dozen. | Prep: 20m | Ready in: 20m

Ingredients

- 8 oz. semisweet chocolate, chopped
- 2 cups miniature marshmallows
- Black or red shoestring licorice
- 24 small round candy-coated milk chocolate balls (such as Hersheys or Sixlets)

Direction

- Microwave chocolate at 50% power in a microwaveable bowl for 1.5 minutes, stirring every 30-second. Stir until the chocolate melts and allow to sit for 5 minutes. Mix in marshmallows. Dollop the mixture by tablespoonfuls onto a baking sheet lined with waxed paper. Cut the licorice into pieces of 2 inches; on each mound, press down 8 pieces to make the legs. Press in each 2 chocolate balls to make eyes.
- Chill in the refrigerator for about 20 minutes to firm up.

Nutrition Information

- Calories: 23 calories
- Total Carbohydrate: 5 g
- Cholesterol: 0 mg
- Total Fat: 1 g
- Fiber: 0 g
- Protein: 0 g
- Sodium: 2 mg

203. Hogs And Kisses

"There is a trend that bacon is a dessert ingredient. The combination of salty and sweet is surprisingly delicious."
Serving: 8 | Prep: 10m | Ready in: 25m

Ingredients

- 8 slices bacon
- 1/2 cup milk chocolate chips

Direction

- Slice bacon in half. Put the bacon in a big, deep skillet, and cook over medium-high heat, flipping sometimes, about 10 mins, until browned evenly. Drain the bacon pieces on a paper towel-lined plate.
- In a microwaveable glass or ceramic bowl, melt the chocolate in 30 second intervals, for 1-3 mins, mixing after each interval (depending on your microwave). To avoid scorching the chocolate, don't overheat. Dip all, except the last inch of each strip of bacon in the melted chocolate. Put bacon on waxed paper and let cool and harden prior to serving.

Nutrition Information

- Calories: 184 calories;
- Total Carbohydrate: 6.5 g
- Cholesterol: 23 mg
- Total Fat: 16.1 g
- Protein: 3.9 g
- Sodium: 251 mg

204. Holiday Bark 4 Ways: Green Tea And Sea Salt Bark

"Have this chocolate candy bar that is made from combination of melted white chocolate and white chocolate mixed with green tea powder. Season it with sea salt then chill."
Serving: 12 | Prep: 20m | Ready in: 1h5m

Ingredients

- Chocolate Bark Base:
- 3 (4 oz.) packages Ghirardelli® White Chocolate Baking Bars, chopped, divided
- Green Tea and Sea Salt Bark:
- 1 tbsp. matcha (green tea powder)
- 2 tsps. sea salt or kosher salt, or more to taste

Direction

- Prepare a baking sheet by lining with parchment paper. Put it on side.
- In the top pan of a double boiler put 2 sliced white chocolate bars and hot not boiling water in the bottom pan. (For alternative, prepare a saucepan half filled with water topped with a glass or metal mixing bowl). Let them melt while stirring occasionally. Take the melted chocolate from heat and set aside to cool for 15 minutes.
- Add into melted chocolate the remaining 1 bar of sliced chocolate; mix until melted and smooth.
- Split in half the melted chocolate then add matcha into one half; stir.
- In prepared baking sheet, transfer white and green chocolate then spread at least 1/4 inch thick. Using a spatula, swirl slowly then season with salt.
- For 30 minutes, refrigerate until firm. Lift candy using parchment then break into smaller pieces. Place candies in between waxed paper sheets in an airtight sealed container at room temperature. It can last for 3 days or 2 weeks if refrigerated.

Nutrition Information

- Calories: 156 calories;
- Total Carbohydrate: 17.6 g
- Cholesterol: 7 mg
- Total Fat: 9.5 g
- Protein: 1.4 g
- Sodium: 314 mg

205. Holiday Bark 4 Ways: Orange Pistachio Bark

"This rich, creamy, and fruity dessert is made with melted dark chocolate and orange zest. Top with orange peel and pistachios, your guests will never get enough of it."
Serving: 12

Ingredients

- Chocolate Bark Base:
- 3 (4 oz.) bars Ghirardelli® 60% Cacao Baking Bars, chopped, divided
- Orange Pistachio Bark:
- 1 tsp. grated orange zest
- 3/4 cup coarsely chopped roasted, salted shelled pistachios
- Orange peel strips

Direction

- Place parchment paper on the surface of a baking sheet, then set aside.
- Chop 2 chocolate bars and place the chopped pieces in the top pan of a double boiler; use hot water, not boiling. (If you don't have a double boiler, you may opt to use a metal or glass mixing bowl positioned on top of a saucepan half filled with hot water.) Wait for the chocolate to melt, occasionally stirring. Once smooth, remove melted chocolate from heat and let cool for 15 minutes.
- Add the 1 remaining chopped chocolate bar. Stir well until chocolate is smooth and completely melted. Add orange zest and stir.

- Place the mixture on the baking sheet. Evenly spread until it's about 1/4 inch-thick. Top with orange peel strips and pistachios.
- Chill in the refrigerator for 30 minutes or until the chocolate becomes firm. Lift the chocolate bar using the parchment paper; slice to make squares or break into pieces. In a container with an airtight lid, store the chocolate bars between sheets of waxed paper up to 3 days at room temperature, or up to 2 weeks inside the refrigerator.

Nutrition Information

- Calories: 191 calories;
- Total Carbohydrate: 17.5 g
- Cholesterol: 0 mg
- Total Fat: 14.2 g
- Protein: 3 g
- Sodium: 34 mg

206. Holiday Bark 4 Ways: Peppermint Bark

"This delicious treat is a combination of dark chocolate, white chocolate and peppermint chunks. What can be a sweeter gift than this?"
Serving: 12 | Prep: 20m | Ready in: 1h5m

Ingredients

- Chocolate Bark Base:
- 3 (4 oz.) bars Ghirardelli® 60% Cacao Baking Bars, chopped
- Peppermint Bark:
- 1 (10 oz.) package Ghirardelli® Holiday Baking Peppermint Chunks
- 2 oz. Ghirardelli® White Chocolate Baking Bar

Direction

- Use parchment paper to line a baking sheet. Set aside.
- Chop down 2 chocolate bars and put them in the top pan of a double boiler over hot water (Remember not to use boiling water here. You

can also fill half a saucepan with water then put a metal or glass mixing bowl on top). Let the chocolate melt, stirring sometimes. Get the double boiler off heat and allow the melted chocolate to sit to cool down for 15 minutes.

- Mix one bar of chopped chocolate into the melted chocolate. Stir till the mixture is melted and smooth.
- Put in 3/4 cup peppermint chunks and stir. Transfer the mixture onto the prepared baking sheet. Spread to make 1/4 inch thick layer. Use the rest of peppermint chunks to sprinkle.
- Put white chocolate in a small microwave safe bowl and microwave on medium power (at 50% power) in half a minute intervals, remember to stir between intervals till the white chocolate is melted.
- Get the bowl out of the microwave and stir. If the chocolate is not melted, put the bowl back to the microwave and repeat heating and stir between half a minute intervals to prevent chocolate from scorching.
- Scoop the white chocolate mixture into a large plastic self-sealing bag. Cut off one corner; drizzle the chocolate over bark.
- Chill for half an hour till it become firm. Lift candy by using parchment; crack into pieces. Place candy between sheets of waxed paper and store in an airtight container in the fridge for up to 2 weeks or at room temperature for up to 3 days.

Nutrition Information

- Calories: 171 calories;
- Total Carbohydrate: 18.1 g
- Cholesterol: 1 mg
- Total Fat: 12.1 g
- Protein: 1.5 g
- Sodium: 3 mg

207. Holiday White Chocolate Fudge

"This creamy fudge is what I serve my family in December aside from the classic chocolate."
Serving: about 3 lbs. (117 pieces) | Prep: 10m | Ready in: 25m

Ingredients

- 1-1/2 tsps. plus 3/4 cup butter, softened, divided
- 3 cups sugar
- 1 can (5 oz.) evaporated milk (about 2/3 cup)
- 1 package (12 oz.) white baking chips
- 1 jar (7 oz.) marshmallow creme
- 1 tsp. vanilla extract

Direction

- Line a 13x9-in. pan using foil; butter foil with 1-1/2 tsps..
- Mix leftover butter, milk and sugar in a heavy saucepan; heat up to a rapid boil over medium heat, mixing continuously. Heat up to a boil for 4 minutes, mixing continuously. Take off from heat; mix in marshmallow crème and baking chips until melted. Mix in vanilla. Put into prepared pan immediately. Chill for 1 to 2 hours until set.
- Take fudge out of pan with foil. Discard foil; slice fudge into 1-inch squares. Put among layers of waxed paper in an airtight container to store.

Nutrition Information

- Calories: 54 calories
- Total Carbohydrate: 8 g
- Cholesterol: 4 mg
- Total Fat: 2 g
- Fiber: 0 g
- Protein: 0 g
- Sodium: 15 mg

208. Homemade Candy Bars

"Enjoy a classic candy bar filled with almond and coconut mixed into chocolate."
Serving: 24 | Prep: 10m | Ready in: 1h

Ingredients

- 1/2 cup butter, softened
- 1 cup white sugar
- 3 eggs
- 1 cup all-purpose flour
- 1/4 cup unsweetened cocoa powder
- 2/3 cup chopped almonds
- 2 cups flaked coconut
- 1 (14 oz.) can sweetened condensed milk
- 1 (16 oz.) container prepared chocolate frosting

Direction

- Set oven to 175°C (350°F) and start preheating. Prepare a 13x9-in. baking pan by greasing.
- Beat white sugar and butter in a bowl. Mix in one egg at a time; mix in cocoa powder and flour. Pat evenly into the greased baking pan.
- Bake at 175°C (350°F) for 15-20 minutes; take out and sprinkle with coconut and almonds. Glaze with sweetened condensed milk. Continue baking.
- Bake for another 15 minutes until it turns golden. Wait until fully cool. Frost and cut into square pieces.

Nutrition Information

- Calories: 266 calories;
- Total Carbohydrate: 37.2 g
- Cholesterol: 39 mg
- Total Fat: 12.4 g
- Protein: 3.8 g
- Sodium: 109 mg

209. Homemade Caramels With Dark Chocolate And Sea Salt

"These buttery caramels are delicious."
Serving: 64 | Prep: 10m | Ready in: 9h50m

Ingredients

- 1 cup white sugar
- 1 cup heavy whipping cream, divided
- 3/4 cup light corn syrup
- 1/2 cup butter
- 1/2 tsp. vanilla extract
- 1 1/4 cups 60% cacao dark chocolate chips
- 3/4 cup semisweet chocolate chips
- 2 tbsps. shortening
- 1 tbsp. sea salt

Direction

- Brush an 8-inch square baking pan with butter.
- In a saucepan, mix butter, light corn syrup, half cup cream and white sugar. Boil over medium heat, mixing often. Stir the remaining half cup cream. Cook without stirring until mixture reaches 242°(117°C) or until when dropped in cold water, a small amount of the caramel mixture forms a firm yet pliable ball. Take out of the heat; stir in vanilla extract.
- Place caramel mixture in a baking pan. Let cool slightly. Use plastic wrap to cover; keep in the fridge for 8 hours or for one night.
- Take baking pan out of the fridge; let the mixture warm up slightly, about half an hour. Using waxed paper, line a baking sheet.
- In a ceramic bowl or microwave-safe glass, combine semisweet and dark chocolate chips with shortening. Microwave; stir after each melting; in 30 seconds interval for about 1 1/2 minutes.
- Cut caramel into 1-inch squares. Submerge caramel squares into melted chocolate, shaking off excess. Arrange on lined baking sheet; top with sea salt. Chill about 1 hour until hardened.

Nutrition Information

- Calories: 77 calories;
- Total Carbohydrate: 9.7 g
- Cholesterol: 9 mg
- Total Fat: 4.7 g
- Protein: 0.3 g
- Sodium: 98 mg

210. Homemade Chocolate Easter Eggs

"These store for up to a week in the fridge."
Serving: 20 | Prep: 25m | Ready in: 5h30m

Ingredients

- 9 oz. 85% dark chocolate, chopped
- 1/4 cup heavy whipping cream
- 3 tbsps. unsalted butter
- 1 tbsp. rum
- 1/4 cup confectioners' sugar, or to taste
- 1/4 cup unsweetened cocoa powder, or as needed
- 1/4 cup coconut flakes, or as needed

Direction

- Put butter, cream and chocolate in top of double boiler above simmering water. Frequently mix, scraping sides down with rubber spatula to prevent scorching, for about 5 minutes till chocolate melts.
- Take off heat; mix rum in then confectioners' sugar. Briefly cool; cover. Cool till firm for about 5 hours in the fridge.
- Form chocolate mixture to oval eggs. Put coconut flakes and cocoa powder to different small bowls. Roll 1/2 chocolate eggs in cocoa powder and other 1/2 into coconut flakes. Put into fridge.

Nutrition Information

- Calories: 111 calories;
- Total Carbohydrate: 10.1 g
- Cholesterol: 9 mg

- Total Fat: 7.9 g
- Protein: 1.1 g
- Sodium: 3 mg

211.Homemade Melt-in-your-mouth Dark Chocolate (paleo)

"With this recipe, you can make chocolate at home. This is made without any waxes or artificial ingredients. You can adjust the sweetness and modify the ingredients to suit your taste."
Serving: 8 | Prep: 10m | Ready in: 1h10m

Ingredients

- 1/2 cup coconut oil
- 1/2 cup cocoa powder
- 3 tbsps. honey
- 1/2 tsp. vanilla extract

Direction

- In a saucepan, gently melt coconut oil over medium-low heat. Mix vanilla extract, honey, and cocoa powder into the melted oil until fully combined. Pour the mixture to a pliable tray or a candy mold. Refrigerate for 60 minutes until cold.

Nutrition Information

- Calories: 157 calories;
- Total Carbohydrate: 9.4 g
- Cholesterol: 0 mg
- Total Fat: 14.7 g
- Protein: 1.1 g
- Sodium: 1 mg

212. Homemade Peanut Butter Cups

"This treat is like candy."
Serving: 30

Ingredients

- 2 cups milk chocolate chips
- 2 tbsps. shortening
- 1/2 cup butter
- 1/2 cup crunchy peanut butter
- 1 cup confectioners' sugar
- 2/3 cup graham cracker crumbs

Direction

- Mix shortening and chocolate chips in 1-quart saucepan. Cook while stirring occasionally over low heat for 3-5 minutes until smooth and melted.
- Loosen top paper cup from stack but not remove from stack to sustain better stability while coating. Coat inside top evenly with about a tsp. of melted chocolate to about 1/8-inch thickness, using a small pain brush; bring coating almost to top of cup, not over the edge. Do the same with other cups until coat 30 cups; keep them in the fridge.
- Mix peanut butter and margarine or butter in 2-quart saucepan. Cook while stirring occasionally over medium heat for 4-6 minutes until melted. Stir in graham cracker crumbs and confectioners' sugar. Press about half tbsp. filling into each chocolate cup.
- Scoop about half tsp. melted chocolate over filling; spread to cover. Freeze for about 2 hours until firm, peel paper cups off carefully. Keep in the fridge.

Nutrition Information

- Calories: 140 calories;
- Total Carbohydrate: 13.6 g
- Cholesterol: 11 mg
- Total Fat: 9.5 g
- Protein: 2 g
- Sodium: 54 mg

213. Homemade Valentine's Chocolates

"A wonderful flavor profile in these truffles!"
Serving: 32 | Prep: 15m | Ready in: 50m

Ingredients

- 1/2 lb. high-quality dark chocolate, chopped
- 1/8 tsp. ground dried chipotle pepper
- 1 pinch salt
- 1/2 cup heavy whipping cream
- 3 tbsps. unsweetened cocoa powder, or as needed

Direction

- Put chocolate in bowl; add salt and chipotle pepper.
- Heat cream in small saucepan on medium low heat till it reaches a boil. Put cream on chocolate; let stand for 3 minutes.
- Gently mix till chocolate mixture is fully smooth. Put chocolate mixture out on plastic wrap sheet on work surface. Pick up a plastic edge; roll chocolate to a rough log shape. Keep rolling and wrapping chocolate in plastic. Refrigerate for 30-60 minutes till firm and chilled.
- Put cocoa in small bowl. Unwrap chocolate; cut in half crosswise. Lengthwise, slice each half to halves. Cut candy to 1/2-in. square "stones" roughly. Put chocolate pieces in cocoa; gently toss to coat.

Nutrition Information

- Calories: 48 calories;
- Total Carbohydrate: 4.9 g
- Cholesterol: 5 mg
- Total Fat: 3.6 g
- Protein: 0.5 g
- Sodium: 2 mg

214. Hot Chocolate Truffles

"Hot chocolate truffles!"
Serving: 20 | Prep: 30m | Ready in: 2h

Ingredients

- 50 NILLA® waters
- 3 (.96 oz.) envelopes Swiss Miss® Simply Cocoa Dark Chocolate Hot Cocoa Mix
- 1 (3.25 oz.) cup Snack Pack® Chocolate Pudding
- 1/2 cup Reddi-wip® Original Dairy Whipped Topping
- 1/2 cup miniature marshmallows
- 1 cup premier white morsels
- 1 tbsp. Pure Wesson® Vegetable Oil
- Coarse colored sugar (optional)

Direction

- Line parchment paper on shallow baking pan; put aside. Pulse cocoa mix and wafers to fine crumbs in a food processor. Add Reddi-wip and pudding; pulse till mixture comes together and makes a ball. Add marshmallows; pulse till marshmallows get cut to small pieces.
- Roll the wafer mixture to 1-inch balls; put on pan. Freeze till set for 30 minutes.
- Put oil and morsels in a small microwave-safe bowl then microwave for 30 seconds on high; mix. Microwave for 30 more seconds till soft on high; mix till completely melted. Roll 1 truffle in mixture till coated evenly; use fork to remove. Let excess drip off. Put on pan; sprinkle colored sugar, if desired, immediately. Repeat with leftover truffles. Refrigerate till firm for 1 hour. Keep in an airtight container in the fridge.

Nutrition Information

- Calories: 133 calories;
- Total Carbohydrate: 17.8 g
- Cholesterol: 5 mg
- Total Fat: 6.3 g
- Protein: 1.3 g

- Sodium: 74 mg

215. Ice Cream Sundae Caramels

"Every holiday's favorite soft caramels!"
Serving: about 3-1/2 lbs.. | Prep: 20m | Ready in: 60m

Ingredients

- 2 cups sugar
- 2 cups (16 oz.) dark corn syrup
- 2 cups (1 pint) vanilla ice cream, melted, divided
- 1 cup butter, cubed
- 8 oz. milk chocolate candy coating, coarsely chopped
- 1/2 cup peanuts, finely chopped

Direction

- In a heavy 4-qt. saucepan, combine the butter, 1 cup of ice cream, corn syrup, and sugar. Cook and stir over low heat until the mixture starts to boil. Raise the heat to medium; cook and stir until it nearly reaches into a firm-ball stage (candy thermometer must read 242°).
- Take it off from the heat; mix in the remaining ice cream slowly. Bring it back onto the heat; cook (do not stir) until it reaches into a firm-ball stage (244°). Pour it into a buttered 13-in. x 9-in. pan immediately without stirring it. Allow it to cool until firm. Flip candy out onto a baking sheet.
- Melt the candy coating in a microwave; mix until smooth. Spread on top of the candy; sprinkle nuts on top. Score the top into 1-in. squares. Let it sit until set. Slice it along the score marks into 1-in. squares. Wrap each in a plastic wrap or waxed paper.

Nutrition Information

- Calories: 61 calories
- Total Carbohydrate: 10 g
- Cholesterol: 5 mg
- Total Fat: 3 g
- Fiber: 0 g

- Protein: 0 g
- Sodium: 25 mg

216. Irish Cream Truffle Fudge

"Amazingly good!"
Serving: 24 | Ready in: 1h45m

Ingredients

- 3 cups semisweet chocolate chips
- 1 cup white chocolate chips
- 1/4 cup butter
- 3 cups confectioners' sugar
- 1 cup Irish cream liqueur
- 1 1/2 cups chopped nuts
- 1 cup semisweet chocolate chips
- 1/2 cup white chocolate chips
- 4 tbsps. Irish cream liqueur
- 2 tbsps. butter

Direction

- Butter an 8x8-inch pan.
- Melt 3 cups of semisweet chocolate chips, 1/4 cup of butter and 1 cup of white chocolate chips in top half of double boiler till soft enough to mix.
- Mix Irish cream and confectioners' sugar in till mixture is smooth. Mix nuts in. Put mixture in the prepared pan; lay plastic wrap sheet on top. Press then smooth the top down.
- Melt leftover chocolates till soft in top half of double boiler. Take off heat; use fork to beat Irish cream and butter in till smooth. Spread topping on cooled fudge using a knife. Put plastic wrap on top if you want a smooth top. Refrigerate for 1-2 hours minimum till firm. You can easily freeze fudge.

Nutrition Information

- Calories: 383 calories;
- Total Carbohydrate: 46.8 g
- Cholesterol: 10 mg
- Total Fat: 20.3 g

- Protein: 3.5 g
- Sodium: 37 mg

217. Jan's Chocolate Coffee Bean Bark

"These candies can be a wonderful gift for those who love coffee and chocolate.""
Serving: 48 | Prep: 20m | Ready in: 40m

Ingredients

- 1/2 cup roasted whole coffee beans
- 1 (11.5 oz.) package milk chocolate chips
- 1 tbsp. shortening, or more if desired (optional)
- 11 1/2 oz. dark chocolate chips

Direction

- Line a silicone baking mat over a 9x14-inch baking sheet.
- Put coffee beans into a food processor and process several times until they are roughly chopped. Heat milk chocolate in the top of a double boiler over simmering water, stirring frequently and scraping down the sides using a rubber spatula to prevent scorching, approximately 5 minutes. Put in shortening to smooth the mixture; whisk until smooth. Whisk coffee beans into the melted milk chocolate until coated.
- Transfer the milk chocolate mixture to the prepared baking sheet; spread mixture to reach the edges. Chill in the fridge.
- Heat dark chocolate in the top of a double boiler over simmering water, stirring frequently and scraping down the sides using a rubber spatula to prevent scorching, approximately 5 minutes. Put in shortening to smooth the melted dark chocolate, mix until smooth. Take out of the heat.
- Stream the melted dark chocolate over the chilled milk chocolate mixture; smooth the surface. Chill, about 10 to 15 minutes, until harden.

- Take off the silicone mat; remove the chocolate mixture to a work surface. Use a sharp knife to divide into pieces. The bark will crack and break while you cut.

Nutrition Information

- Calories: 66 calories;
- Total Carbohydrate: 8.8 g
- Cholesterol: 0 mg
- Total Fat: 4.1 g
- Protein: 0.3 g
- Sodium: 2 mg

218. Janaan's Fudge

"This is sweet chocolaty treat that is assembled right away."
Serving: 2-1/2 dozen. | Prep: 20m | Ready in: 30m

Ingredients

- 2-1/4 cups sugar
- 3/4 cup evaporated milk
- 16 large marshmallows
- 1/4 cup butter, cubed
- 1/4 tsp. salt
- 1 cup (6 oz.) semisweet chocolate chips
- 1 cup chopped walnuts
- 1 tsp. vanilla extract

Direction

- Mix the first 5 ingredients in a heavy saucepan. Cook and mix over medium heat until the blend boils. Boil and mix for another 5 minutes. Take away from the heat. Toss in chocolate chips until melted. Mix in vanilla and nuts. Distribute in a buttered 8-inch square pan. Cool. Slice into squares. Keep in the fridge.

Nutrition Information

- Calories: 144 calories
- Total Carbohydrate: 23 g
- Cholesterol: 6 mg

- Total Fat: 6 g
- Fiber: 1 g
- Protein: 2 g
- Sodium: 44 mg

219. Layered Mint Chocolate Fudge

"Chocolate fudge is layered with white or hued mint fudge in this beautiful occasion sweets."
Serving: 30 | Prep: 20m | Ready in: 2h20m

Ingredients

- 2 cups semi-sweet chocolate chips
- 1 (14 oz.) can EAGLE BRAND® Sweetened Condensed Milk, divided
- 2 tsps. vanilla extract
- 6 oz. white confectioners coating* or premium white chocolate chips
- 1 tbsp. peppermint extract
- Green or red food coloring (optional)

Direction

- Melt the 1 cup sweetened condensed milk with chocolate chips in a big saucepan over low heat; put in vanilla. Spread half of the blend into 8- or 9-inch square wax-paper-lined pan; chill for 10 minutes or until firm. Keep the leftover chocolate blend at room temperature.
- Melt the leftover sweetened condensed milk with white confectioners coating in heavy saucepan over low heat (blend will be thick). Put in food coloring (optional) and peppermint extract.
- Spread over chilled chocolate layer; chill until firm, about another 10 minutes.
- Spread reserved chocolate blend over the mint layer. Chill until firm, about 2 hours. Move to the cutting board; peel off the paper then slice into squares. Keep, covered, the remainder in the fridge.

Nutrition Information

- Calories: 146 calories;
- Total Carbohydrate: 14.6 g
- Cholesterol: 6 mg
- Total Fat: 6.6 g
- Protein: 1.3 g
- Sodium: 25 mg

---

220. Layered Peanut Butter Chocolate Fudge

"A traditional blend of chocolate and peanut butter in this creamy and smooth fudge."
Serving: About 2-1/2 lbs.. | Prep: 25m | Ready in: 25m

Ingredients

- 1-1/2 tsps. butter, softened
- 2-2/3 cups milk chocolate chips
- 1 cup creamy peanut butter, divided
- 2 tbsps. shortening, divided
- 2-2/3 cups vanilla or white chips

Direction

- Using foil, line a 13-in. x 9-in. tray; butter the foil and put aside. Melt a tbsp. shortening, half cup peanut butter and the milk chocolate chips in a big heavy saucepan over low heat; cook and mix continuously until smooth. Put into lined pan. Chill for 10 minutes or until set.
- In the meantime, melt the shortening, the leftover peanut butter and vanilla chips in the microwave at 70% power for a minute; mix. Microwave at extra 10- to 20-second intervals, mixing until smooth.
- Put over the chocolate layer evenly. Chill for half an hour or until set. Take fudge out of the pan using foil. Discard the foil gently; slice into 1-in. squares.

Nutrition Information

- Calories: 56 calories
- Total Carbohydrate: 5 g
- Cholesterol: 2 mg

- Total Fat: 4 g
- Fiber: 0 g
- Protein: 1 g
- Sodium: 17 mg

---

221. Lemon Cream Bonbons

"These treats can be served year-round."
Serving: about 4 dozen. | Prep: 30m | Ready in: 30m

Ingredients

- 2 packages (8 oz. each) cream cheese, softened
- 2 tbsps. grated lemon zest
- 3 tbsps. lemon juice
- 1 tsp. lemon extract
- 1 cup confectioners' sugar
- 1 lb. dark chocolate candy coating, melted
- 4 oz. white candy coating, melted

Direction

- Beat lemon extract, juice and zest, and cream cheese in a large bowl. Whisk in confectioners' sugar gradually. Freeze for 2 hours with a cover.
- Drop mixture by 1-in. balls onto baking sheets lined with waxed paper, using a small ice cream scoop. Freeze with a cover for an hour.
- Working with a few frozen balls at a time, coat with melted chocolate; let any excess drip off. Place on baking sheets lined with waxed paper. Allow to rest until set.
- Scoop melted candy coating into a heavy-duty resealable plastic bag. Slice a small hole in the corner of the bag; drizzle coating on top of candies. Keep in the fridge. Take the candies out of the fridge right before serving.

Nutrition Information

- Calories: 105 calories
- Total Carbohydrate: 11 g
- Cholesterol: 10 mg
- Total Fat: 7 g
- Fiber: 0 g

- Protein: 1 g
- Sodium: 28 mg

222. Lemon Drop Bark

"Use high quality ingredients for this recipe."
Serving: 12 | Prep: 10m | Ready in: 42m

Ingredients

- 1 (12 oz.) package white chocolate chips (such as Nestle®)
- 3/4 cup lemon drop candies (such as Brach's®)

Direction

- In microwave-safe 2-cup measuring cup, put white chocolate chips. Heat till melted for 2 minutes in microwave; mix till smooth.
- Put lemon drop candies in resealable plastic bag. Put bag into another resealable bag, making a double bag so candies don't puncture bag. Use mallet/rolling pin to crack candies till broken to small pieces.
- Mix cracker candies in melted white chocolate. On aluminum foil piece, smooth mixture to 1/4-inch thick. Chill in the fridge for at least 30 minutes till set. Break bark to small pieces; keep in the fridge in airtight container.

Nutrition Information

- Calories: 219 calories;
- Total Carbohydrate: 30.7 g
- Cholesterol: 6 mg
- Total Fat: 10 g
- Protein: 2 g
- Sodium: 36 mg

223. Les Truffles Au Chocolat

"These dipped balls combine orange and chocolate."
Serving: 3 dozen. | Prep: 40m | Ready in: 45m

Ingredients

- 1 cup (6 oz.) semisweet chocolate chips
- 1 cup (6 oz.) milk chocolate chips
- 5 tbsps. butter, cubed
- 1 cup plus 2 tbsps. confectioners' sugar
- 3 tbsps. heavy whipping cream
- 3 tbsps. thawed orange juice concentrate
- 1 tsp. vanilla extract
- 3 tbsps. baking cocoa

Direction

- Mix butter and chocolate chips in a small heavy saucepan. Cook while stirring over low heat until melted and smooth. Take out of the heat. Stir in vanilla, orange juice concentrate, cream and confectioners' sugar. Keep in the fridge, covered, until firm or for 3 hours.
- Quickly form into 1-in. balls; coat in cocoa. Keep in an airtight container in the fridge.

Nutrition Information

- Calories: 84 calories
- Total Carbohydrate: 10 g
- Cholesterol: 7 mg
- Total Fat: 5 g
- Fiber: 1 g
- Protein: 1 g
- Sodium: 16 mg

224. Light Chocolate Truffles

"I love giving this as gifts."
Serving: about 1-1/2 dozen. | Prep: 25m | Ready in: 25m

Ingredients

- 1/3 cup semisweet chocolate chips
- 4 oz. reduced-fat cream cheese
- 1/3 cup plus 2 tsps. baking cocoa, divided

- 1-1/4 cups plus 2 tsps. confectioners' sugar, divided

Direction

- Melt chocolate chips in microwave; mix till smooth. Put aside.
- Beat cream cheese till fluffy in small bowl. Beat melted chocolate and 1/3 cup cocoa in. Beat 1 1/4 cups confectioners' sugar in slowly. Coat hands lightly with confectioners' sugar then roll chocolate mixture to 1-in. balls. Roll in confectioners' sugar/leftover cocoa. Cover; refrigerate for 1 hour minimum.

Nutrition Information

- Calories: 62 calories
- Total Carbohydrate: 11 g
- Cholesterol: 4 mg
- Total Fat: 2 g
- Fiber: 0 g
- Protein: 1 g
- Sodium: 24 mg

---

225. Liquor-infused Chocolate Strawberries

"This absolutely delectable and rich treat takes a little time but it's worth it. Inject the strawberries with orange brandy then dip them in rich dark chocolate."
Serving: 16 | Prep: 15m | Ready in: 15m

Ingredients

- 16 large fresh strawberries with leaves
- 1/2 cup brandy-based orange liqueur (such as Grand Marnier®)
- 1 lb. bittersweet chocolate, chopped
- 2 tbsps. shortening
- 2 tbsps. heavy cream
- 1/4 cup brandy-based orange liqueur (such as Grand Marnier®)
- 1 (1 oz.) square chopped white chocolate

Direction

- Rinse then dry the strawberries thoroughly. Inject about 2 tsp of brandy into each berry using a clean marinade injector or a syringe. Place on a baking sheet and store in the fridge for 30 minutes.
- Combine shortening and bittersweet chocolate in a metal bowl set over a pan filled with simmering water. Occasionally stir till smooth and melted. Stir in 1/4 cup of brandy and heavy cream. In another bowl, place the white chocolate. Once the dark chocolate has melted, set the white chocolate bowl over the pan filled with simmering water and stir occasionally till smooth. Make sure to take away from the heat as soon as the chocolate is mostly melted, white chocolate can be sensitive.
- Dip the strawberries into chocolate, allow the excess drip off into the bowl then put on a waxed paper till set. Once all the strawberries have been dipped in chocolate, dip a fork into the white chocolate then drizzle over the berries back and forth to stripe.

Nutrition Information

- Calories: 231 calories;
- Total Carbohydrate: 23.3 g
- Cholesterol: 4 mg
- Total Fat: 12.5 g
- Protein: 2.2 g
- Sodium: 5 mg

---

226. Luscious Chocolate Truffles

"Top with whatever toppings you like such as sprinkles or colored sugar."
Serving: 72 | Prep: 10m | Ready in: 3h

Ingredients

- 3 cups semi-sweet chocolate chips
- 1 (14 oz.) can sweetened condensed milk
- 1 tbsp. vanilla extract

Direction

- Melt sweetened condensed milk and chocolate chips in big saucepan; take off heat. Mix vanilla in. Put mixture in a medium bowl; cover. Chill till firm for 2-3 hours.
- Form mixture to 1-inch balls. Decorate and/roll in desired covering. Refrigerate in tightly covered dish.

Nutrition Information

- Calories: 53 calories;
- Total Carbohydrate: 7.5 g
- Cholesterol: 2 mg
- Total Fat: 2.5 g
- Protein: 0.9 g
- Sodium: 7 mg

227. Made-in-minutes No-cook Fudge

"Wonderful fudge with no heating and cooking. Put almonds, chopped walnuts and other flavorings if you prefer."
Serving: 16 | Prep: 15m | Ready in: 1h15m

Ingredients

- 1 cup virgin coconut oil, room temperature
- 1 cup unsweetened cocoa powder
- 1/2 cup honey

Direction

- Slightly grease 8x8 inch baking dish.
- Put the coconut oil into a bowl, then sift in the cocoa, mixing to evenly combine. Mix in the honey and stir until smooth. Lather mixture evenly into greased dish, and chill no less than an hour. Slice into 1-inch squares.

Nutrition Information

- Calories: 162 calories;
- Total Carbohydrate: 11.6 g
- Cholesterol: 0 mg

- Total Fat: 14.4 g
- Protein: 1.1 g
- Sodium: 2 mg

228. Maine Potato Candy

"This candy reminds you of old-school flavors."
Serving: 2 lbs.. | Prep: 30m | Ready in: 30m

Ingredients

- 4 cups confectioners' sugar
- 4 cups sweetened shredded coconut
- 3/4 cup cold mashed potatoes (without added milk and butter)
- 1-1/2 tsps. vanilla extract
- 1/2 tsp. salt
- 1 lb. dark chocolate candy coating, coarsely chopped

Direction

- Mix the first 5 ingredients in large bowl. Using foil, line a 9-in. square pan; butter the foil. Spread coconut mixture into pan. Chill with a cover overnight. Cut into 2-in. x 1-in. rectangles. Freeze with a cover.
- Melt candy coating in a microwave; stir until smooth. Coat bars with coating; let any excess drip off. Transfer to waxed paper to set. Keep in an airtight container.

Nutrition Information

- Calories: 155 calories
- Total Carbohydrate: 25 g
- Cholesterol: 0 mg
- Total Fat: 7 g
- Fiber: 1 g
- Protein: 1 g
- Sodium: 55 mg

229. Mamie Eisenhower's Fudge

"My mom has known this recipe 40 years ago, you must make it to see how great it is."
Serving: about 6 lbs.. | Prep: 20m | Ready in: 20m

Ingredients

- 1 tbsp. plus 1/2 cup butter, divided
- 3 milk chocolate candy bars (two 7 oz., one 1.55 oz.), broken into pieces
- 4 cups (24 oz.) semisweet chocolate chips
- 1 jar (7 oz.) marshmallow creme
- 1 can (12 oz.) evaporated milk
- 4-1/2 cups sugar
- 2 cups chopped walnuts

Direction

- Line a 13-in. x 9-in. pan using foil and grease the foil with a tbsp. butter; put aside. Mix the marshmallow crème, chocolate chips and candy bars in a big heat-proof bowl; put aside.
- Over medium-low heat, combine the leftover butter, sugar and milk in a big heavy saucepan. Heat up to a boil, mixing frequently. Boil and mix for 4-1/2 minutes. Pour on top of chocolate mixture; mix until chocolate is melted, and mixture is creamy and smooth. Mix in walnuts. Pour into lined and greased pan. Cover and chill until set.
- Lift fudge out of pan with foil; slice into 1-inch squares. Put in an airtight container in the fridge to store.

Nutrition Information

- Calories: 107 calories
- Total Carbohydrate: 16 g
- Cholesterol: 4 mg
- Total Fat: 5 g
- Fiber: 1 g
- Protein: 1 g
- Sodium: 17 mg

230. Maple Cream Bonbons

"My family consistently grins when I fix these chocolates."
Serving: 5 dozen. | Prep: 30m | Ready in: 30m

Ingredients

- 1 cup butter, softened
- 3-1/2 cups confectioners' sugar
- 3 tbsps. maple flavoring
- 2 cups chopped walnuts
- 2 cups semisweet chocolate chips
- 1 cup butterscotch chips

Direction

- Cream the maple flavoring, sugar and butter in a big bowl until smooth. Mix in the walnuts. Form into balls of 1-inch; put onto baking sheets lined with waxed paper. Freeze till firm.
- Melt the chips in a microwave; mix till smooth. Dip the balls into chocolate; let the excess drip off. Put onto baking sheets lined with waxed paper. Refrigerate until set. Keep in the fridge.

Nutrition Information

- Calories: 131 calories
- Total Carbohydrate: 14 g
- Cholesterol: 8 mg
- Total Fat: 8 g
- Fiber: 1 g
- Protein: 1 g
- Sodium: 35 mg

231. Maple Peanut Delights

"This candy recipe is wonderful."
Serving: about 8 dozen. | Prep: 30m | Ready in: 30m

Ingredients

- 1 package (8 oz.) cream cheese, softened
- 1/2 cup butter, softened
- 6 cups confectioners' sugar
- 1 tsp. maple flavoring

- 2 lbs. dark chocolate candy coating, coarsely chopped
- 1 cup chopped peanuts

Direction

- Beat flavoring, confectioners' sugar, butter and cream cheese in a large bowl until smooth. Keep in the fridge with a cover for an hour.
- Form into 1-in. balls. Melt candy coating in a microwave; stir often. Submerge the balls into coating; top with peanuts. Arrange on baking sheets lined with waxed paper. Keep in the fridge.

Nutrition Information

- Calories: 208 calories
- Total Carbohydrate: 29 g
- Cholesterol: 10 mg
- Total Fat: 11 g
- Fiber: 1 g
- Protein: 2 g
- Sodium: 46 mg

232. Maple-bacon White Chocolate Fudge

"Attempt my formula with white chips, maple seasoning and bacon."
Serving: about 2-1/2 lbs.. | Prep: 10m | Ready in: 10m

Ingredients

- 1 tsp. plus 1/4 cup butter, cubed, divided
- 10 slices ready-to-serve fully cooked bacon
- 2 packages (10 to 12 oz. each) white baking chips
- 1 can (14 oz.) sweetened condensed milk
- 3/4 tsp. maple flavoring

Direction

- Line a 9-inch square pan using foil; coat the foil with 1 tsp. butter. Heat the bacon based on the direction of the package. Crumble bacon the put aside.

- Mix the leftover butter, flavoring, condensed milk and baking chips in a big microwave-safe bowl. Microwave on high for 1 minute; mix until smooth. (If the chips are not fully melted, microwave until melted in 10 to 20-second intervals; mix to smooth). Mix in the bacon; pour over the prepared pan. Refrigerate with a cover for 2 hours, until firm.
- Lift fudge out of the pan with foil. Discard the foil; slice the fudge into 1-inch squares.
- To Prepare Ahead: Keep the fudge in an airtight container in the refrigerator, layered between waxed paper. Enjoy at room temperature.
- Enclose fudge in waxed paper, and in the foil. Put into the freezer containers then freeze. Take the wrapped fudge to room temperature to thaw.

233. Marbled Almond Roca

"I always make these candies to give out as gifts in winter."
Serving: 1-1/2 lbs.. | Prep: 25m | Ready in: 40m

Ingredients

- 1/2 cup slivered almonds
- 1 cup butter, cubed
- 1 cup sugar
- 3 tbsps. boiling water
- 2 tbsps. light corn syrup
- 1/2 cup semisweet chocolate chips
- 1/2 cup white baking chips

Direction

- Grease a 15x10x1-in. baking pan and use almonds to sprinkle on the greased pan. Put the pan into the oven and bake at 300 degrees for 15 minutes or till almonds are toasted and turn to golden brown; get the baking pan out of oven and set aside.
- Put sugar and butter in a large saucepan and cook on low heat for 5 minutes. Pour in corn syrup and water. Bring the mixture to a boil over medium heat; cook and stir sometimes till

a candy thermometer reaches 300 degrees (this is the hard crack stage). Pour the mixture over almonds quickly. Use chips to sprinkle on top, allow the mixture to sit for a minute or two or till chips are melted. Spread and swirl chocolate over candy. Completely cool; break into pieces.

Nutrition Information

- Calories: 306 calories
- Total Carbohydrate: 29 g
- Cholesterol: 42 mg
- Total Fat: 22 g
- Fiber: 1 g
- Protein: 2 g
- Sodium: 166 mg

234. Marian's Fudge

"My family has been loving this recipe for years."
Serving: 20 | Prep: 10m | Ready in: 1h10m

Ingredients

- 2 (1 oz.) squares unsweetened baking chocolate
- 1 tbsp. butter
- 1 cup milk
- 2 cups white sugar
- 1 pinch salt
- 1 tsp. vanilla extract

Direction

- Butter a 9x9 inch dish.
- Mix milk, butter and chocolate in a medium saucepan over medium heat. Bring to boiling; allow to boil for a minute. Stir in salt and sugar until they dissolve. Heat while stirring constantly to between 234 and 240°F (112 to 116°C), or until when you drop a small amount of syrup into cold water, it forms a soft ball that becomes flat when taken out of the water and transferred to a flat surface. Take out of the heat; stir in vanilla. Allow to cool for 10 minutes.

- Using a spoon, whisk fudge until its gloss disappears. Quickly transfer to the prepared dish. Keep in the fridge until firm, about half an hour.

Nutrition Information

- Calories: 103 calories;
- Total Carbohydrate: 21.4 g
- Cholesterol: 3 mg
- Total Fat: 2.3 g
- Protein: 0.8 g
- Sodium: 10 mg

235. Marshmallow Chocolate-covered Cherries

"My husband likes these candies the most."
Serving: about 4-1/2 dozen. | Prep: 25m | Ready in: 25m

Ingredients

- 1/2 cup butter, softened
- 2 cups marshmallow creme
- Pinch salt
- 1 tsp. almond extract
- 4 cups confectioners' sugar
- 1 jar (16 oz.) maraschino cherries, well drained
- 2 cups (12 oz.) semisweet chocolate chips
- 2 tbsps. shortening

Direction

- Cream butter in a bowl. Add sugar, extract, salt and marshmallow crème; combine well. Knead into a large ball; chill for an hour. Shape into 1-in. balls; make them into 2-in. flat circles. Wrap around cherries with circles and form into balls carefully. Arrange in a baking sheet lined with waxed paper. Loosely cover; keep in the fridge for 4 hours or overnight. In a microwave-safe bowl or a double boiler, melt shortening and chocolate chips. Coat cherries with chocolate; arrange on waxed paper to harden. Keep in a container with cover in the fridge for 1-2 weeks before serving.

Nutrition Information

- Calories: 106 calories
- Total Carbohydrate: 19 g
- Cholesterol: 5 mg
- Total Fat: 4 g
- Fiber: 0 g
- Protein: 0 g
- Sodium: 24 mg

236. Marshmallow Flowers

"These vanilla-flavored puffs are the best treat for your kids."
Serving: 21 (3-inch) flowers. | Prep: 30m | Ready in: 30m

Ingredients

- 2 envelopes unflavored gelatin
- 1/2 cup cold water
- 2 cups sugar
- 3/4 cup hot water
- 1 cup light corn syrup, divided
- 1 tsp. vanilla extract
- Confectioners' sugar
- 1-1/2 lbs. white candy coating, melted
- Red and yellow paste food coloring
- 1/2 cup miniature semisweet chocolate chips

Direction

- Coat cooking spray over a 9-inch square pan and a 13-inch x 9-inch pan. Put aside. Combine gelatin and cold water in a bowl; allow to stand for 5 mins. In the meantime, combine half a cup of corn syrup, hot water and sugar in a saucepan. Boil, stirring constantly, over medium heat. Cook until a candy thermometer registers 238° (soft-ball stage), without stirring. Discard from heat, then mix in remaining corn syrup.
- Transfer to a large bowl. Then beat on high speed; put in gelatin mixture by tablespoonfuls gradually until well blended. Keep beating for 10 mins or until thickened and fluffy. Mix in vanilla; stir well. Transfer to

the prepared pans. Allow to stand, uncovered, up to overnight.
- Use flower-shaped cookie cutter coated with the cooking spray to cut. Submerge the flowers in the confectioners' sugar and brush all the excess off. Melt candy coating in a heavy saucepan or microwave. Let cool for 5 mins. Portion the candy coating in 1/2; tint 1 portion yellow and the other pink. Cover flowers with the candy coating, using an icing knife. Arrange on the waxed paper-lined pans. Scatter the chocolate chips in middle of flowers; allow to dry.

237. Marshmallow Puffs

"Kids love these treats."
Serving: 3 dozen. | Prep: 10m | Ready in: 10m

Ingredients

- 36 large marshmallows
- 1-1/2 cups semisweet chocolate chips
- 1/2 cup chunky peanut butter
- 2 tbsps. butter

Direction

- Using foil, line a 9-in. square pan; butter the foil. Place marshmallow in pan. Melt butter, peanut butter and chocolate chips in a microwave; stir until smooth. Pour over the marshmallows and spread. Chill completely. Cut into 1-1/2-in. squares.

Nutrition Information

- Calories: 83 calories
- Total Carbohydrate: 11 g
- Cholesterol: 2 mg
- Total Fat: 5 g
- Fiber: 1 g
- Protein: 1 g
- Sodium: 28 mg

238. Martha Washington Candy

"This formula is a loved family custom."
Serving: about 5-1/2 dozen. | Prep: 45m | Ready in: 45m

Ingredients

- 1 cup butter, softened
- 4 cups confectioners' sugar
- 1 can (14 oz.) sweetened condensed milk
- 1 tsp. vanilla extract
- 3 cups sweetened shredded coconut
- 2 cups chopped pecans, toasted
- 6 cups (36 oz.) semisweet chocolate chips
- 1/4 cup shortening

Direction

- Beat the vanilla, milk, confectioners' sugar and butter in a big bowl. Mix in the pecans and coconut. Split the dough in half; refrigerate with the cover for 1 hour.
- With half the dough at a time, form the blend into 1-inch balls; put them onto waxed paper-lined baking sheets. Refrigerate for another 30 minutes.
- Melt the shortening and chocolate chips in a metal bowl over barely simmering water or in top of a double boiler; mix until smooth. Dip the balls in melted chocolate; let excess drip off. Bring back to waxed paper. Refrigerate until set.
- To prepare in advance: Store in an airtight container in the fridge.
- Freeze choice: In freezer containers, freeze the candy layered between pieces of waxed paper. Thaw in the fridge for 2 hours prior to serving.

Nutrition Information

- Calories: 196 calories
- Total Carbohydrate: 23 g
- Cholesterol: 9 mg
- Total Fat: 13 g
- Fiber: 1 g
- Protein: 2 g
- Sodium: 43 mg

239. Marzipan Harvest Table Topper

"This can be a dessert or just a centerpiece for decoration."
Serving: 1-1/4 cups. | Prep: 60m | Ready in: 60m

Ingredients

- 7 oz. almond paste
- 1/4 cup light corn syrup
- 1-1/4 cups confectioners' sugar
- Liquid or paste food coloring
- Baking cocoa (optional for acorn coloring)
- Cutting board or other protected work surface
- Cutting board or other protected work surface
- Assorted mini craft baskets and small wooden wagon
- Excelsior
- Cloves
- Leaf-shaped cookie cutters (1 to 2 inches)

Direction

- Marzipan: In a large bowl, break almond paste into crumbles. Knead in corn syrup. Add confectioners' sugar gradually; after each addition, knead well until blended thoroughly. Break off piece of marzipan to preferred size and knead in a little color at a time to tint with food coloring (add baking cocoa if preferred for brown.)
- Shaping: For each Acorn: Shape a 1/4-1/2-in. slightly oblong ball of brown marzipan.
- About the cap, add more baking cocoa or food coloring to tint a small piece of marzipan until it turns to a slightly darker brown. Shape into a flat circle; press onto top of acorn. For stem, insert brown marzipan or a whole clove into cap. Dot the cap gently with knife point or toothpick for texture.
- For apple: Shape a 3/4-in. ball of red marzipan. Slightly curve slides. Gently pinch bottom to taper. Indent apple's bottom and top with sharp knife or toothpick. For steam,

shape a brown marzipan stem or insert a whole clove; press into top indentation.

- For ear of corn: Shape a 1/2-in. ball of yellow marzipan into along cylinder shape about 1-1/2 in. long. Tapper an end slightly to shape the cob's top. Shape small pieces of yellow marzipan into balls for kernels. Press the balls in rows onto cob. Roll ball of green marzipan to 1/8-in. thickness between waxed paper for corn husks. On waxed paper, place on green marzipan's top, create 3 1-3/4-in. long x 1/2-in.-wide elongated leaf shapes. Peel top layer of waxed paper away; cut husks out onto the cob's sides with a knife; overlapping at center front's bottom, then 1 to cover the cob's back, overlap side's edges. Curve top points of every husk out gently.
- For leaves: Knead the same portions of orange, yellow and red marzipan together a few times to make marble effect. Between pieces of waxed paper, roll out to 1/8-in. thickness. Using cookie cutter, cut leaves out. Score veins on the leaves with a sharp knife or toothpick. For stem, form a brown marzipan stem then insert or insert a whole clove. Top with sugar if preferred.
- For pumpkins: Shape orange marzipan into 1/2 in. to 1-1/2 in balls. Slightly depress to make bottom and top flat. Create shallow ridges around sides from center top to bottom with sharp knife or toothpick. For stem, form one of each from brown marzipan stem then insert or insert a whole clove into the center top of each pumpkin.

Nutrition Information

- Calories: 172 calories
- Total Carbohydrate: 31 g
- Cholesterol: 0 mg
- Total Fat: 6 g
- Fiber: 1 g
- Protein: 2 g
- Sodium: 12 mg

240. Melt In Your Mouth Toffee

"It's so easy to make."
Serving: 48 | Prep: 10m | Ready in: 1h

Ingredients

- 1 lb. butter
- 1 cup white sugar
- 1 cup packed brown sugar
- 1 cup chopped walnuts
- 2 cups semisweet chocolate chips

Direction

- Combine brown sugar, white sugar and butter in a heavy saucepan. Over medium heat, cook, stirring constantly until boiled. Boil, without stirring, to 300°F (150°C) (brittle stage). Discard from the heat.
- Put chocolate chips and nuts into 9x13-in. dish. Add over chocolate and nuts with the hot mixture. Allow the mixture cool, then break into pieces. Enjoy!

Nutrition Information

- Calories: 153 calories;
- Total Carbohydrate: 13.6 g
- Cholesterol: 20 mg
- Total Fat: 11.3 g
- Protein: 1 g
- Sodium: 56 mg

241. Microwave Mint Fudge

""Add mint and chocolate to this quick fudge recipe if you love them.""
Serving: 2-1/4 lbs.. | Prep: 15m | Ready in: 15m

Ingredients

- 1-1/2 cups sugar
- 1 can (5 oz.) evaporated milk
- 1/4 cup butter, cubed
- 5 cups miniature marshmallows
- 1 package (10 oz.) mint chocolate chips

- 1 packet (1 oz.) pre-melted baking chocolate
- 1/2 cup chopped walnuts
- 1 tsp. vanilla extract
- 1/2 tsp. peppermint extract

Direction

- Mix butter, milk and sugar together in a 2-qt. microwave-safe bowl. Microwave on high, stirring after 2 1/2 minutes, till the mixture comes to a full rolling boil. Cook for 3 more minutes, stirring after 1 minutes. Put in marshmallows; mix till melted. Mix in chocolate and chips till smooth. Mix in extracts and nuts. Transfer to a greased 11x7-in. pan immediately. Chill till firm. Cut into squares. Refrigerate for storing.

Nutrition Information

- Calories: 75 calories
- Total Carbohydrate: 12 g
- Cholesterol: 3 mg
- Total Fat: 3 g
- Fiber: 0 g
- Protein: 0 g
- Sodium: 12 mg

242. Microwave Truffles

"It's just super easy but luscious!"
Serving: 2 dozen. | Prep: 15m | Ready in: 35m

Ingredients

- 1/3 cup finely chopped pecans, toasted, divided
- 8 oz. semisweet chocolate
- 1/4 cup butter
- 1/4 cup heavy whipping cream
- 1/4 tsp. almond extract

Direction

- Put 24 small foil candy cups on a baking sheet or in miniature muffin cups. Put half a tsp. of

the pecans into each. Put the remaining pecans and cups aside.

- Combine butter and chocolate in a 2-quart microwave-safe bowl. Microwave for 1 minute at 50% power, until melted. Mix in extract and cream. Using an electric mixer, beat until they are thickened slightly, occasionally scraping sides of the bowl. Transfer to prepared cups immediately. Sprinkle with the remaining pecans. Place in the refrigerator until set.

Nutrition Information

- Calories: 86 calories
- Total Carbohydrate: 2 g
- Cholesterol: 17 mg
- Total Fat: 9 g
- Fiber: 0 g
- Protein: 1 g
- Sodium: 40 mg

243. Milk Chocolate Raspberry Truffles

"Super easy recipe!"
Serving: 2-1/2 dozen. | Prep: 10m | Ready in: 20m

Ingredients

- 1/2 cup evaporated milk
- 1/4 cup sugar
- 1 package (11-1/2 oz.) milk chocolate chips
- 1/4 cup seedless raspberry preserves
- 1/2 tsp. instant coffee granules
- 3/4 cup finely chopped almonds, toasted

Direction

- Put sugar and milk to a rolling boil in big heavy saucepan on medium heat; mix and boil for 3 minutes. Take off heat; mix coffee, preserves and chocolate chips in till mixture is smooth and chill for an hour.
- Roll to 1-inch balls then roll in almonds. Put onto waxed paper-lined baking sheets and chill till firm; cover. Keep in the fridge.

Nutrition Information

- Calories: 186 calories
- Total Carbohydrate: 22 g
- Cholesterol: 7 mg
- Total Fat: 10 g
- Fiber: 2 g
- Protein: 3 g
- Sodium: 26 mg

244. Milk Chocolate Fudge

Serving: Makes 64 (1-inch) pieces | Prep: 15m

Ingredients

- 1 lb. fine-quality milk chocolate, chopped
- 1/2 stick (1/4 cup) unsalted butter
- 1 (14-oz.) can sweetened condensed milk
- 3/4 tsp. salt

Direction

- Preparation: Use wax paper or parchment paper to line the bottom of a square baking pan (8-inch).
- Place the ingredients in a metal bowl set over a pan of just simmering water until smooth, whisking occasionally.
- Transfer to the baking pan and chill with no cover for about 4 hours, until firm. Use a knife to run around edges of the pan and reverse fudge onto a work surface. Take off the parchment paper and slice fudge into squares (1-inch). Serve chilled.

Nutrition Information

- Calories: 64
- Total Carbohydrate: 8 g
- Cholesterol: 6 mg
- Total Fat: 3 g
- Fiber: 0 g
- Protein: 1 g
- Sodium: 33 mg
- Saturated Fat: 2 g

245. Milk Chocolate Truffles

"Easy and quick truffles."
Serving: 3 dozen. | Prep: 30m | Ready in: 30m

Ingredients

- 3 cups (18 oz.) milk chocolate chips
- 1 carton (8 oz.) frozen whipped topping, thawed
- 1/2 cup vanilla wafer crumbs (about 15 wafers)

Direction

- In double boiler/microwave, melt chocolate chips; cool. Beat whipped topping and melted chocolate in a bowl. Form to 1/2-in. balls. Roll into vanilla wafer crumbs then freeze/refrigerate.

Nutrition Information

- Calories: 96 calories
- Total Carbohydrate: 11 g
- Cholesterol: 3 mg
- Total Fat: 6 g
- Fiber: 1 g
- Protein: 1 g
- Sodium: 17 mg

246. Million Dollar Fudge

"I have made this delicious fudge recipe for years."
Serving: 48

Ingredients

- 4 1/2 cups white sugar
- 1 pinch salt
- 2 tbsps. butter
- 1 (12 fluid oz.) can evaporated milk
- 2 cups chopped nuts
- 1 (12 oz.) package semisweet chocolate chips
- 12 (1 oz.) squares German sweet chocolate

- 2 cups marshmallow creme

Direction

- Grease two 9-inch square baking pan with butter; put aside.
- Place nuts, marshmallow creme, German chocolate, and chocolate chips in a large mixing bowl. Put aside.
- Mix evaporated milk, butter, salt, and sugar in a 4-quart saucepan. Stir mixture over low heat until sugar is dissolved. Heat to a boil, and cook for 6 minutes.
- Pour boiling syrup into the bowl of ingredients; stir well to melt chocolate. Transfer mixture to the buttered pans. Allow mixture to stand for a couple of hours before slicing.

Nutrition Information

- Calories: 206 calories;
- Total Carbohydrate: 32.8 g
- Cholesterol: 4 mg
- Total Fat: 8.9 g
- Protein: 2.1 g
- Sodium: 18 mg

247. Million-dollar Chocolate Fudge

"This good old chocolate candy recipe gives off a fancy taste."
Serving: about 3 lbs.. | Prep: 20m | Ready in: 30m

Ingredients

- 1-1/2 tsps. plus 1/4 cup butter, divided
- 2-1/4 cups sugar
- 3/4 cup plus 2 tbsps. evaporated milk
- 1/2 tsp. salt
- 1 cup marshmallow creme
- 8 oz. German sweet chocolate, chopped
- 3 milk chocolate candy bars with almonds (1.45 oz. each), chopped
- 1 cup (6 oz.) semisweet chocolate chips

- 2 cups chopped blanched almonds
- 1-1/2 tsps. vanilla extract

Direction

- Use foil to line a 13x9-inch pan and butter foil with 1-1/2 tsps. butter; put aside. Mix together the rest of butter, salt, milk and sugar in a heavy saucepan. Put over medium heat; cook, while stirring, to dissolve sugar. Bring mixture to a rapid boil, whisking frequently for 5 minutes. Take away from the heat.
- Mix in chips, candy bars, chocolate and marshmallow creme until combined and chocolate melts. Fold vanilla and almonds into mixture. Transfer immediately to the prepared pan and spread out. Allow to cool. Take the fudge out of the pan by lifting with foil. Remove foil and slice fudge into square pieces. Keep in a dry and cool place to store.

Nutrition Information

- Calories: 104 calories
- Total Carbohydrate: 14 g
- Cholesterol: 4 mg
- Total Fat: 5 g
- Fiber: 1 g
- Protein: 2 g
- Sodium: 37 mg

248. Mint Chocolate Bark

"A simple recipe my friends and family love."
Serving: 1-1/2 lbs.. | Prep: 15m | Ready in: 15m

Ingredients

- 1 tsp. plus 3 tbsps. shortening, divided
- 1 package (10 oz.) Andes creme de menthe baking chips
- 2 cups white baking chips
- 1/2 cup crushed peppermint candies

Direction

- Line foil on 13x9-in. pan; use 1 tsp. shortening to grease foil.
- Melt 1 tbsp. shortening and Andes baking chips in microwave; mix till smooth. Put in prepped pan; refrigerate till set for 10 minutes.
- Melt leftover shortening and baking chips in top of double boiler/metal bowl above barely simmering water. Stir till smooth. Spread on chocolate layer; sprinkle crushed candies. Cool; refrigerate till firm for 2 hours.
- Break to small pieces; keep in airtight container.

Nutrition Information

- Calories: 161 calories
- Total Carbohydrate: 17 g
- Cholesterol: 3 mg
- Total Fat: 10 g
- Fiber: 0 g
- Protein: 1 g
- Sodium: 19 mg

249. Mint Chocolate Cookie Crunch

"It is easy to make with the kids."
Serving: about 8 dozen. | Prep: 5m | Ready in: 10m

Ingredients

- 3 packages (12 oz. each) semisweet chocolate chips
- 1 to 1-1/2 tsps. peppermint extract
- 1 package (20 oz.) chocolate cream-filled sandwich cookies, coarsely crushed
- 4 cups crisp rice cereal

Direction

- Use waxed paper to line baking sheets; put aside. In a heavy saucepan or microwave, melt chocolate chips. Mix in extract. Combine cereal and cookies in a large bowl. Add in the chocolate mixture and mix until well coated. Drop onto the prepared baking sheets by

tablespoonfuls; let cool. Keep at room temperature in airtight containers.

Nutrition Information

- Calories: 83 calories
- Total Carbohydrate: 12 g
- Cholesterol: 0 mg
- Total Fat: 4 g
- Fiber: 1 g
- Protein: 1 g
- Sodium: 51 mg

250. Mint Chocolate Fudge

"This fudge is a marvelous combination of mint and chocolate."
Serving: 28 | Prep: 10m | Ready in: 45m

Ingredients

- 2 cups semisweet chocolate chips
- 1 (14 oz.) can sweetened condensed milk, divided
- 2 tsps. vanilla extract
- 1 cup white confectioners' coating
- 1 tbsp. peppermint extract
- 1 drop green food coloring (optional)

Direction

- Use waxed paper to line a 9 or 8 inch square pan.
- Put vanilla, chocolate chips and a cup of sweetened condensed milk in a heavy saucepan and melt the mixture on low heat. Use 1/2 of the mixture to spread into the prepared pan; chill the mixture for 10 minutes or till firm. Reserve the rest of the chocolate mixture at room temperature.
- Put the rest of sweetened condensed milk and white confectioners' coating in a different heavy saucepan and melt mixture on low heat (keep in mind that the mixture will be thick). Mix in food coloring, peppermint extract. Use the peppermint mixture to spread on the

chilled chocolate layer; chill it for 10 minutes or till firm.

- Use the reserved chocolate mixture to spread over the mint layer; chill for 2 hours or till firm.

Nutrition Information

- Calories: 137 calories;
- Total Carbohydrate: 18.8 g
- Cholesterol: 6 mg
- Total Fat: 6.8 g
- Protein: 2 g
- Sodium: 25 mg

251. Mint Truffles

"Pretty chocolate candies!"
Serving: about 1 dozen. | Prep: 20m | Ready in: 20m

Ingredients

- 1 cup (6 oz.) milk chocolate chips
- 3/4 cup whipped topping
- 1/4 tsp. peppermint extract
- 2 tbsps. baking cocoa

Direction

- Melt chocolate chips in a small microwave-safe bowl; let cool for 7 minutes to lukewarm. Beat extract and whipped topping in; put in freezer till firm enough to shape to balls for 15 minutes. Form to 1-inch balls then roll into cocoa. Keep in a covered container in the fridge.

Nutrition Information

- Calories: 91 calories
- Total Carbohydrate: 10 g
- Cholesterol: 3 mg
- Total Fat: 5 g
- Fiber: 1 g
- Protein: 1 g
- Sodium: 11 mg

252. Minty Chocolate Crackles

"I guarantee you these chewy mint morsels will disappear in a blink of an eye whenever you serve them."
Serving: about 4 dozen. | Prep: 25m | Ready in: 40m

Ingredients

- 1 cup (6 oz.) semisweet chocolate chips
- 1/2 cup plus 4-1/2 tsps. shortening
- 3/4 cup sugar
- 1 egg
- 1/4 cup light corn syrup
- 1 tsp. peppermint extract
- 1 tsp. vanilla extract
- 2 cups all-purpose flour
- 1/2 tsp. baking soda
- 1/4 tsp. salt
- 1/4 cup crushed peppermint candy
- Additional sugar

Direction

- Melt chocolate chips in a double boiler or a microwave; slightly cool the melted chocolate. Cream sugar and shortening in a bowl, beat in extract and melted chocolate, corn syrup and egg. Mix salt, baking soda and flour; add the flour mixture to the cream mixture slowly. Fold in candy. Make 1-in. balls by rolling the mixture then roll I sugar. Place balls 2 in. apart from each other on ungreased baking sheets. Put baking sheets into the oven and bake for 12 to 14 minutes at 350 degrees till surface cracks and edges becomes firm (the center will still be soft). Cool it for 5 minutes then transfer to wire racks.

Nutrition Information

- Calories: 157 calories
- Total Carbohydrate: 22 g
- Cholesterol: 9 mg
- Total Fat: 7 g
- Fiber: 1 g
- Protein: 2 g

- Sodium: 59 mg

253. Mocha Truffles

"Just a favorite chocolate truffle, delicious bite-sized dessert designed for you to enjoy."
Serving: 66 | Prep: 30m | Ready in: 2h35m

Ingredients

- Truffle:
- 1 (24 oz.) bag semi-sweet chocolate chips
- 8 oz. cream cheese, softened
- 3 tbsps. instant coffee granules
- 2 tsps. water
- Coating:
- 6 oz. semi-sweet chocolate chips
- 1 tbsp. shortening

Direction

- Line a baking sheet with the waxed paper.
- In a ceramic or microwave-safe glass bowl melt 24 oz. of chocolate chips for 1 to 3 minutes in 30-second intervals. Stir the chocolate after each melting. Add coffee granules, cream cheese, and water into the melted chocolate and stir until smooth. Let the chocolate mixture cool down about 30 minutes, until it's hard enough to shape.
- Make 1-inch balls from the chocolate mixture, placing them on the baking sheet. Chill for at least 1 to 2 hours until truffles are firm.
- In a ceramic bowl or microwave-safe glass melt 6 oz. of chocolate chips and shortening for 1 to 3 minutes in 30-second intervals. Stir after each melting.
- Dip truffles in the melted chocolate mixture and place on waxed paper. Set aside for at least 30 minutes until truffles are firm.

Nutrition Information

- Calories: 75 calories;
- Total Carbohydrate: 8 g
- Cholesterol: 4 mg
- Total Fat: 5.3 g

- Protein: 0.9 g
- Sodium: 11 mg

254. Morgan's Amazing Peppermint Bark

"Snack that you can easily be eating in less than 30 minutes. Let's try this out!"
Serving: 15 | Prep: 15m | Ready in: 1h16m

Ingredients

- 1 (6 oz.) package white chocolate, chopped
- 3 peppermint candy canes

Direction

- With waxed paper, line a baking sheet. Set it aside.
- In a microwave-safe bowl, melt white chocolate by microwaving it for 60 to 90 seconds. Whisk it until smooth.
- Create a double layer bag by placing one-gallon sized resealable bag inside a second gallon sized bag. Put candy canes inside the inner bag and seal it. Use rolling pin to crush candy canes. Mix crushed candy canes with the melted white chocolate.
- Transfer white chocolate mixture into the set aside baking sheet. Chill it for 1 hour until it hardens.

Nutrition Information

- Calories: 83 calories;
- Total Carbohydrate: 12.2 g
- Cholesterol: 2 mg
- Total Fat: 3.6 g
- Protein: 0.7 g
- Sodium: 12 mg

255. Mounds Balls

"It's a yummy treat!"
Serving: about 7 dozen candies. | Prep: 40m | Ready in:
40m

Ingredients

- 1/2 lb. unsalted butter
- 3-3/4 cups confectioners' sugar
- 1 lb. sweetened shredded coconut
- 1/2 cup sweetened condensed milk
- 1 cup chopped walnuts
- 1 tsp. vanilla extract
- CHOCOLATE COATING:
- 2 cups (12 oz.) semisweet chocolate chips
- 4 oz. unsweetened chocolate
- 2 -inch x 1-inch x 1/2-inch piece paraffin wax
- Round wooden toothpicks
- Styrofoam sheets

Direction

- Cream sugar and butter together in bowl. Put in vanilla, walnuts, milk and coconut. Then stir until blended. Let chill until firm slightly. Form into the walnut-sized balls. Put a toothpick into each ball. Arrange balls on the baking sheets. Place in the freezer. In double boiler, melt paraffin wax, chocolate squares and chocolate chips over the simmering water. Over the hot water, keep warm. Submerge the frozen balls into the chocolate mixture with picks as handles. Stick the picks upright into the wax paper-wrapped Styrofoam sheet. Let chill until firm. Discard package candy and picks in the individual paper liners. (It may also be frozen.)

Nutrition Information

- Calories: 111 calories
- Total Carbohydrate: 12 g
- Cholesterol: 7 mg
- Total Fat: 7 g
- Fiber: 1 g
- Protein: 1 g
- Sodium: 18 mg

256. My Christmas Fudge

"This is the richest fudge I ever tasted."
Serving: 5-3/4 lbs. (96 pieces). | Prep: 15m | Ready in:
25m

Ingredients

- 4-1/2 cups sugar
- 1 can (12 oz.) evaporated milk
- 1/2 cup butter, cubed
- 2 packages (11-1/2 oz. each) milk chocolate chips
- 4-1/2 cups miniature marshmallows
- 2 oz. unsweetened chocolate, chopped
- 3 cups chopped walnuts, toasted
- 2 tsps. vanilla extract
- 4 oz. white baking chocolate, melted

Direction

- Using foil, line a 13x9-in. pan; use cooking spray to coat.
- Mix butter, milk and sugar in a heavy Dutch oven. Bring to a rapid boil; stir constantly over medium heat. Cook while stirring for 5 minutes. Take out of the heat.
- Stir in chopped chocolate, marshmallows and chocolate chips until melted. Fold in vanilla and walnuts. Spread into lined pan immediately. Drizzle with melted white baking chocolate; cool completely.
- Lift fudge out of pan with foil. Get rid of foil; cut fudge into 96 squares. Keep squares between layers of waxed paper; keep in airtight containers.

Nutrition Information

- Calories: 127 calories
- Total Carbohydrate: 17 g
- Cholesterol: 6 mg
- Total Fat: 6 g
- Fiber: 1 g
- Protein: 2 g
- Sodium: 18 mg

257. Nana's Rocky Road Fudge

"Treat yourself with this incredible Rocky Road-style fudge recipe anytime you want!"
Serving: about 2-1/2 lbs.. | Prep: 15m | Ready in: 20m

Ingredients

- 1-1/2 tsps. plus 1 tbsp. butter, divided
- 2 cups (12 oz.) semisweet chocolate chips
- 1 can (14 oz.) sweetened condensed milk
- 2 cups salted peanuts
- 1 package (10-1/2 oz.) miniature marshmallows

Direction

- Use an aluminum foil to line a 13x9-inch baking pan then use 1 1/2 tsps. of butter to grease the aluminum foil; put it aside.
- Mix the milk, remaining butter and chocolate chips together in a big saucepan. Let the mixture cook over medium heat setting while stirring it until it is smooth in consistency. Remove the pan away from the heat then add in the peanuts and mix well. In a big bowl, put in the marshmallows followed by the prepared chocolate mixture and mix everything together thoroughly. Distribute the marshmallow mixture evenly onto the prepared baking pan and keep it in the fridge until the mixture becomes firm.
- Use the aluminum foil lining to remove the fudge out of the baking pan. Slice the fudge into square shapes that are 1 1/2 inches in size.

Nutrition Information

- Calories: 153 calories
- Total Carbohydrate: 20 g
- Cholesterol: 4 mg
- Total Fat: 8 g
- Fiber: 1 g
- Protein: 3 g
- Sodium: 39 mg

258. Neapolitan Fudge

"This fudge has full flavors of chocolate, strawberry and vanilla."
Serving: about 6-1/2 lbs.. | Prep: 35m | Ready in: 35m

Ingredients

- 1-1/2 tsps. butter
- 1 package (8 oz.) cream cheese, softened
- 3 cups confectioners' sugar
- 16 oz. milk chocolate, melted and cooled
- VANILLA LAYER:
- 1 package (8 oz.) cream cheese, softened
- 3 cups confectioners' sugar
- 16 oz. white baking chocolate, melted and cooled
- 1 tbsp. vanilla extract
- RASPBERRY LAYER:
- 1 package (8 oz.) cream cheese, softened
- 3 cups confectioners' sugar
- 16 oz. white baking chocolate, melted and cooled
- 1 tbsp. raspberry extract
- 8 to 10 drops red food coloring, optional

Direction

- Using foil, line a 13x9-in. pan, use butter to grease foil. Whisk cream cheese in a large bowl until fluffy. Whisk in confectioners' sugar gradually. Whisk in melted milk chocolate. Transfer into lined pan and spread. Keep in the fridge for 10 minutes.
- To prepare vanilla layer, whisk cream cheese until fluffy in large bowl. Whisk in confectioners' sugar gradually. Whisk in vanilla and melted white chocolate. Place and spread on top of chocolate layer. Keep in the fridge for 10 minutes.
- To prepare raspberry layer, whisk cream cheese until fluffy in a large bowl. Whisk in confectioners' sugar gradually. Whisk in raspberry extract and melted white chocolate. Tint with food coloring if preferred. Place over top and spread. Keep in the fridge with a cover for at least 8 hours or overnight.

- Lift fudge out of pan with foil. Get rid of foil; cut fudge into 1-in. squares. Keep squares between layers of waxed paper in an airtight container in the fridge.

Nutrition Information

- Calories: 114 calories
- Total Carbohydrate: 16 g
- Cholesterol: 7 mg
- Total Fat: 5 g
- Fiber: 0 g
- Protein: 1 g
- Sodium: 20 mg

---

259. Never-fail Fudge

"A fudgey and glorious treat."
Serving: 12 | Prep: 15m | Ready in: 45m

Ingredients

- 4 cups confectioners' sugar
- 1/2 cup unsweetened cocoa powder
- 6 tbsps. butter
- 1/4 cup milk
- 1 tbsp. vanilla extract
- 1/4 tsp. salt
- 1 cup chopped pecans

Direction

- Butter a 9x9 inch dish.
- In a double boiler's top over simmering water, combine salt, vanilla, milk, butter, cocoa and sugar. Cook and stir, until smooth. Take off the heat and beat until mixture is no longer glossy. Mix in chopped nuts and quickly pour into the prepared pan.
- Cool thoroughly before slicing into squares.

Nutrition Information

- Calories: 283 calories;
- Total Carbohydrate: 43.4 g
- Cholesterol: 16 mg
- Total Fat: 12.9 g

- Protein: 1.8 g
- Sodium: 93 mg

---

260. No Fail Chocolate Fudge

"Make this appetizing fudge for your guests during the holidays. Assure that the highest temperature of this mixture is 238°.""
Serving: 30

Ingredients

- 1 1/2 cups confectioners' sugar
- 1/3 cup skim milk
- 6 tbsps. butter
- 1 cup semisweet chocolate chips
- 3/4 cup marshmallow creme
- 1/4 tsp. vanilla extract
- 3 tbsps. cocoa

Direction

- Lightly coat an 8-inch square pie pan with oil; put aside.
- Combine butter, milk, and powdered sugar in a heavy saucepan over medium heat. Stir well, whisk constantly, until a candy thermometer registers 238°F (112°C).
- Turn off the heat; put in cocoa, vanilla, marshmallow creme, and chocolate chips. Quickly whisk everything together and transfer to the prepared pan. Allow to cool before serving. Chill in an airtight container.

Nutrition Information

- Calories: 100 calories;
- Total Carbohydrate: 14.1 g
- Cholesterol: 6 mg
- Total Fat: 4.7 g
- Protein: 0.8 g
- Sodium: 20 mg

261. No-bake Chocolate Cookie Triangles

"You will be surprised by how fast these bars are to make. With no baking required, you will have a creamy and rich treat ready in no time."
Serving: 32 cookies. | Prep: 15m | Ready in: 15m

Ingredients

- 3/4 cup butter, cubed
- 8 oz. semisweet chocolate, chopped
- 20 vanilla wafers, coarsely crushed
- 1/2 cup chopped pecans

Direction

- Microwave chocolate and butter until melted and stir until the mixture is smooth. Allow to cool slightly. Mix in pecans and wafer crumbs. In an 8-inch square pan greased and lined with foil, add mixture. Chill, while covered, until the mixture is firm, 2 hours.
- Take the cookies out of the pan by lifting with foil. Remove the foil and slice cookies into triangular pieces. Keep leftovers in the refrigerator.

Nutrition Information

- Calories: 96 calories
- Total Carbohydrate: 6 g
- Cholesterol: 12 mg
- Total Fat: 8 g
- Fiber: 1 g
- Protein: 1 g
- Sodium: 38 mg

262. No-bake Cookie Dough Truffles

"One of my favorite treats to make,"
Serving: 50 | Prep: 30m | Ready in: 3h30m

Ingredients

- 3/4 cup firmly packed brown sugar
- 1/2 cup butter, softened
- 1 tsp. vanilla extract
- 2 cups all-purpose flour
- 1 (14 oz.) can sweetened condensed milk
- 1/2 cup miniature semisweet chocolate chips
- 1 cup finely chopped pecans
- 1 1/2 lbs. chocolate almond bark (chocolate confectioners' coating)

Direction

- Line waxed paper on baking sheets.
- Use an electric mixer to beat butter and brown sugar in big bowl till creamy and smooth; add vanilla extract. Beat till smooth. Beat flour slowly into creamed butter mixture till smooth; add sweetened condensed milk. Beat till smooth. Fold pecans and chocolate chips in cookie dough mixture; form to 1-inch balls. Put on the prepared baking sheets; refrigerate the cookie dough balls for 2 hours till chilled.
- In top of a double boiler above simmering water, melt chocolate bark, frequently mixing and using a rubber spatula to scrape sides down to prevent scorching. In melted chocolate, use 2 forks to hold a ball and dip each cookie dough ball in. Put dipped ball on waxed paper; repeat with leftover chocolate and balls. Chill for 1 hour minimum in the fridge till set.

Nutrition Information

- Calories: 160 calories;
- Total Carbohydrate: 19.1 g
- Cholesterol: 8 mg
- Total Fat: 9.9 g
- Protein: 2.5 g
- Sodium: 25 mg

263. No-bake Fudge Bar

"This dessert is easy and elegant."
Serving: 24 | Prep: 30m | Ready in: 3h15m

Ingredients

- 2 1/2 cups finely crushed chocolate sandwich cookie crumbs
- 2/3 cup unsalted butter, melted
- 1/2 tsp. kosher salt
- 2 3/4 cups Ghirardelli® Dark Chocolate 60% Cacao Baking Chips
- 1 cup heavy cream
- 2 tbsps. unsalted butter
- 1 tbsp. Ghirardelli® Semi-Sweet Chocolate Mini Baking Chips
- 3 chocolate sandwich cookies or wafers, crushed

Direction

- Stir salt, melted butter and cookie crumbs together in a medium bowl. Press into the bottom and up sides of an 11x8-inch rectangular or 9-inch square tart pan with a removable bottom. Chill with a cover while making the filling.
- To prepare filling: In a large, heatproof bowl, place dark chocolate chips. Heat 2 tbsps. of butter and cream in a small saucepan until just simmering and butter is melted. Place over chips. Stir once. Allow to stand 5 minutes, do not stir. Stir until smooth. Place into crust.
- Top with crushed cookies and mini chips evenly. Chill with a cover until set, at least 2 hours or overnight.
- Rest at room temperature 45- 60 minutes before serving. To serve, cut into small squares.

Nutrition Information

- Calories: 235 calories;
- Total Carbohydrate: 17.5 g
- Cholesterol: 30 mg
- Total Fat: 19.2 g
- Protein: 2.1 g

- Sodium: 91 mg

264. No-cook Never-fail Fudge

"This fudge recipe is a hit!"
Serving: 40 | Prep: 20m | Ready in: 20m

Ingredients

- 1 lb. processed cheese food, cubed
- 1 lb. butter
- 1 cup unsweetened cocoa powder
- 4 lbs. confectioners' sugar
- 3 cups chopped walnuts
- 1 tbsp. vanilla extract

Direction

- In a nonstick saucepan, melt butter and cheese together; stir until smooth. Keep the mixture over low heat. Sift cocoa and confectioners' sugar together in a mixing bowl until combine thoroughly and no lumps left.
- Combine melted cheese and butter with sugar mixture. Stir until very smooth. Stir in vanilla and nuts. Press into 2 lightly buttered or sprayed 9x13 inch pans; allow to cool until firm. Cut into small squares. You can freeze this fudge.

Nutrition Information

- Calories: 359 calories;
- Total Carbohydrate: 48.6 g
- Cholesterol: 32 mg
- Total Fat: 18 g
- Protein: 4.1 g
- Sodium: 176 mg

265. No-fuss Truffles

"You only need 3 ingredients for this recipe!"
Serving: about 4-1/2 dozen. | Prep: 50m | Ready in: 50m

Ingredients

- 2 packages (10 to 12 oz. each) milk chocolate or butterscotch chips
- 1 carton (8 oz.) frozen whipped topping, thawed
- 1-1/4 cups ground toasted almonds, graham cracker crumbs or finely chopped salted peanuts

Direction

- Melt chips in microwave-safe bowl; mix till smooth. Cool for 30 minutes, mixing several times, to room temperature.
- Fold whipped topping in; drop on waxed paper-lined baking sheets by rounded teaspoonfuls. Freeze till firm or for 1 1/2 hours.
- Form to balls; roll in peanuts/crumbs/almonds. Refrigerate/freeze in airtight container. Remove from freezer about 30 minutes prior to serving if frozen.

Nutrition Information

- Calories: 103 calories
- Total Carbohydrate: 9 g
- Cholesterol: 2 mg
- Total Fat: 7 g
- Fiber: 1 g
- Protein: 2 g
- Sodium: 9 mg

266. Nut Fruit Bark

"A sophisticated version of fruit bark."
Serving: 1-1/2 lbs.. | Prep: 15m | Ready in: 15m

Ingredients

- 1 lb. dark chocolate, coarsely chopped

- 1 tsp. instant espresso powder
- 1/2 cup dried cherries or blueberries, divided
- 1/2 cup macadamia nuts, chopped and divided
- 1/2 cup chopped cashews, divided
- 1/2 tsp. coarse sea salt, optional

Direction

- Line a 15x10x1-inch baking pan's sides and bottom with parchment paper; grease the paper and put aside.
- Liquefy chocolate in a metal bowl over hot water or double boiler; mix till smooth. Mix in half of the cherries and nuts and espresso powder. Spread into prepped pan; put leftover cherries and nuts on top; pan will not be full. Scatter salt if preferred. Chill for 15 minutes till firm.
- Shatter into pieces. Keep in an airtight container.

Nutrition Information

- Calories: 147 calories
- Total Carbohydrate: 14 g
- Cholesterol: 1 mg
- Total Fat: 10 g
- Fiber: 2 g
- Protein: 2 g
- Sodium: 26 mg

267. Nutty Chocolate Caramels

"Nothing is more perfect than caramels to give as holiday gifts. This is the recipe from my grandma that I always trust.""
Serving: 4 dozen (about 1-3/4 lbs.). | Prep: 5m | Ready in: 45m

Ingredients

- 2 tsps. plus 1/4 cup butter, divided
- 3/4 cup light corn syrup
- 1/4 cup cold water
- 1-1/2 cups sugar
- 3 oz. semisweet chocolate, chopped

- 1/2 tsp. salt
- 1 cup half-and-half cream
- 2 tsps. vanilla extract
- 1 cup chopped walnuts

Direction

- Use foil to line an 8x8-inch pan. Use 1 tsp. butter to grease the pan and put aside. Grease a heavy saucepan's sides using 1 tsp. butter; add remaining butter, salt, chocolate, sugar, water and corn syrup. Cook while stirring for 6 minutes on medium heat until combined and smooth.
- Mix in cream, little by little. Cook while stirring for 25 minutes until mixture reaches firm-ball stage at 245 degrees. Put off the heat; mix in walnuts and vanilla. Transfer to the prepped pan.
- Allow to cool, then slice into squares. Keep refrigerated in a sealed container to store. Take out of the refrigerator for an hour, then serve.

Nutrition Information

- Calories: 74 calories
- Total Carbohydrate: 11 g
- Cholesterol: 5 mg
- Total Fat: 3 g
- Fiber: 0 g
- Protein: 1 g
- Sodium: 45 mg

268. Nutty Chocolate Fudge

"I altered the original recipe to make it less sweet. You can try it with butterscotch chips or peanut butter."
Serving: 2-2/3 lbs. (81 pieces). | Prep: 25m | Ready in: 25m

Ingredients

- 1 jar (7 oz.) marshmallow creme
- 2/3 cup fat-free evaporated milk
- 1/2 cup butter, cubed
- 2 tsps. vanilla extract
- 3 cups (18 oz.) semisweet chocolate chips

- 2 cups chopped pecans or walnuts, toasted

Direction

- Line a 9-in. square pan using foil and grease foil with cooking spray; put aside.
- Mix the butter, evaporated milk and marshmallow creme in a big saucepan. Cook and mix over medium heat until smooth. Heat up to a boil; boil for 5 minutes, mixing frequently. Take off from the heat; put in vanilla. Mix in chocolate chips until melted. Put in pecans. Add to lined and greased pan. Chill for 2 hours or until set.
- Lift fudge from pan using foil; tear off foil slowly. Slice into 1-inch squares. Put in the fridge to store.

Nutrition Information

- Calories: 70 calories
- Total Carbohydrate: 7 g
- Cholesterol: 3 mg
- Total Fat: 5 g
- Fiber: 1 g
- Protein: 1 g
- Sodium: 16 mg

269. Nutty Chocolate Marshmallow Puffs

"A big fluffy marshmallow inside the coating of chocolate and nut."
Serving: 40 candies. | Prep: 20m | Ready in: 20m

Ingredients

- 2 cups milk chocolate chips
- 1 can (14 oz.) sweetened condensed milk
- 1 jar (7 oz.) marshmallow creme
- 40 large marshmallows
- 4 cups coarsely chopped pecans (about 1 lb.)

Direction

- In a heavy saucepan, heat marshmallow creme, milk, and chocolate chips until just melted; mix until smooth (mixture will become thick).

- Use tongs to dip marshmallows immediately into the chocolate mixture, one at a time; let the excess drip off. Quickly roll them in the pecans. Transfer onto the baking sheets lined with waxed paper (if necessary, reheat the mixture of chocolate for easier coating.), chill in the refrigerator until firm. Keep in an airtight container and store it inside the fridge.

Nutrition Information

- Calories: 208 calories
- Total Carbohydrate: 24 g
- Cholesterol: 6 mg
- Total Fat: 12 g
- Fiber: 1 g
- Protein: 3 g
- Sodium: 31 mg

270. Nutty Chocolate Peanut Clusters

"Simple chocolatey nut clusters that will be a great treat for parties."
Serving: 2-3/4 lbs.. | Prep: 10m | Ready in: 20m

Ingredients

- 1 lb. white candy coating, chopped
- 2 cups (12 oz.) semisweet chocolate chips
- 1 jar (16 oz.) dry roasted peanuts

Direction

- Melt chocolate chips and candy coating in a metal bowl or double boiler over hot water; mix until smooth. Take off from the heat; mix in peanuts.
- Dollop by rounded teaspoonfuls onto waxed paper-lined baking sheets. Chill for 10-15 minutes or until firm. Put in airtight containers to store.

271. Nutty Chocolate Truffles

"No need to bake! Use different fruit preserves for a change."
Serving: 4 dozen. | Prep: 10m | Ready in: 10m

Ingredients

- 1 package (8 oz.) cream cheese, softened
- 1 cup (6 oz.) semisweet chocolate chips, melted and cooled
- 1 cup crushed vanilla wafers (about 30 wafers)
- 1/4 cup strawberry preserves
- 1-1/4 cups chopped almonds, toasted

Direction

- Beat cream cheese till smooth in big bowl; beat strawberry preserves, wafer crumbs and chocolate in. Cover; refrigerate till easy to handle or for 1 hour minimum.
- Form to 1-in. balls; roll into almonds. Keep in the fridge.

Nutrition Information

- Calories: 68 calories
- Total Carbohydrate: 6 g
- Cholesterol: 5 mg
- Total Fat: 5 g
- Fiber: 1 g
- Protein: 1 g
- Sodium: 22 mg

272. Nutty White Fudge

"One of my friends shared this soft fudge recipe with me a couple of years ago.""
Serving: about 1 lb.. | Prep: 20m | Ready in: 20m

Ingredients

- 3 oz. cream cheese, softened
- 1 tbsp. whole milk
- 2 cups confectioners' sugar
- 2 oz. white baking chocolate

- 1/2 tsp. vanilla extract
- 1/8 tsp. salt
- 1 cup chopped walnuts

Direction

- Beat milk and cream cheese in a large mixing bowl until smooth. Slowly add sugar. Whisk in melted chocolate. Put in salt and vanilla; stir well. Mix in walnuts. Spread mixture into an 8x8-inch pan greased with butter. Refrigerate for 4 to 5 hours before slicing. Keep chilled in the fridge

Nutrition Information

- Calories: 34 calories
- Total Carbohydrate: 4 g
- Cholesterol: 2 mg
- Total Fat: 2 g
- Fiber: 0 g
- Protein: 1 g
- Sodium: 9 mg

273. Old Fashioned Fudge

"Without additional toppings, this fudge already tastes good on its own."
Serving: 50 | Prep: 15m | Ready in: 45m

Ingredients

- 1/2 cup unsweetened cocoa powder
- 2 cups white sugar
- 1/4 tsp. salt
- 1 tbsp. light corn syrup
- 1 cup milk
- 1 tbsp. vanilla extract
- 2 tbsps. butter

Direction

- Mix together salt, sugar and cocoa powder in a medium saucepan. Whisk in milk and corn syrup until thoroughly combined. Put in butter and heat until the mixture reaches 112-116°C (234-240°F); or until a little bit syrup

dropped into cold water turns into a soft ball that flattens when taken out of water and put on a flat surface, that can spread out flat. Mix once in a while.

- Take away from the heat, use a wooden spoon to beat until the mixture is no longer glossy and becomes thickened. Mix in vanilla and transfer to a 9-inch square baking dish greased with butter. Allow to cool until set. Slice into small square pieces before serving.

Nutrition Information

- Calories: 41 calories;
- Total Carbohydrate: 9 g
- Cholesterol: 2 mg
- Total Fat: 0.7 g
- Protein: 0.3 g
- Sodium: 17 mg

274. Old-time Butter Crunch Candy

"This recipe can't be lack in our collection for the season."
Serving: about 2 lbs.. | Prep: 15m | Ready in: 40m

Ingredients

- 1 cup butter
- 1-1/4 cup sugar
- 2 tbsps. light corn syrup
- 2 tbsps. water
- 2 cups finely chopped toasted almonds
- 8 milk chocolate candy bars (1.55 oz. each)

Direction

- Using foil, line a 13x9-in. pan; put aside. Grease the sides of a large heavy saucepan with part of the butter. Add the rest of the butter to the saucepan; over low heat, melt. Add water, corn syrup and sugar. Over medium heat, cook while stirring until a candy thermometer registers 300° (hard-crack stage).
- Take out of the heat; stir in almonds. Transfer to the lined pan quickly; spread to cover the bottom of the pan. Completely cool. Turn the

pan upside down carefully to remove the candy in one piece; get rid of foil.

- In a microwave-safe bowl or double boiler, melt 1/2 of the chocolate; top over candy. Allow to cool. Turn candy over and do the same with the rest of the chocolate; cool. Break into 2-in. pieces. Keep in an airtight container.

Nutrition Information

- Calories: 375 calories
- Total Carbohydrate: 34 g
- Cholesterol: 35 mg
- Total Fat: 26 g
- Fiber: 3 g
- Protein: 5 g
- Sodium: 137 mg

275. One Bowl Chocolate Fudge

"This chocolaty fudge dessert is popular among kids. Cut into small pieces, and it becomes easier to bite and munch on. For a nutty twist, add peanut butter by spoonsful into chocolate mixture, and cut before refrigerating."
Serving: 48 | Prep: 15m | Ready in: 2h18m

Ingredients

- 16 oz. semisweet chocolate
- 1 (14 oz.) can sweetened condensed milk
- 2 tsps. vanilla extract
- 1 1/2 cups chopped walnuts

Direction

- Place aluminum foil in an 8 x 8-inch square dish.
- In a large microwave safe bowl, place chopped chocolate and add condensed milk. Heat in the microwave for 2 to 3 minutes on high power, stirring once or twice, until chocolate softens. Remove and continue to stir until mixture is smooth. Add walnuts and vanilla. Spread evenly in the prepared dish.
- Chill in the refrigerator for 2 hours, or until firm. Cut into squares before serving.

Nutrition Information

- Calories: 98 calories;
- Total Carbohydrate: 10.3 g
- Cholesterol: 3 mg
- Total Fat: 6.2 g
- Protein: 1.9 g
- Sodium: 10 mg

276. One Bowl Chocolate Fudge With Pecans

"Microwave fudge made with semi-sweet chocolate and improved dense milk."
Serving: 48 | Prep: 15m | Ready in: 2h17m

Ingredients

- 16 oz. semisweet chocolate, chopped
- 1 (14 oz.) can sweetened condensed milk
- 1 1/2 cups chopped pecans
- 2 tsps. vanilla extract
- 1 tsp. instant coffee granules
- 1/2 tsp. sea salt

Direction

- Line an 8-inch square dish using aluminum foil.
- In a microwave-safe bowl, mix the sweetened condensed milk and chocolate. Heat in the microwave on high, mixing once or twice, for 2 to 3 minutes, until the chocolate is soft.
- Mix sea salt, coffee granules, vanilla and pecans into chocolate mixture until smooth; distribute into the prepared dish.
- Refrigerate for 2 hours, until firm. Slice into squares for serving.

Nutrition Information

- Calories: 97 calories;
- Total Carbohydrate: 10.3 g
- Cholesterol: 3 mg
- Total Fat: 6.2 g
- Protein: 1.6 g
- Sodium: 29 mg

277. One Two Three Fudge

"This rich fudge makes certain to satisfy any gathering of chocolate-lovin' people."
Serving: 36

Ingredients

- 1/2 cup butter
- 2 cups semisweet chocolate chips
- 1 (16 oz.) package chocolate fudge frosting

Direction

- Grease a 9x13 pan with butter. Put aside.
- Melt the chocolate chips and butter together over low heat in a medium saucepan. Take away from the heat and mix in the frosting. Stir well.
- Pour into the prepared pan. Refrigerate for about 2 hours. Slice into squares. Store with the cover in a fridge.

Nutrition Information

- Calories: 149 calories;
- Total Carbohydrate: 17.6 g
- Cholesterol: 7 mg
- Total Fat: 8.6 g
- Protein: 1.1 g
- Sodium: 42 mg

278. Orange Chocolate Meltaways

"Wonderful and easy holiday gifts."
Serving: 6 dozen. | Prep: 30m | Ready in: 30m

Ingredients

- 1 package (11-1/2 oz.) milk chocolate chips
- 1 cup (6 oz.) semisweet chocolate chips
- 3/4 cup heavy whipping cream
- 1 tsp. grated orange zest
- 2-1/2 tsps. orange extract
- 1-1/2 cups finely chopped toasted pecans

- COATING:
- 1 cup (6 oz.) milk chocolate chips
- 2 tbsps. shortening

Direction

- Put chocolate chips in bowl; put aside. Gently boil orange zest and cream in saucepan; put on chips immediately. Let stand for a minute; whisk till smooth. Add extract; cover. Chill till mixture starts to thicken for 35 minutes.
- Beat mixture till just lightens in color for 10-15 seconds, don't overbeat. Put rounded teaspoonfuls on waxed paper-lined baking sheets and cover. Chill for 5 minutes.
- Form to balls gently; roll 1/2 into nuts. Melt shortening and chocolate in microwave; mix till smooth. Dip leftover balls into chocolate; let excess drip off. Put onto waxed paper; let stand till set. Keep in fridge.

Nutrition Information

- Calories: 76 calories
- Total Carbohydrate: 6 g
- Cholesterol: 5 mg
- Total Fat: 6 g
- Fiber: 1 g
- Protein: 1 g
- Sodium: 7 mg

279. Orange Flavored Fudge

"Quick and easy orange-flavored fudge made in a microwave. Orange liqueur and orange peel make this fudge super delicious."
Serving: 36 | Prep: 5m | Ready in: 2h16m

Ingredients

- 1 1/3 cups white sugar
- 1 (5 oz.) can evaporated milk
- 1/2 cup butter, melted
- 2 1/2 cups miniature marshmallows
- 1 cup semisweet chocolate chips
- 1 cup finely chopped pecans
- 1 tsp. grated orange peel

- 2 tbsps. orange liqueur

Direction

- Mix butter and sugar evaporated milk in a 2-quart microwavable dish. Microwave for 8 minutes on high.
- Stir and add chocolate chips and marshmallows; heat for 3 minutes on high, until melted.
- Add in orange liqueur and peel. Chill until firm for 2 hours and cut into pieces.

Nutrition Information

- Calories: 115 calories;
- Total Carbohydrate: 14.4 g
- Cholesterol: 8 mg
- Total Fat: 6.4 g
- Protein: 0.8 g
- Sodium: 27 mg

---

280. Orange-almond Chocolate Logs

"A fantastic holiday recipe."
Serving: 2 dozen. | Prep: 30m | Ready in: 30m

Ingredients

- 1/3 cup butter, softened
- 1/4 cup almond paste
- 2 tsps. grated orange zest, divided
- 9 oz. white baking chocolate, chopped
- 2 tbsps. orange juice
- 3 tbsps. coarse sugar
- 1-1/2 cups dark chocolate chips
- 1-1/2 tsps. shortening

Direction

- Cream 1/2 tsp. orange zest, almond paste and butter till fluffy and light in small bowl. Melt white baking chocolate in microwave; mix till smooth. Add to creamed mixture slowly. Mix orange juice in slowly; beat till smooth. Cover;

refrigerate till easy to handle, occasionally mixing, for 20 minutes.
- Form to 2-in. logs; put onto waxed paper-lined baking sheets. Cover loosely; refrigerate till firm for 30 minutes. Mix leftover orange zest and coarse sugar; put aside.
- Melt shortening and chocolate chips in microwave; mix till smooth. Dip logs into chocolate; let excess drip off. Put onto waxed paper-lined sheets. Sprinkle sugar mixture on. Let stand till firm.

Nutrition Information

- Calories: 182 calories
- Total Carbohydrate: 18 g
- Cholesterol: 9 mg
- Total Fat: 12 g
- Fiber: 0 g
- Protein: 2 g
- Sodium: 29 mg

---

281. Orange-fruit Nut Truffles

"These flavors are hit!"
Serving: 36

Ingredients

- 1 1/2 cups walnuts
- 1 cup orange-essence dried plums (prunes)
- 1/2 cup dried cranberries
- 1/2 cup chocolate-covered raisins (or plain raisins)
- 1 tsp. cinnamon
- 1/4 tsp. ground ginger
- 1 tsp. vanilla extract

Direction

- Blend all in a food processor with the knife blade until it forms a dough-like ball. Shape into 1-inch balls with your hands. Place walnut piece on top if preferred.

Nutrition Information

- Calories: 55 calories;
- Total Carbohydrate: 7 g
- Cholesterol: < 1 mg
- Total Fat: 3.1 g
- Protein: 0.9 g
- Sodium: 1 mg

---

282. Oreos And Candy Cane Chocolate Bark

"Super easy treats."
Serving: about 1-1/2 lbs.. | Prep: 15m | Ready in: 15m

Ingredients

- 2 packages (10 oz. each) dark chocolate chips
- 10 candy cane or chocolate mint creme Oreo cookies, split and chopped
- 1/3 cup white baking chips
- 1/8 tsp. peppermint extract
- 2 candy canes, crushed

Direction

- Line parchment paper on 15x10x1-in. baking pan. Melt dark chocolate in top of double boiler/metal bowl above hot water; mix till smooth. Take off heat; mix cookies in. Spread on prepped pan.
- Microwave white baking chips, mixing every 30 seconds, on high till melted. Mix extract in; drizzle dark chocolate mixture on. Sprinkle crushed candy canes on; cool. Refrigerate till set for an hour.
- Break to pieces; keep in airtight container.

Nutrition Information

- Calories: 141 calories
- Total Carbohydrate: 19 g
- Cholesterol: 0 mg
- Total Fat: 8 g
- Fiber: 2 g
- Protein: 2 g
- Sodium: 32 mg

---

283. Oreo™ Cookie Bark

"So delicious!"
Serving: 50

Ingredients

- 1 (20 oz.) package chocolate sandwich cookies with creme filling
- 2 (18.5 oz.) packages white chocolate

Direction

- Line waxed paper on 10x15-inch jellyroll pan. Use nonstick vegetable spray to coat paper; put aside.
- Break 1/2 of the cookies to coarse pieces using back of wooden spoon/fingers in big mixing bowl.
- Melt 1 white chocolate package following package directions in a microwave safe glass/ceramic mixing bowl. Remove from microwave. Fold broken cookie pieces in quickly. Put mixture in prepped pan; spread to cover 1/2 of the pan.
- Repeat the process with leftover cookies and chocolates, spreading mixture into the other 1/2 of pan. Refrigerate for 1 hour till solid.
- Take bark out of pan. Peel waxed paper off carefully. Put bark on big cutting board; use big chef's knife to cut. Keep in airtight container.

Nutrition Information

- Calories: 59 calories;
- Total Carbohydrate: 8.7 g
- Cholesterol: < 1 mg
- Total Fat: 2.5 g
- Protein: 0.7 g
- Sodium: 55 mg

284. Peanut Butter And Banana Chocolate Truffles

"My own yummy recipe!"
Serving: 24 | Prep: 15m | Ready in: 3h50m

Ingredients

- 12 oz. semisweet chocolate
- 1 banana, mashed
- 1/3 cup heavy whipping cream
- 2 tbsps. peanut butter
- 1/4 cup sifted confectioners' sugar, or as needed

Direction

- Mix and cook peanut butter, cream, banana and chocolate in saucepan on medium heat for 5-10 minutes till melted, it'll be a bit lumpy because of peanut butter. Put mixture in bowl; refrigerate for 2 1/2-3 hours till firm.
- Use melon baller to scoop chocolate mixture; roll to 1-in. balls. Put confectioner's sugar into shallow bowl; coat the truffles with confectioner's sugar. Refrigerate for 1-2 hours more till firm.

Nutrition Information

- Calories: 99 calories;
- Total Carbohydrate: 10.8 g
- Cholesterol: 5 mg
- Total Fat: 6.4 g
- Protein: 1.5 g
- Sodium: 8 mg

285. Peanut Butter Candy Bars

"The best dish ever."
Serving: 35 | Prep: 20m | Ready in: 30m

Ingredients

- 1 1/2 cups margarine, melted
- 2 cups peanut butter
- 4 1/2 cups confectioners' sugar

- 2 cups graham cracker crumbs
- 1/2 cup margarine
- 2 cups semisweet chocolate chips

Direction

- Coat a 15"x10" pan with grease. Mix together graham cracker crumbs, confectioners' sugar, peanut butter and 1 1/2 cups of melted margarine in a big bowl, then spread the mixture into the prepped pan.
- In a medium saucepan, mix together chocolate chips and 1/2 cup of margarine on moderately low heat. Stir sometimes until smooth and melted, then spread over the peanut butter mixture. Allow to cool thoroughly prior to cutting into bars.

Nutrition Information

- Calories: 305 calories;
- Total Carbohydrate: 28.1 g
- Cholesterol: 0 mg
- Total Fat: 21.1 g
- Protein: 4.5 g
- Sodium: 218 mg

286. Peanut Butter Chocolate Balls

"A lovely treat."
Serving: 16 servings. | Prep: 30m | Ready in: 30m

Ingredients

- 1 cup peanut butter and milk chocolate chips
- 3/4 cup whipped topping
- 1 cup milk chocolate chips
- 1 tbsp. shortening
- 1/4 cup chopped salted peanuts

Direction

- Melt chocolate chips and peanut butter in small saucepan on low heat. Put in small bowl; cool for about 7 minutes to lukewarm. Beat whipped topping in; put in freeze till firm enough to shape to balls for 15 minutes.

- Form to 1-in. balls. Melt shortening and milk chocolate chips in small microwave-safe bowl; mix till smooth. Dip balls into chocolate; put onto waxed paper-lined baking sheet then sprinkle peanuts on. Refrigerate till firm; keep in airtight container in the fridge.

Nutrition Information

- Calories: 154 calories
- Total Carbohydrate: 16 g
- Cholesterol: 2 mg
- Total Fat: 10 g
- Fiber: 1 g
- Protein: 1 g
- Sodium: 43 mg

287. Peanut Butter Chocolate Bark

"A super good recipe."
Serving: 36 | Prep: 10m | Ready in: 41m

Ingredients

- 16 oz. white chocolate chips
- 1 1/2 cups peanut butter
- 8 oz. semi-sweet chocolate chips
- 1 tsp. vanilla extract (optional)

Direction

- Grease baking sheet; line using parchment paper.
- Heat peanut butter and white chocolate chips in microwave-safe bowl in microwave for 30-60 seconds till half-melted; mix.
- Heat semi-sweet chocolate chips in microwave-safe bowl in microwave for 15-30 seconds till half-melted. Mix vanilla extract into the half-melted semi-sweet chocolate.
- On prepped baking sheet, spread peanut butter mixture. Distribute melted semi-sweet chocolate evenly on peanut butter mixture; use tip of sharp knife to drag semisweet chocolate through the peanut butter mixture to make marble pattern.

- Refrigerate for 30 minutes – 2 hours till set. Cut to pieces; keep in airtight container.

Nutrition Information

- Calories: 164 calories;
- Total Carbohydrate: 13.1 g
- Cholesterol: 3 mg
- Total Fat: 11.7 g
- Protein: 3.8 g
- Sodium: 63 mg

288. Peanut Butter Chocolate Cups

"Your kids will very like this!"
Serving: 1 dozen. | Prep: 20m | Ready in: 20m

Ingredients

- 1 milk chocolate candy bar (7 oz.)
- 1/4 cup butter
- 1 tbsp. shortening
- 1/4 cup creamy peanut butter

Direction

- Melt shortening, butter and chocolate in a microwave. Stir until they become smooth. Put paper miniature baking cups or foil into miniature muffin tin. Add one tbsp. chocolate mixture to each cup.
- Melt peanut butter in a microwave. Stir until they become smooth. Pour into cups. Add the remaining chocolate mixture on top. If necessary, remelt the chocolate mixture. Place in the refrigerator until firm, about half an hour.

Nutrition Information

- Calories: 93 calories
- Total Carbohydrate: 3 g
- Cholesterol: 11 mg
- Total Fat: 9 g
- Fiber: 0 g
- Protein: 2 g
- Sodium: 66 mg

289. Peanut Butter Chocolate Fudge

"Let's cook a wonderful meal with your lovely family!"
Serving: 4 lbs. (117 pieces). | Prep: 20m | Ready in: 40m

Ingredients

- 2 tsps. butter
- CHOCOLATE LAYER:
- 2 cups sugar
- 1 can (5 oz.) evaporated milk (2/3 cup)
- 5 tbsps. butter, cubed
- 1/2 tsp. salt
- 1 jar (7 oz.) marshmallow creme
- 1/2 tsp. vanilla extract
- 2 cups (12 oz.) semisweet chocolate chips
- PEANUT BUTTER LAYER:
- 2 cups sugar
- 1 can (5 oz.) evaporated milk (2/3 cup)
- 5 tbsps. butter, cubed
- 1/2 tsp. salt
- 1 jar (7 oz.) marshmallow creme
- 1/2 cup creamy peanut butter
- 1 tsp. vanilla extract
- Coarsely chopped chocolate-covered or salted peanuts, optional

Direction

- Line foil on a pan, about 13x9 inches. Coat the foil with 2 tsps. of the butter.
- To make chocolate layer: Combine salt, butter, milk and sugar in a large heavy saucepan. Over medium heat, bring to a rapid boil, stirring constantly. Then cook while stirring for 4 mins or until the candy thermometer registers 234° (soft-ball stage). Discard from the heat. Mix in vanilla and marshmallow creme until they are blended. Mix in the chocolate chips until melted. Spread into the prepared pan immediately.
- To make peanut butter layer: Combine salt, butter, milk and sugar in another large heavy saucepan. Over medium heat, bring to a rapid boil, stirring constantly. Then cook while stirring for 4 mins or until the candy thermometer registers 234° (soft-ball stage). Discard from the heat. Mix in vanilla, peanut butter and marshmallow creme until they are blended. Spread over the chocolate layer immediately. Top with peanuts, if desired. Place in the refrigerator until firm, about 3 hours. When cooled, cover.
- Take fudge out of the pan by lifting foil. Discard the foil; slice the fudge into 1-inch squares. Preserve in airtight container between layers of the waxed paper.

Nutrition Information

- Calories: 71 calories
- Total Carbohydrate: 12 g
- Cholesterol: 4 mg
- Total Fat: 3 g
- Fiber: 0 g
- Protein: 1 g
- Sodium: 40 mg

290. Peanut Butter Clusters

"A yummy treats but healthy as well, using chocolate, whole-grain cereals, spices, nuts, and dried fruits"
Serving: 36

Ingredients

- 1 (10 oz.) package Reese's Peanut Butter Chips
- 1/2 cup dry-roasted unsalted peanuts
- 1/2 cup regular oats, uncooked
- 1/2 cup raisins
- 1 tsp. cinnamon

Direction

- Place chips in a bowl and microwave on high power for 1 1/2 minutes until melted. Mix. Put in the rest of ingredients; stir well. Firmly roll into 1-inch balls with your hands. Let cool.

Nutrition Information

- Calories: 65 calories;
- Total Carbohydrate: 6.7 g
- Cholesterol: 0 mg
- Total Fat: 3.2 g
- Protein: 2.3 g
- Sodium: 19 mg

291. Peanut Butter Cocoa Fudge

"This recipe only needs 5 ingredients to prepare."
Serving: about 2 lbs.. | Prep: 10m | Ready in: 10m

Ingredients

- 1 cup plus 3 tbsps. chunky peanut butter
- 1 cup butter, cubed
- 3-1/2 cups confectioners' sugar
- 3 tbsps. baking cocoa
- 1 tbsp. vanilla extract

Direction

- Mix butter and peanut butter in a saucepan. Cook while stirring until blended over medium heat. Take out of the heat; stir in vanilla, cocoa and confectioners' sugar. Spread into 8-in. square pan brushed with butter. Freeze for half an hour or until just firm; cut into squares. Keep at room temperature.

Nutrition Information

- Calories: 80 calories
- Total Carbohydrate: 8 g
- Cholesterol: 8 mg
- Total Fat: 5 g
- Fiber: 0 g
- Protein: 1 g
- Sodium: 52 mg

292. Peanut Butter Honeybees

"Making these tasty snacks with your children is kind of fun."
Serving: 4 dozen. | Prep: 30m | Ready in: 30m

Ingredients

- 1/2 cup creamy peanut butter
- 2 tbsps. butter, softened
- 1/2 cup confectioners' sugar
- 3/4 cup graham cracker crumbs
- 1 oz. semisweet chocolate
- 1/3 cup sliced almonds, toasted

Direction

- Beat butter and peanut butter in a small mixing bowl together with confectioners' sugar until no lumps remain. Mix in crumbs.
- Form 1 teaspoonful of dough into 1 1/2-inch oval; arrange on a baking sheet lined with waxed paper. Put chocolate into a small microwaveable bowl; microwave for 1 minute on high power until melted. Allow to sit for 5 minutes.
- Pour melted chocolate into a resealable plastic bag; snip a tiny hole in 1 corner of the bag. Pipe 3 stripes on each bee. Attach 2 almonds into each bee to make wings. Poke holes for eyes using a toothpick. Keep chilled in the fridge.

Nutrition Information

- Calories: 112 calories
- Total Carbohydrate: 10 g
- Cholesterol: 4 mg
- Total Fat: 7 g
- Fiber: 1 g
- Protein: 3 g
- Sodium: 76 mg

293. Peanut Butter Truffles

"Peanut butter truffles with crunchy granola."
Serving: 3 dozen. | Prep: 25m | Ready in: 25m

Ingredients

- 5 oz. white candy coating, coarsely chopped, divided
- 2/3 cup creamy peanut butter
- 1/2 cup confectioners' sugar
- 3 tsps. vanilla extract
- 2/3 cup crushed granola cereal with oats and honey
- 6 oz. semisweet chocolate, chopped
- 2 tbsps. shortening

Direction

- At 70% power, melt 3-oz. white candy coating for 1 minute in microwave; mix. Microwave at extra 10-20 sec intervals, mixing till smooth. Mix peanut butter in till smooth. Add cereal, vanilla and confectioners' sugar; chill till easy to handle for 2-3 hours.
- Form to 1-in. balls; put aside. Melt shortening and chocolate in microwave; mix till smooth. In chocolate, dip balls; let excess drip off. Put on wire rack above waxed paper; let stand for 15 minutes till set.
- Melt leftover coating; cool it for 5 minutes. Drizzle on truffles; chill till set for 5-10 minutes. Cover; keep in the fridge.

Nutrition Information

- Calories: 149 calories
- Total Carbohydrate: 14 g
- Cholesterol: 0 mg
- Total Fat: 10 g
- Fiber: 1 g
- Protein: 3 g
- Sodium: 46 mg

294. Peanut Choc-scotch Fudge

"The best fudge ever."
Serving: 24 | Prep: 10m | Ready in: 45m

Ingredients

- 3/4 cup butter
- 3 cups white sugar
- 3/4 cup milk
- 3/4 cup peanut butter
- 1 cup semisweet chocolate chips
- 1 cup butterscotch chips
- 1 tsp. vanilla extract
- 1 (7 oz.) jar marshmallow creme

Direction

- Grease a 9x13 inch dish lightly.
- In a 2-quart saucepan, combine milk, sugar and butter over medium heat. Heat until boiling, stir continuously. Heat up to between 112 to 116°C (234 and 240°F), or until when a small amount of syrup is dropped into cold water, it creates a soft ball that will flatten when taken out of the water onto a flat surface. Take off the heat and mix in butterscotch chips, chocolate chips and peanut butter until melted. Mix in vanilla. Fold in marshmallow creme. Transfer to prepared pan. Refrigerate until firm.

Nutrition Information

- Calories: 300 calories;
- Total Carbohydrate: 42.4 g
- Cholesterol: 16 mg
- Total Fat: 14.1 g
- Protein: 2.7 g
- Sodium: 96 mg

295. Pecan Carmel Clusters

"Chocolate candy that tastes great!"
Serving: 54 | Prep: 30m | Ready in: 50m

Ingredients

- 1 (14 oz.) package individually wrapped caramels, unwrapped
- 3 tbsps. butter
- 2 tbsps. water
- 2 cups chopped pecans
- 1 lb. dark chocolate, broken into small pieces

Direction

- In a microwavable bowl, add water, butter and caramels, then place in the microwave to cook on high setting for 3 minutes while stirring after each half a minute, until smooth. Add pecans, stir.
- Drop onto parchment paper with caramel pecan mixture by spoonfuls, then put in the freezer about 15-20 minutes.
- In a microwavable bowl, add chocolate and microwave on high setting for 1-2 minutes while stirring after each 15 seconds, until chocolate is smooth and melted. Use a fondue fork to dip into chocolate with each caramel cluster until coated, then arrange on parchment paper to let it dry. Refrigerate until firm, if needed.

Nutrition Information

- Calories: 103 calories;
- Total Carbohydrate: 11.8 g
- Cholesterol: 2 mg
- Total Fat: 6.6 g
- Protein: 1.2 g
- Sodium: 25 mg

296. Pecan Chocolate Candies

"Treats you don't have to bake."
Serving: 3 dozen. | Prep: 25m | Ready in: 30m

Ingredients

- 1 can (5 oz.) evaporated milk
- 1/2 cup sugar
- 1 cup (6 oz.) semisweet chocolate chips
- 2 tsps. vanilla extract
- 2-1/2 cups crushed vanilla wafers (about 75 wafers)
- 1-1/2 cups chopped pecans, divided

Direction

- Boil sugar and milk in big saucepan on medium heat; take off heat. Mix vanilla and chocolate chips in till smooth. Add 1/3 cup pecans and vanilla wafers; mix till combined well. Put in bowl; refrigerate till set for 30 minutes.
- Form to 3/4-in. balls. Coat by rolling in leftover pecans. Put onto waxed paper-lined baking sheets then refrigerate till set.

Nutrition Information

- Calories: 108 calories
- Total Carbohydrate: 13 g
- Cholesterol: 2 mg
- Total Fat: 6 g
- Fiber: 1 g
- Protein: 1 g
- Sodium: 29 mg

297. Pecan Delights

"This one is a must-try!"
Serving: about 4 dozen. | Prep: 15m | Ready in: 01h15m

Ingredients

- 2-1/4 cups packed brown sugar
- 1 cup butter, cubed
- 1 cup light corn syrup

- 1/8 tsp. salt
- 1 can (14 oz.) sweetened condensed milk
- 1 tsp. vanilla extract
- 1-1/2 lbs. whole pecans
- 1 cup (6 oz.) semisweet chocolate chips
- 1 cup milk chocolate chips
- 2 tbsps. shortening

Direction

- Combine first 4 ingredients in a large saucepan. Over medium heat, cook until all the sugar dissolves. Put in milk gradually and mix well. Keep cooking till a candy thermometer registers 248° (firm-ball stage).
- Discard from heat; mix in the vanilla until it is blended. Then fold in pecans. Drop onto a parchment-lined or oiled baking sheets by tablespoonfuls. Let chill until firm. Then loosen from the paper.
- In a microwave-safe bowl, melt shortening and chocolate chips. Drizzle over every cluster. Allow to cool.

Nutrition Information

- Calories: 255 calories
- Total Carbohydrate: 26 g
- Cholesterol: 14 mg
- Total Fat: 17 g
- Fiber: 2 g
- Protein: 2 g
- Sodium: 71 mg

298. Pecan Fudge

"Creamy fudge recipe that I love making every Christmas!"
Serving: about 4 lbs.. | Prep: 15m | Ready in: 25m

Ingredients

- 3 cups sugar
- 3/4 cup butter, cubed
- 1 can (5 oz.) evaporated milk
- 2 cups (12 oz.) semisweet chocolate chips
- 30 caramels, quartered

- 1 jar (7 oz.) marshmallow creme
- 1 cup pecan halves
- 1 tsp. vanilla extract

Direction

- Mix the first 3 ingredients in a big heavy saucepan. Cook and mix over low heat until sugar dissolves. Heat up to a full rolling boil. Boil and mix about 5 minutes until a candy thermometer registers 234°.
- Take off from the heat; mix in caramels and chocolate chips until melted. Mix in leftover ingredients until thoroughly combined. Put into a greased 13-in. x 9-in. pan. Refrigerate until set. Slice into squares.

Nutrition Information

- Calories: 82 calories
- Total Carbohydrate: 13 g
- Cholesterol: 5 mg
- Total Fat: 4 g
- Fiber: 0 g
- Protein: 1 g
- Sodium: 26 mg

299. Peppermint Candy

"Let's enjoy a great meal!"
Serving: about 1-1/2 lbs. (64 pieces). | Prep: 25m | Ready in: 25m

Ingredients

- 1 cup semisweet chocolate chips
- 1 can (14 oz.) sweetened condensed milk, divided
- 1 cup white baking chips
- 3 tsps. peppermint extract
- 2 to 3 drops green food coloring

Direction

- Melt the chocolate chips with 3/4 cup of the condensed milk in a small saucepan over low heat, stirring occasionally. Line waxed paper on an 8-inch square dish; coat the paper with butter.

- Spread pan with 1/2 melted chocolate mixture; let chill for 5 to 10 mins (allow the remaining melted chocolate mixture to stand at the room temperature).
- Melt the white baking chips in another saucepan. Mix in the remaining condensed milk until they become smooth. Discard from heat. Put in food coloring and extract. Place in the refrigerator until set. Spread over chocolate layer; spread with reserved chocolate mixture. Place in the refrigerator until set. Cut into 1-inch pieces.

Nutrition Information

- Calories: 51 calories
- Total Carbohydrate: 7 g
- Cholesterol: 3 mg
- Total Fat: 2 g
- Fiber: 0 g
- Protein: 1 g
- Sodium: 11 mg

---

300. Peppermint Fudge

""Bring holiday spirit to your fudge with a touch of peppermint""
Serving: 24 | Prep: 10m | Ready in: 2h15m

Ingredients

- 1 2/3 cups granulated sugar
- 2/3 cup NESTLE® CARNATION® Evaporated Milk
- 2 tbsps. butter or margarine
- 1/4 tsp. salt
- 2 cups miniature marshmallows
- 1 1/2 cups NESTLE® TOLL HOUSE® Semi-Sweet Chocolate Morsels
- 1/2 tsp. vanilla extract
- 1/4 tsp. peppermint extract
- 1/4 cup crushed, hard peppermint candy

Direction

- Use foil to line an 8-in square baking pan.
- In a medium heavy-duty saucepan, mix together salt, butter, evaporated milk and sugar. Put over medium heat and bring to a full rolling boil while stirring continuously. Boil for 4-5 minutes while stirring continuously. Put off the heat.
- Whisk in peppermint extract, vanilla extract, morsels and marshmallows. Vigorously whisk to melt marshmallows, about a minute. Transfer to the lined baking pan and allow to cool for a minute. Place candy on top, lightly press into the mixture. Put in the refrigerator to firm up for 2 hours. Take out of the pan and discard foil. Slice into 48 pieces.

Nutrition Information

- Calories: 150 calories;
- Total Carbohydrate: 27.3 g
- Cholesterol: 5 mg
- Total Fat: 4.6 g
- Protein: 1.3 g
- Sodium: 45 mg

---

301. Peppermint Mocha Chocolate Bark

"Turn plain chocolate into this delicious treat with this chocolate bark recipe. Mix peppermint candies and chocolate-covered espresso beans in and it's perfect as a gift."
Serving: 36 | Ready in: 45m

Ingredients

- 2 cups chopped bittersweet or semisweet chocolate (or chips)
- 30 peppermint candies, coarsely chopped
- ¼ cup chocolate-covered espresso beans, coarsely chopped

Direction

- Using foil, line a rimmed baking sheet. (Make sure to avoid wrinkles.)
- In medium microwaveable bowl, add chocolate; microwave for a minute on Medium. Mix, then keep microwaving on Medium, mixing every 20 seconds, until melted. (Or put on top of a double boiler over hot, but not boiling, water. Mix until melted.)
- In a small bowl, mix espresso beans and candy together. Mix half of the mixture into the melted chocolate. Scrape the chocolate onto the foil and spread it into a 9-inch square. Scatter with the leftover candy mixture, forcing any big pieces in. Chill about half an hour until firm.
- Turn the bark and foil to a cutting board. Cut into 1 1/2-inch pieces with a sharp knife.

Nutrition Information

- Calories: 60 calories;
- Total Carbohydrate: 10 g
- Cholesterol: 0 mg
- Total Fat: 3 g
- Fiber: 1 g
- Protein: 0 g
- Sodium: 0 mg
- Sugar: 7 g
- Saturated Fat: 2 g

302. Peppermint Pretzel Dippers

"It's just so delicious!"
Serving: about 4 dozen. | Prep: 15m | Ready in: 15m

Ingredients

- 2 cups (12 oz.) semisweet chocolate chips
- 1 tbsp. shortening
- 1 package (10 oz.) pretzel rods
- 40 red and/or green hard mint candies, crushed

Direction

- Melt shortening and chocolate chips in a microwave. Then stir until they become smooth. Crack each pretzel rod in 1/2. Submerge the broken end halfway into the melted chocolate; let the excess drip off. Then roll in the crushed candies. Arrange on the waxed paper-lined baking sheet. Let chill until set.

Nutrition Information

- Calories: 75 calories
- Total Carbohydrate: 13 g
- Cholesterol: 0 mg
- Total Fat: 3 g
- Fiber: 1 g
- Protein: 1 g
- Sodium: 80 mg

303. Perfect Peppermint Patties

"When making large batches of candies for holiday gifts, it is nice to have this quick and easy recipe."
Serving: 5 dozen. | Prep: 20m | Ready in: 20m

Ingredients

- 3-3/4 cups confectioners' sugar
- 3 tbsps. butter, softened
- 2 to 3 tsps. peppermint extract
- 1/2 tsp. vanilla extract
- 1/4 cup evaporated milk
- 2 cups (12 oz.) semisweet chocolate chips
- 2 tbsps. shortening

Direction

- Mix together the first 4 ingredients in a big bowl. Pour in milk and stir thoroughly. Form into 1-in balls and put in a baking sheet lined with waxed paper. Use a glass to flatten to 1/4 inch thick. Freeze while covered for half an hour.
- Heat shortening and chocolate chips on high in the microwave to melt; mix until smooth.

Dip patties in and wait for excess to drip off. Allow to set on waxed paper.

Nutrition Information

- Calories: 67 calories
- Total Carbohydrate: 11 g
- Cholesterol: 2 mg
- Total Fat: 3 g
- Fiber: 0 g
- Protein: 0 g
- Sodium: 7 mg

304. Popcorn And Peanut Truffles

"Amazing!"
Serving: 24 | Prep: 15m | Ready in: 1h15m

Ingredients

- 6 cups popped popcorn
- 1 cup salted, roasted peanuts
- 1 (12 oz.) bag semi-sweet chocolate chips
- 1/2 cup honey

Direction

- Line waxed paper on baking sheet.
- Mix peanuts and popcorns in big bowl.
- In microwave-safe glass/ceramic bowl, melt chocolate chips in 30-sec intervals, mixing after every melting, for 1-3 minutes.
- Put honey in microwave-safe bowl; heat in microwave for 10 seconds till pourable and warm; mix into melted chocolate.
- Put chocolate-honey mixture on popcorn mixture, mixing till coated evenly. Use small ice cream scoop to scoop chocolate-popcorn mixture; press mixture to scoop then release mixture on prepped baking sheet. Refrigerate the truffles for 1 hour till firm.

Nutrition Information

- Calories: 132 calories;
- Total Carbohydrate: 17.5 g
- Cholesterol: 0 mg

- Total Fat: 7.3 g
- Protein: 2.3 g
- Sodium: 51 mg

305. Potato Chip Clusters

"You don't need an oven to make these unique lovely candies. They don't even melt when you pack them in containers to be on the move with you."
Serving: about 3 dozen. | Prep: 15m | Ready in: 15m

Ingredients

- 9 oz. white baking chocolate, chopped
- 2 cups coarsely crushed ridged potato chips
- 1/2 cup chopped pecans

Direction

- Put white chocolate in a big microwave safe bowl and melt the chocolate. Put in pecans and potato chips. Use waxed paper to line baking sheets then drop tablespoonfuls of the mixture on the prepared baking sheets. Chill candies in the fridge till they are set.

Nutrition Information

- Calories: 33 calories
- Total Carbohydrate: 2 g
- Cholesterol: 0 mg
- Total Fat: 3 g
- Fiber: 0 g
- Protein: 0 g
- Sodium: 19 mg

306. Pretzel Sparklers

""For different decorations, you just need to change the sprinkles. This is so fun and easy for children to make.""
Serving: about 2 dozen. | Prep: 30m | Ready in: 30m

Ingredients

- 8 oz. white baking chocolate, chopped

- 1 package (10 oz.) pretzel rods
- Colored candy stars or sprinkles

Direction

- Microwave chocolate in a microwaveable bowl at 70% power for a minute and whisk. Heat for additional 10-20-second intervals while whisking until smooth.
- Plunge each pretzel rod halfway into chocolate; wait for excess to drip off. Sprinkle stars on top. Allow to dry on waxed paper.

Nutrition Information

- Calories: 105 calories
- Total Carbohydrate: 20 g
- Cholesterol: 1 mg
- Total Fat: 2 g
- Fiber: 1 g
- Protein: 3 g
- Sodium: 311 mg

307. Pretzel Turtles®

"Turtles® candies that is simple and quick. This dessert is made of pecans, caramel covered chocolate candies and mini pretzels."
Serving: 20 | Prep: 10m | Ready in: 14m

Ingredients

- 20 small mini pretzels
- 20 chocolate covered caramel candies
- 20 pecan halves

Direction

- Set oven to 300°F (150°C) to preheat.
- Put the pretzels in one layer on a parchment lined cookie sheet. Put a chocolate covered caramel candy on each pretzel.
- Bake for 4 minutes. On each candy covered pretzel, press down a pecan half while it's still warm. Let cool completely before putting in an airtight container to store.

Nutrition Information

- Calories: 82 calories;
- Total Carbohydrate: 14.1 g
- Cholesterol: < 1 mg
- Total Fat: 2.2 g
- Protein: 1.7 g
- Sodium: 263 mg

308. Pumpkin Truffles

"You can use very strong coffee for coffee liqueur."
Serving: 48 | Prep: 15m | Ready in: 1h50m

Ingredients

- 1 1/4 cups almonds
- 2 1/2 cups crushed vanilla wafers
- 1/2 cup confectioners' sugar
- 2 tsps. ground cinnamon
- 1 cup semi-sweet chocolate chips, melted
- 1/2 cup pumpkin puree (such as Libby's®)
- 1/3 cup coffee-flavored liqueur
- 1/2 cup semi-sweet chocolate chips, or as needed

Direction

- Preheat an oven to 200°C/400°F then spread almonds on baking sheet.
- In preheated oven, bake for 5-10 minutes till almonds are toasted and fragrant. Remove from oven; cool. In food processor, grind till almonds texture are like flour.
- Mix cinnamon, confectioners' sugar, crushed vanilla wafers and ground almonds in bowl. Mix coffee liqueur, pumpkin and 1 cup melted chocolate chips in vanilla wafer mixture. Form mixture to 1-in. balls; put on baking sheet. Freeze/refrigerate truffles for 1-2 hours till solid.
- In top of double boiler above simmering water, melt 1/2 cup of chocolate chips, frequently mixing and scraping sides down with rubber spatula to prevent scorching. In

melted chocolate, dip truffles; put on baking sheet to let harden.

Nutrition Information

- Calories: 103 calories;
- Total Carbohydrate: 13 g
- Cholesterol: 0 mg
- Total Fat: 5.3 g
- Protein: 1.4 g
- Sodium: 36 mg

309. Raspberry Truffle Fudge

"A wonderful recipe for that special someone."
Serving: 40 | Prep: 10m | Ready in: 1h20m

Ingredients

- 3 cups semi-sweet chocolate chips
- 1 (14 oz.) can sweetened condensed milk
- 1 1/2 tsps. vanilla extract
- salt to taste
- 1/4 cup heavy cream
- 1/4 cup raspberry flavored liqueur
- 2 cups semi-sweet chocolate chips

Direction

- Spray nonstick cooking spray on 9x9-in. pan; line wax paper.
- Mix sweetened condensed milk and 3 cup chocolate chips in microwave-safe bowl; heat in microwave, occasionally mixing, till chocolate melts. Don't let scorch; mix vanilla and salt in. Spread in pan; cool it down to room temperature.
- Heat 2 cups chocolate chips, liqueur and cream in microwave-safe bowl in microwave till chocolate melts; mix till smooth. Cool to lukewarm; put on fudge layer. Refrigerate for about 1 hour till both layers set completely. Cut to 1-in. pieces.

Nutrition Information

- Calories: 149 calories;

- Total Carbohydrate: 19.7 g
- Cholesterol: 5 mg
- Total Fat: 7.5 g
- Protein: 2.3 g
- Sodium: 13 mg

310. Raspberry Truffles

"One of my favorite Christmas recipes."
Serving: 4 dozen. | Prep: 40m | Ready in: 40m

Ingredients

- 1 tbsp. butter
- 2 tbsps. heavy whipping cream
- 1-1/3 cups semisweet chocolate chips
- 7-1/2 tsps. seedless raspberry jam
- 6 oz. white candy coating or dark chocolate candy coating, coarsely chopped
- 2 tbsps. shortening

Direction

- Cook chocolate chips, cream and butter in small heavy saucepan on low heat till chocolate melts for 4-5 minutes. Take off heat; mix jam in till combined. Put into small freezer container; cover. Freeze till mixture is thick and can be scooped.
- By teaspoonfuls, drop on foil-lined baking sheet. Freeze it for 15 minutes. Roll to balls; freeze it till very firm.
- Put wire rack above big waxed paper sheet. Melt shortening and candy coating in microwave; mix till smooth. Slightly cool; put on balls. Put onto prepped wire rack. Let stand till set for 15 minutes. Keep in airtight container in the fridge.

Nutrition Information

- Calories: 105 calories
- Total Carbohydrate: 12 g
- Cholesterol: 3 mg
- Total Fat: 7 g
- Fiber: 1 g

- Protein: 0 g
- Sodium: 6 mg

311.Raspberry-mocha Chocolate Bark

"A yummy candy bark recipe."
Serving: 1 lb.. | Prep: 10m | Ready in: 10m

Ingredients

- 1-1/4 cups white baking chips
- 1 tsp. shortening, divided
- 1/4 cup seedless raspberry preserves
- 4 tbsps. finely crushed chocolate-covered espresso beans, divided
- 1 cup plus 2 tbsps. dark chocolate chips, divided

Direction

- Line foil on 9-in. square pan; put aside. Melt 1/2 tsp. shortening and white baking chips in microwave; mix till smooth. Spread in prepped pan.
- Microwave preserves till melted in 10-20-sec. intervals; mix till smooth. By teaspoonfuls, drop preserves on top; use knife to cut through layer to swirl. Sprinkle 2 tbsp. espresso beans. Refrigerate till firm for 10 minutes.
- Melt leftover shortening and 1 cup dark chocolate chips in microwave; mix till smooth. Spread on white chocolate layer. Chop leftover dark chocolate chips finely. Sprinkle leftover espresso beans and chips on top; refrigerate till firm. Break to small pieces. Keep in airtight container.

312. Raw Strawberry-filled Chocolate Truffles

"Raw no-bake truffles."
Serving: 32 | Prep: 10m | Ready in: 35m

Ingredients

- Chocolate:
- 2 cups coconut oil, melted
- 1 cup unsweetened cocoa powder
- 1/2 cup raw honey, melted
- 2 tbsps. stevia powder (optional)
- Strawberry Filling:
- 3/4 cup strawberries
- 1/4 cup coconut oil
- 1/4 cup sunflower seed butter
- 2 tbsps. raw honey
- 1/2 lemon, juiced
- 1 vanilla bean, split lengthwise and seeds scraped
- 1/4 tsp. Himalayan rock salt

Direction

- Whisk stevia powder, 1/2 cup of honey, cocoa powder and 2 cups of coconut oil till smooth in a bowl.
- Blend rock salt, vanilla bean seeds, lemon juice, 2 tbsps. of honey, sunflower seed butter, 1/4 cup of coconut oil and strawberries till smooth in food processor; put into bowl. Refrigerate.
- Put 1/2 chocolate mixture in bottom of ice cube trays/truffle molds; freeze for 10 minutes till partially hardened. Keep leftover chocolate at room temperature.
- Put 1 1/2 tsp. – 1 tbsp. of strawberry filling on frozen chocolate; put leftover chocolate on top of each, filling molds to top. Freeze truffles for 15 more minutes till set.

Nutrition Information

- Calories: 176 calories;
- Total Carbohydrate: 8.7 g

- Cholesterol: 0 mg
- Total Fat: 17.1 g
- Protein: 1 g
- Sodium: 29 mg

- Total Fat: 4 g
- Fiber: 0 g
- Protein: 1 g
- Sodium: 39 mg

313. Ribbon Fantasy Fudge

"A great combination between peanut butter and chocolate."
Serving: 49 pieces. | Prep: 10m | Ready in: 20m

Ingredients

- 2 tsps. plus 3/4 cup butter, cubed, divided
- 3 cups sugar
- 1 can (5 oz.) evaporated milk
- 1 jar (7 oz.) marshmallow creme
- 1 cup (6 oz.) semisweet chocolate chips
- 1 tsp. vanilla extract, divided
- 1/2 cup peanut butter

Direction

- Use foil to line a 9-in. square pan; with 2 tsps. of butter, grease the foil; put aside. Mix the rest of the butter, milk and sugar in a large heavy saucepan. Bring to a full rolling boil; stir constantly. Boil over medium heat for 4 minutes; stir to prevent scorching. Take out of the heat; put aside.
- Split marshmallow crème into 2 heat-resistant bowls; add half tsp. vanilla and chocolate chips to one bowl, the rest of vanilla and peanut butter to the second one. Place 1/2 of sugar mixture into each bowl.
- Stir chocolate mixture until smooth; transfer to lined pan; mix peanut butter mixture; pour over chocolate layer carefully. Keep in the fridge until firm.
- Lift fudge out of pan with foil. Get rid of foil; slice fudge into 1-1/4-in. squares.

Nutrition Information

- Calories: 99 calories
- Total Carbohydrate: 15 g
- Cholesterol: 7 mg

314. Rich Candy Bar Fudge

"This fudge is rich and delightful."
Serving: 4 lbs. (about 7 dozen). | Prep: 20m | Ready in: 20m

Ingredients

- 6 Snickers candy bars (2.07 oz. each)
- 3 cups sugar
- 3/4 cup butter, cubed
- 2/3 cup evaporated milk
- 2 cups (12 oz.) semisweet chocolate chips
- 1 jar (7 oz.) marshmallow creme
- 1 tsp. vanilla extract

Direction

- Using foil, line a 9-in. square pan. Butter the foil; put pan aside. Slice candy bars into 1/2-in. slices; put aside.
- Boil milk, butter and sugar over medium heat in a heavy saucepan. Cook while stirring about 3 minutes until a candy thermometer registers 234° (soft-ball stage). Take out of the heat. Stir in vanilla, marshmallow crème and chocolate chips until smooth.
- Transfer 1/2 into lined pan. Top with candy bar slices. Place the rest of the chocolate mixture on top; spread evenly. Allow to stand at room temperature to cool. Lift out of pan; get rid of foil. Cut into squares.

Nutrition Information

- Calories: 75 calories
- Total Carbohydrate: 12 g
- Cholesterol: 5 mg
- Total Fat: 3 g
- Fiber: 0 g
- Protein: 0 g

- Sodium: 23 mg

315. Rich Truffle Wedges

"A wonderful decadent dessert."
Serving: 12 servings. | Prep: 30m | Ready in: 55m

Ingredients

- 1/2 cup butter
- 6 oz. semisweet chocolate, chopped
- 3 eggs
- 2/3 cup sugar
- 1 tsp. vanilla extract
- 1/4 tsp. salt
- 2/3 cup all-purpose flour
- GLAZE:
- 1/4 cup butter
- 2 oz. semisweet chocolate, chopped
- 2 tsps. honey
- SAUCE:
- 2 cups fresh or frozen unsweetened raspberries
- 2 tbsps. sugar
- Whipped cream, fresh raspberries and mint, optional

Direction

- Melt chocolate and butter in microwave/double boiler; mix till smooth. Cool for 10 minutes. Beat salt, vanilla, sugar and eggs for 4 minutes till thick in bowl. Blend chocolate mixture in; mix flour in. Stir well.
- Put in 9-in. greased and floured springform pan. Bake for 25-30 minutes at 350° till an inserted toothpick in middle exits clean. On wire rack, completely cool.
- Mix glaze ingredients in small saucepan; mix and cook on low heat till smooth and melted. Slightly cool. Run knife around springform pan edges to loosen. Transfer cake to serving plate; spread glaze on sides and top. Put aside.
- Sauce: In food processor/blender, puree raspberries. If desired, press through sieve; discard seeds. Mix sugar in; chill till serving.

- Put sauce on individual servings. Use mint (optional), raspberries and whipped cream to garnish.

Nutrition Information

- Calories: 246 calories
- Total Carbohydrate: 25 g
- Cholesterol: 84 mg
- Total Fat: 16 g
- Fiber: 2 g
- Protein: 3 g
- Sodium: 181 mg

316. Rocky Road Candies

"Very quick and easy to make this treat."
Serving: 24 | Prep: 5m | Ready in: 2h10m

Ingredients

- 1 (12 oz.) package semisweet chocolate chips
- 1/8 cup butter
- 1 (14 oz.) can sweetened condensed milk
- 2 1/2 cups dry-roasted peanuts
- 1 (16 oz.) package miniature marshmallows

Direction

- Use wax paper to line a 13"x9" pan.
- Melt butter and chocolate in a microwave-safe bowl in the microwave until melted. Stir sometimes until chocolate is smooth, then add in condensed milk, stir. Mix marshmallows and peanuts together, then stir into the chocolate mixture. Put into prepped pan and refrigerate until firm. Cut into squares.

Nutrition Information

- Calories: 284 calories;
- Total Carbohydrate: 36.3 g
- Cholesterol: 8 mg
- Total Fat: 14.1 g
- Protein: 5.5 g
- Sodium: 53 mg

317. Rocky Road Fudge

Ingredients

- 2 cups one 12 oz. bag nestle semisweet morsels
- 1 can sweetened condensed milk, 14 oz.
- 1 tsp. vanilla extract
- 2 cups mini marshamallows, rounded
- 1 1/2 cups salted coctail peanuts, coarsely chopped, flat, instead do fw salted toasted almonds

Direction

- Preparation:
- LINE 13 x 9-inch baking pan using foil; lightly grease. MICROWAVE the sweetened condensed milk and morsels on HIGH (100%) power in a big, uncovered, microwave-safe bowl for a minute; MIX. Some of morsels may retain their original form. Microwave for another 10 to 15-second intervals if needed, mixing until morsels are melted. Mix in the vanilla extract. Fold in nuts and marshmallows. PUSH the blend into the prepared baking pan. Refrigerate until ready to eat. Take out of the pan; discard the foil. Slice into pieces.
- We prefer in 7 x 11 Pyrex plate (so I reduce the marshmallows from 3 cups in the original recipe to 2).
- I process in the microwave at 50% power.
- Distribute in a pan with green spatula, after an hour in the refrigerator, cut quickly 8 by 4, lifted using med offset then place in the containers, return to the refrigerator.
- The longer it sets the better. In other words, the time should be more than 2 hours, or else the consistency will too soft.

318. Salted Caramel And Toasted Pecan Truffles

"Fancy candies!"
Serving: 12 | Prep: 8m | Ready in: 4h

Ingredients

- 1/2 cup chopped pecans
- 1/2 cup granulated sugar
- 6 tbsps. heavy cream
- 9 (1 oz.) squares semi-sweet baking chocolate, divided
- 1/8 tsp. Diamond Crystal® Kosher Salt or Coarse Sea Salt
- 1/2 tsp. vanilla extract

Direction

- In dry skillet, toast pecans on medium heat for about 1 minute till fragrant and golden. Put aside; cool.
- Heat sugar in heavy pan/Dutch oven on medium high heat, constantly mixing. When sugar starts to melt, mix and cook till sugar is rich golden color. Caramel flavor will be faint if color is too light.
- Take caramelized sugar off heat; mix cream in. Put back on heat; lower heat to low. Mix and cook till caramel dissolves well into cream. Take off heat; mix 1/2 chocolate, vanilla and salt in. Mix till chocolate melts. Mix toasted pecan bits in.
- Put mixture into bowl; slightly cool. Cover; refrigerate for about 1 hour till set.
- Roll/shape to 24 small balls, 3/4-1-in. Put on parchment-lined baking sheet; chill for an hour.
- Put leftover chocolate in microwave-safe bowl; microwave for about 15 seconds on high; mix. Microwave till chocolate melts in 15-sec intervals.
- Roll balls in melted chocolate with a fork; put onto parchment-lined bake sheet. Sprinkle truffles quickly with few grains of coarse sea

salt/Diamond Crystal Kosher salt. Chill for about 1 hour to set.

Nutrition Information

- Calories: 195 calories;
- Total Carbohydrate: 21.2 g
- Cholesterol: 10 mg
- Total Fat: 12.8 g
- Protein: 2.1 g
- Sodium: 23 mg

319. Shortcut Fudge

"I have been making this recipe for 35 years and it's still one of my favorite recipes till this day."
Serving: 3/4 lb. (about 1-1/2 dozen). | Prep: 15m | Ready in: 15m

Ingredients

- 1 package (3.4 oz.) cook-and-serve chocolate pudding mix
- 1 cup sugar
- 1/2 cup evaporated milk
- 1 tbsp. butter, softened
- 1 cup chopped pecans

Direction

- Mix butter, milk, sugar, and dry pudding mix together in a heavy saucepan. Boil and stir for 3 minutes until a candy thermometer reaches 224°. Take away from heat and quickly whisk for 1 minute. Add pecans; keep whisking until the mixture has thickened a bit. Drop onto cookie sheets lined with waxed papers by tablespoonfuls. Chill for 45 minutes until firm.

Nutrition Information

- Calories: 122 calories
- Total Carbohydrate: 17 g
- Cholesterol: 4 mg
- Total Fat: 6 g
- Fiber: 1 g
- Protein: 1 g

- Sodium: 37 mg

320. Simple And Amazing Peanut Butter-chocolate Fudge

"To make this dish, you only need a few ingredients."
Serving: 24 | Prep: 10m | Ready in: 6h10m

Ingredients

- 1 cup semi-sweet chocolate chips
- 1 cup peanut butter
- 3/4 cup maple syrup

Direction

- In a double boiler over medium heat, melt chocolate chips with maple syrup and peanut butter; continually stir until smooth. Pour into a dish lined with parchment paper; keep in the fridge for 6 hours to overnight before cutting. Serve.

Nutrition Information

- Calories: 124 calories;
- Total Carbohydrate: 13.3 g
- Cholesterol: 0 mg
- Total Fat: 7.5 g
- Protein: 3.2 g
- Sodium: 50 mg

321. Simple Macadamia Nut Fudge

"You can make this candy with whatever type of nut you like and it is still amazing with the recipe I have."
Serving: about 5 lbs.. | Prep: 15m | Ready in: 15m

Ingredients

- 2 tsps. plus 1/2 cup butter, divided
- 4-1/2 cups granulated sugar
- 1 can (12 oz.) evaporated milk
- 3 cups chopped macadamia nuts, divided
- 12 oz. German sweet chocolate, chopped

- 1 package (12 oz.) semisweet chocolate chips
- 1 jar (7 oz.) marshmallow creme
- 2 tsps. vanilla extract
- 1/2 tsp. salt, optional

Direction

- Line two 9-inch square pans with aluminum foil. Brush the foil with 2 tsp. butter. Put to one side.
- Combine remaining butter, milk, and sugar in a large heavy saucepan. Bring the mixture to a gentle boil. Cook and stir continuously for 5 minutes. Turn off the heat; mix in vanilla, marshmallow creme, chocolate chips, chopped chocolate, 2 cups of nuts and salt if desired.
- Transfer fudge to the two pans; scatter remaining nuts on top and press them lightly into the mixture. Chill until firm. Once firm, lift the fudge out of the pans using foil. Remove the foil; slice fudge into 1-inch square bars. Preserve them in an air-tight container.

Nutrition Information

- Calories: 72 calories
- Total Carbohydrate: 10 g
- Cholesterol: 2 mg
- Total Fat: 4 g
- Fiber: 0 g
- Protein: 1 g
- Sodium: 14 mg

322. Soda Cracker Candy

"A dish with soda crackers and if you like almond roca, you'll love this recipe."
Serving: 8 | Prep: 10m | Ready in: 20m

Ingredients

- 1 (10 oz.) package saltine crackers
- 1 1/2 cups butter
- 1 1/2 cups packed brown sugar
- 2 (12 oz.) packages semisweet chocolate chips
- 2 cups chopped almonds

Direction

- Set an oven to preheat to 200°C (400°F). Use aluminum foil to line a 10x15-inch cookie sheet.
- Put the crackers on the prepped cookie sheet in a single layer. Use fewer or more crackers as necessary to cover the pan's bottom.
- Mix together the brown sugar and butter in a small saucepan over low heat, then boil. Let it boil for 3 minutes, then pour it on top of the crackers.
- Let it bake for 5 minutes in the preheated oven. Evenly sprinkle the chocolate chips on the top. Sprinkle the almonds on top of the chocolate chips, then press the nuts into the chocolate using the back of a wooden spoon.
- Let it chill in the fridge for a minimum of 3 hours or until it becomes set. Break into pieces and store it in the fridge, sealed.

Nutrition Information

- Calories: 1151 calories;
- Total Carbohydrate: 123 g
- Cholesterol: 92 mg
- Total Fat: 75.7 g
- Protein: 12.2 g
- Sodium: 641 mg

323. Soda Cracker Chocolate Candy

"We often make this treats as holiday gifts for everybody."
Serving: about 5 dozen. | Prep: 15m | Ready in: 25m

Ingredients

- 35 to 40 soda crackers
- 1 cup butter, cubed
- 1 cup packed brown sugar
- 1-1/2 cups semisweet chocolate chips
- 1-1/2 cups coarsely chopped walnuts

Direction

- Using foil, line a 15x10x1-in. baking pan and use cooking spray to coat. Arrange crackers in rows on foil. Melt butter in a saucepan; add brown sugar; boil. Broil for 3 minutes. Add over crackers; spread until cover completely. Bake for 5 minutes at 350° (crackers should float.) Take out of the oven. Turn the oven off. Top with walnuts and chocolate chips over crackers. Place back in the oven for about 3-5 minutes until chocolate is melted. Take out of the oven; press walnuts into chocolate with a greased spatula. While it is still warm, cut into 1 in. squares. Completely cool; take the candy out of foil.

Nutrition Information

- Calories: 173 calories
- Total Carbohydrate: 16 g
- Cholesterol: 16 mg
- Total Fat: 12 g
- Fiber: 1 g
- Protein: 2 g
- Sodium: 108 mg

324. Speculoos Cups

"This recipe is brilliant."
Serving: 12 | Prep: 15m | Ready in: 1h

Ingredients

- 6 oz. dark chocolate, coarsely chopped
- 1/2 cup cookie butter (speculoos spread)
- 1/2 cup crushed speculoos cookies (European caramelized cookies)

Direction

- In top of a double boiler, over simmering water, place chocolate; heat and stir frequently, scraping down the sides, for about 5 minutes until smooth and melted.
- Spoon 1 1/2 tsp. melted chocolate into 12 paper or silicon cupcake liners; spread around the bottom evenly and use a spoon to partway up to sides. Chill for 10-15 minutes until set.
- In a small bowl, combine crushed cookies and cookie butter together to make filling.
- Drop filling over chilled chocolate by teaspoonfuls. Add the rest of the melted chocolate to cover; using a spoon to smooth tops. Chill for half an hour until set.

Nutrition Information

- Calories: 155 calories;
- Total Carbohydrate: 16.5 g
- Cholesterol: 1 mg
- Total Fat: 9.4 g
- Protein: 0.9 g
- Sodium: 19 mg

325. Speedy Oven Fudge

"This recipe will wow your family."
Serving: 3 lbs.. | Prep: 10m | Ready in: 25m

Ingredients

- 1/2 cup milk
- 1 cup butter
- 2/3 cup baking cocoa
- 2 lbs. confectioners' sugar
- 2 tsps. vanilla extract
- 1 cup chopped nuts

Direction

- In a 3-quart baking dish, put first 4 ingredients in order listed (without stirring). Bake for 15 mins in a 350° oven, until the butter melts.
- Place into a bowl carefully. Put in vanilla, then beat for 2 mins on high. Mix in nuts. Transfer to a buttered 11x7-inch dish. Let cool. Cut and serve.

Nutrition Information

- Calories: 128 calories
- Total Carbohydrate: 20 g
- Cholesterol: 11 mg

- Total Fat: 5 g
- Fiber: 0 g
- Protein: 1 g
- Sodium: 40 mg

326. Spiced Chocolate Truffles

"Pumpkin spice truffles."
Serving: about 2 dozen. | Prep: 45m | Ready in: 50m

Ingredients

- 12 oz. milk chocolate baking bars, divided
- 1/2 cup heavy whipping cream
- 2 tbsps. canned pumpkin
- 1/4 tsp. ground cinnamon
- 1/4 tsp. ground ginger
- 1/4 tsp. ground nutmeg
- Dash ground cloves
- Baking cocoa
- Candy eyeballs, optional

Direction

- Chop 10-oz. chocolate finely; put in small bowl. Heat spices, pumpkin and cream to just a boil in small heavy saucepan. Put on chocolate; let stand for 5 minutes.
- Use a whisk to mix till smooth. Cool it to room temperature; refrigerate for minimum of 4 hours, covered.
- Grate leftover chocolate finely; put in small microwave-safe bowl. Form chocolate mixture to 1-in. balls with hands lightly dusted with baking cocoa. Roll in grated chocolate, it'll be soft and the truffles may slightly flatten when standing. Melt leftover grated chocolate in microwave if desired to attach eyeballs. Keep in airtight container in the fridge.

Nutrition Information

- Calories: 89 calories
- Total Carbohydrate: 9 g
- Cholesterol: 10 mg
- Total Fat: 6 g

- Fiber: 0 g
- Protein: 1 g
- Sodium: 7 mg

327. Spook-tacular Chocolate-dipped Pretzels

"Those chocolate-dipped pretzel rods are beautiful and delicious.""
Serving: 30 | Prep: 15m | Ready in: 45m

Ingredients

- Wax paper
- 1 1/3 cups NESTLE® TOLL HOUSE® Semi-Sweet Chocolate Morsels, melted according to package directions in 8- or 9-inch microwave-safe dish
- 1 (10 oz.) bag pretzel rods
- 3 pieces NESTLE® CRUNCH® Candy Bars, chopped
- 3 pieces NESTLE® BUTTERFINGER® Bites Candy, chopped
- WONKA Halloween Candies such as Spooky NERDS and SweeTARTS Skulls n' Bones*

Direction

- Line waxed paper on a baking sheet. Lay candies individually in different sheets of waxed paper.
- Immerse pretzel rods halfway into chocolate, dripping off excess. Roll pretzel rods in candies (use 1 type of candy for 1 pretzel rod); arrange rolled pretzels on the waxed paper-lined baking sheet.
- Put into the fridge and allow to chill for about half an hour to set. Once hardened, take out of the baking sheets; place pretzels between layers of waxed papers; cover and store pretzels in a cool area.

Nutrition Information

- Calories: 107 calories;
- Total Carbohydrate: 17.6 g

- Cholesterol: < 1 mg
- Total Fat: 3.6 g
- Protein: 1.8 g
- Sodium: 213 mg

328. Stovetop Dark Chocolate Popcorn

"This sweet popcorn recipe is cooked in a popcorn kettle."
Serving: 12 | Prep: 5m | Ready in: 15m

Ingredients

- 1/2 cup unpopped popcorn
- 1/4 cup vegetable oil
- 1/3 cup white sugar, or to taste
- 1 tbsp. cocoa powder

Direction

- Heat a pot or popcorn kettle over medium heat. Add the cocoa powder, sugar, oil and popcorn. Cook while gently turning the handle until the popping slows to 3 seconds between pops.

Nutrition Information

- Calories: 94 calories;
- Total Carbohydrate: 12 g
- Cholesterol: 0 mg
- Total Fat: 5 g
- Protein: 1.1 g
- Sodium: < 1 mg

329. Strawberry Chocolate Truffles

"I love giving these truffles as gifts."
Serving: 3-1/2 dozen. | Prep: 40m | Ready in: 45m

Ingredients

- 4 milk chocolate candy bars (7 oz. each), halved
- 1 cup heavy whipping cream

- 1/4 cup strawberry spreadable fruit
- 1-1/2 tsps. vanilla extract
- 1-1/4 cups chopped almonds, toasted

Direction

- Process chocolate in food processor till chopped, covered. Put cream to just a boil in small saucepan. Put on chocolate; cover. Process till smooth. Mix vanilla and spreadable fruit in till combined. Put in small bowl; cool, occasionally mixing, to room temperature. Refrigerate for 3 hours till firm.
- Form to 1-in. balls then roll into almonds.

Nutrition Information

- Calories: 147 calories
- Total Carbohydrate: 13 g
- Cholesterol: 12 mg
- Total Fat: 10 g
- Fiber: 1 g
- Protein: 2 g
- Sodium: 17 mg

330. Stuffed Cherries Dipped In Chocolate

""I prepare these delightful cherry treats in early summer when the cherries are in season and ripe. Well-loved during summertime, they freeze super great and are a pretty treat to present visitors throughout the summer.""
Serving: 5 dozen. | Prep: 40m | Ready in: 45m

Ingredients

- 1-1/2 lbs. fresh dark sweet cherries with stems
- 1 package (8 oz.) cream cheese, softened
- 2 tbsps. ground hazelnuts
- 2 tbsps. maple syrup
- 2 cups white baking chips
- 12 tsps. shortening, divided
- 1-1/2 cups milk chocolate chips
- 1-1/2 cups semisweet chocolate chips

Direction

- Through the sides, pit cherries, keeping stems intact. Whisk cream cheese in a small bowl until smooth. Mix in syrup and hazelnut. Then pipe into cherries. Dissolve 5 tsps. shortening and vanilla chips in a small microwave-safe bowl at 70%. Microwave at extra 10-20 seconds intervals, whisking until smooth. Repeat with 3-1/2 tsps. shortening and milk chocolate chips in a separate bowl. Do the same with remaining shortening and semisweet chips. Dunk a third of the filled cherries while holding the stem, into dissolved white chocolate; let excess to drip off. Set on waxed paper; allow to stand until set. Continue with remaining cherries and semisweet chocolate and milk chocolate. Dunk the white-coated cherries a second time to fully coat; allow to stand until set.
- Heat again the remaining dissolved chocolate if needed. Pour white chocolate over cherries dipped in semisweet or milk chocolate. Pour semisweet or milk chocolate over white chocolate-dipped cherries. Keep in an airtight container and refrigerate.

Nutrition Information

- Calories: 105 calories
- Total Carbohydrate: 11 g
- Cholesterol: 6 mg
- Total Fat: 7 g
- Fiber: 1 g
- Protein: 1 g
- Sodium: 20 mg

331. Sugar-free Chocolate Fudge

"For those who can't eat sugar and are constantly craving, this fudge is what you should always keep in hand."
Serving: 16 servings. | Prep: 10m | Ready in: 10m

Ingredients

- 2 packages (8 oz. each) cream cheese, softened

- 2 oz. unsweetened chocolate, melted and cooled
- 24 packets aspartame sweetener (equivalent to 1 cup sugar)
- 1 tsp. vanilla extract
- 1/2 cup chopped pecans

Direction

- Beat vanilla, sweetener, chocolate and cream cheese in a small bowl to form a smooth mixture. Mix in pecans. Transfer to a foil-lined 8-inch square dish. Chill, while covered, overnight. Slice into 16 square pieces. Serve while chilled.

Nutrition Information

- Calories: 150 calories
- Total Carbohydrate: 4 g
- Cholesterol: 31 mg
- Total Fat: 15 g
- Fiber: 1 g
- Protein: 3 g
- Sodium: 84 mg

332. Surprise Chocolate Fudge

"This recipe will surprise you."
Serving: about 3-1/2 lbs.. | Prep: 20m | Ready in: 20m

Ingredients

- 1 can (15 oz.) pinto beans, rinsed and drained
- 1 cup baking cocoa
- 3/4 cup butter, melted
- 1 tbsp. vanilla extract
- 7-1/2 cups confectioners' sugar
- 1 cup chopped walnuts

Direction

- Use a fork to mash beans, in a microwave-safe dish, until they become smooth, then microwave, covered, until heated through, about 90 secs. Put in vanilla, butter and cocoa. (It will be thick.) Stir in sugar slowly; put in nuts. Then press into a 9-inch square pan coated with the cooking spray. Place in the refrigerator, covered, until firm. Slice into 1-inch pieces.

Nutrition Information

- Calories: 76 calories
- Total Carbohydrate: 13 g
- Cholesterol: 4 mg
- Total Fat: 3 g
- Fiber: 1 g
- Protein: 1 g
- Sodium: 20 mg

333. Swedish Chocolate Balls (or Coconut Balls)

""*A classic recipe adored by every Swede. It is loved by everyone, and it is among the first recipes learnt by kids. The balls may be prepared in various sizes depending on the preference of the cook. The flavor is appreciated on the addition of extra cocoa powder or chocolate.*""
Serving: 48 | Prep: 20m | Ready in: 2h20m

Ingredients

- 4 cups regular rolled oats
- 1 1/4 cups white sugar
- 1/2 cup unsweetened cocoa powder
- 1 cup butter or margarine, softened
- 2 tbsps. strong coffee
- 1 tsp. vanilla extract
- 2 (1 oz.) squares unsweetened baking chocolate, melted
- 1/3 cup coconut flakes

Direction

- In a bowl, combine the cocoa, oats and sugar. Put in butter and mix the ingredients together with your hands to form dough with considerable thickness. Add the chocolate, vanilla and coffee until it mixes thoroughly.
- Pour the coconut flakes in a small bowl. Roll small amounts of dough between your hands

to form small balls of diameter about 1 1/2 inches. Roll the balls in the coconut flakes. Balls are already edible, or may be chilled for 2 hours to become firmer.

Nutrition Information

- Calories: 90 calories;
- Total Carbohydrate: 10.9 g
- Cholesterol: 10 mg
- Total Fat: 5.2 g
- Protein: 1.3 g
- Sodium: 30 mg

334. Sweet Pretzel Stacks

"So tasty!"
Serving: 18

Ingredients

- 2 cups crushed pretzels
- 1/4 cup peanuts
- 2/3 cup sweetened condensed milk
- 1/2 cup semisweet chocolate chips
- 1/2 cup butterscotch chips
- 1/4 tsp. vanilla extract

Direction

- Combine peanuts and pretzels in a large mixing bowl. Put aside.
- Mix butterscotch chips, chocolate chips and condensed milk together in a medium saucepan. Cook for 5 mins over low heat until the chips melt, stirring constantly. Discard pan from the heat; mix in vanilla extract.
- Add the saucepan mixture over peanut/pretzel mixture. Stir until they are coated thoroughly. Drop onto foil or waxed paper by rounded tsps.. Let chill (or cool) until firm. Preserve in a covered container in fridge (or cool place).

Nutrition Information

- Calories: 133 calories;

- Total Carbohydrate: 20 g
- Cholesterol: 4 mg
- Total Fat: 5.1 g
- Protein: 2.4 g
- Sodium: 181 mg

335. Sweet Tooth Treats

"I recollect Mom would have these yummy bites hanging tight for us kids when we returned home from school."
Serving: 2-1/2 dozen. | Prep: 20m | Ready in: 25m

Ingredients

- 1 cup peanut butter
- 1/2 cup light corn syrup
- 1/2 cup confectioners' sugar
- 1/4 cup sweetened shredded coconut
- 2 cups Cheerios
- 1 cup (6 oz.) semisweet chocolate chips
- 1 tbsp. shortening

Direction

- Mix the coconut, sugar, corn syrup and peanut butter in a big bowl until combined. Mix in the cereal. Form into balls of 1-1/2 inches.
- Melt the shortening and chocolate chips in a microwave; mix until smooth. Dip the balls in chocolate halfway; let excess drip off. Put onto the baking sheets lined with waxed paper; allow to stand until set.

Nutrition Information

- Calories: 232 calories
- Total Carbohydrate: 26 g
- Cholesterol: 0 mg
- Total Fat: 14 g
- Fiber: 2 g
- Protein: 5 g
- Sodium: 135 mg

336. Sweetheart Fudge

"This rich cocoa fudge makes certain to charm somebody you cherish."
Serving: about 5 dozen. | Prep: 30m | Ready in: 30m

Ingredients

- 1-1/2 tsps. plus 1/4 cup butter, divided
- 3 cups sugar
- 2/3 cup baking cocoa
- 1/8 tsp. salt
- 1-1/2 cups milk
- 1 tsp. vanilla extract

Direction

- Line an 8-inch square pan using foil then coat the foil using 1-1/2 tsps. butter; put aside. Mix salt, cocoa and sugar in a heavy saucepan. Mix in milk until smooth; bring to a rapid boil over medium heat, mixing constantly. Cook without mixing until reaching 234 ° (soft-ball stage) on a candy thermometer. Take away from the heat; put in the leftover butter and vanilla (don't blend).
- Cool down to 110 ° (for 5 minutes). Beat using a spoon until the fudge becomes thick and starts losing its gloss. Spread instantly into prepared pan. Cool. Lift the fudge out of the pan with foil. Remove the foil; slice fudge into 1-inch squares.

Nutrition Information

- Calories: 106 calories
- Total Carbohydrate: 22 g
- Cholesterol: 6 mg
- Total Fat: 2 g
- Fiber: 0 g
- Protein: 1 g
- Sodium: 33 mg

337. The Best White Chocolate Almond Bark

"A great treat to give out in the holidays."
Serving: 24 | Prep: 5m | Ready in: 1h17m

Ingredients

- 1 1/4 cups whole almonds
- 3 cups white chocolate melting wafers
- 3 tbsps. butter
- 1 tsp. almond extract

Direction

- Preheat the oven to 375°F (190°C). Line parchment paper on two baking sheets.
- In the preheated oven, roast almonds on a baking sheet in about 10 minutes, stirring occasionally, till toasted.
- In a microwave-safe bowl, microwave butter and white chocolate melting wafers on medium-high in about 90 seconds; stir. Microwave for 20-30 more seconds, until well melted. Put in almond extract and mix until smooth. Mix in toasted almonds.
- On the second baking sheet, spread evenly the chocolate mixture. Allow to chill in the fridge in about 1 hour, until hardened. Using hands to break into small pieces.

Nutrition Information

- Calories: 171 calories;
- Total Carbohydrate: 14 g
- Cholesterol: 8 mg
- Total Fat: 12 g
- Protein: 2.8 g
- Sodium: 29 mg

338. The Ultimate Chocolate Bar

"Rich chocolate squares filled with nuts and marshmallows."
Serving: 30

Ingredients

- 1/2 cup butter
- 1 (1 oz.) square unsweetened chocolate
- 1 cup white sugar
- 1 cup all-purpose flour
- 1/2 cup chopped walnuts
- 1 tsp. baking powder
- 1 tsp. vanilla extract
- 2 eggs
- 6 oz. cream cheese, softened
- 1/2 cup white sugar
- 2 tbsps. all-purpose flour
- 1 egg
- 1/2 tsp. vanilla extract
- 2 cups miniature marshmallows
- 1/3 cup butter
- 2 (1 oz.) squares unsweetened chocolate
- 1/3 cup milk
- 2 oz. cream cheese
- 4 cups confectioners' sugar
- 1 tsp. vanilla extract

Direction

- Set oven to 350°F (175°C) to preheat. Grease and flour a 13x9 inch pan lightly.
- Melt 1 oz chocolate and 1/2 cup butter in a big saucepan over low heat. Take off from heat, mix in 2 eggs, 1 tsp. vanilla, baking powder, walnuts, 1 cup flour, and a cup white sugar, then blend thoroughly. Lather chocolate base into greased and floured pan evenly.
- Mix half a tsp. vanilla, an egg, 2 tbsps. flour, half a cup white sugar and 6 oz cream cheese in a small bowl. With an electric mixer, whip for a minute at medium speed, or until smooth and fluffy. Spread cream cheese filling on top of chocolate mixture.
- At 350°F (175°C), bake filling and base for 25 to 35 minutes.

- In the meantime, make frosting. In a big saucepan, melt 2 oz cream cheese, milk, 2 oz chocolate and 1/3 cup butter over low heat. Take off from heat and put in confectioners' sugar and a tsp. vanilla; whip thoroughly. With heat, soften if it starts to dry before ready to use.
- Scatter marshmallows on top of the chocolate bar in pan. Pour warm frosting on top of marshmallows. With kitchen knife, mix the two slightly. Allow to cool to room temperature. Put foil over to cover when cooled and chill overnight. Slice cold into small pieces.

Nutrition Information

- Calories: 237 calories;
- Total Carbohydrate: 33.8 g
- Cholesterol: 41 mg
- Total Fat: 11.1 g
- Protein: 2.5 g
- Sodium: 87 mg

339. Three-chip English Toffee

"Rich and flavorful toffee that melts in your mouth! You can dribble 3 different melted chips on top then sprinkle with walnuts. Just place them in decorative tins to present them as gifts."
Serving: about 2-1/2 lbs.. | Prep: 15m | Ready in: 45m

Ingredients

- 1/2 tsp. plus 2 cups butter, divided
- 2 cups sugar
- 1 cup slivered almonds
- 1 cup milk chocolate chips
- 1 cup chopped walnuts
- 1/2 cup semisweet chocolate chips
- 1/2 cup white baking chips
- 1-1/2 tsps. shortening

Direction

- Spread a half tsp. of butter in a 15-in by 10-in by 1-in pan. On medium-low heat, boil the

remaining butter and sugar together in a heavy pot while constantly stirring; cover and cook for 2-3 minutes.
- Remove the cover then put in almonds; cook and mix using a clean spoon until golden brown and an inserted candy thermometer registers 300 degrees or at hard-crack stage.
- Transfer in the buttered pan but avoid scraping the sides of the pot; the top will be buttery. Cool for 1-2 minutes then spread milk chocolate chips on top; set aside for 1-2 minutes then slather the chocolate on top. Spread walnuts then gently press them down using the back of a spoon. Refrigerate for 10 minutes.
- Melt the semisweet chips in the microwave then mix until smooth; dribble on top of the walnuts. Place in the refrigerator for 10 minutes. Melt shortening and vanilla chips; mix until smooth then dribble on top of the walnuts. Cover then place in the refrigerator for 1-2 hours. Break into pieces.

Nutrition Information

- Calories: 397 calories
- Total Carbohydrate: 32 g
- Cholesterol: 52 mg
- Total Fat: 30 g
- Fiber: 1 g
- Protein: 4 g
- Sodium: 197 mg

340. Three-chocolate Fudge

"What a wonderful recipe to treat your friends and neighbors at Christmas time."
Serving: about 5-1/2 lbs.. | Prep: 15m | Ready in: 35m

Ingredients

- 1 tbsp. butter
- 3-1/3 cups sugar
- 1 cup packed dark brown sugar
- 1 can (12 oz.) evaporated milk
- 1 cup butter, cubed

- 32 large marshmallows, halved
- 1 tsp. vanilla extract
- 2 cups (12 oz.) semisweet chocolate chips
- 14 oz. milk chocolate, chopped
- 2 oz. semisweet chocolate, chopped
- 2 cups chopped pecans, toasted

Direction

- Line foil over a 15x10x1-inch pan; use 1 tbsp. butter to grease the foil.
- Combine cubed butter, milk, and sugar in a heavy large saucepan. Heat over medium heat, stirring constantly, until mixture comes to a rolling bowl; cook while stirring, for 5 minutes. Turn off the heat. Mix in vanilla and marshmallows until combined.
- Slowly whisk in chopped chocolate and chocolate chips until melted. Mix in pecans. Instantly pour mixture into the buttered pan, spreading evenly. Chill in the fridge until set, about 1 hour. Take fudge out of the pan using foil. Take off the foil; divide the fudge into squares about 1 inch. Place fudges between layers of waxed paper in an airtight container to store.

Nutrition Information

- Calories: 79 calories
- Total Carbohydrate: 11 g
- Cholesterol: 5 mg
- Total Fat: 4 g
- Fiber: 0 g
- Protein: 1 g
- Sodium: 16 mg

341. Tiger Butter Candy

"This candy is so fun to make."
Serving: about 1-1/2 lbs.. | Prep: 20m | Ready in: 20m

Ingredients

- 1 lb. white candy coating, coarsely chopped
- 1/2 cup chunky peanut butter
- 1/2 cup semisweet chocolate chips

- 4 tsps. half-and-half cream

Direction

- Melt peanut butter and coating in a microwave. Stir until they become smooth. Transfer to foil-lined baking sheet coated with the cooking spray. Then spread into thin layer.
- Repeat with cream and chips. Pour while swirling over the peanut butter layer. Place in the freezer until set, about 5 mins. Crack into small pieces.

Nutrition Information

- Calories: 225 calories
- Total Carbohydrate: 25 g
- Cholesterol: 1 mg
- Total Fat: 14 g
- Fiber: 1 g
- Protein: 2 g
- Sodium: 40 mg

342. Toasted Coconut Truffles

"Tempting and wonderful truffles."
Serving: about 5-1/2 dozen. | Prep: 30m | Ready in: 30m

Ingredients

- 4 cups (24 oz.) semisweet chocolate chips
- 1 package (8 oz.) cream cheese, softened and cubed
- 3/4 cup sweetened condensed milk
- 3 tsps. vanilla extract
- 2 tsps. water
- 1 lb. white candy coating, coarsely chopped
- 2 tbsps. sweetened shredded coconut, finely chopped and toasted

Direction

- Melt chocolate chips in a microwave-safe bowl; mix till smooth. Add water, vanilla, milk and cream cheese; use hand mixer to beat till blended. Cover; refrigerate for 1 1/2 hours till easy to handle.

- Form to 1-inch balls; put on waxed paper-lined baking sheets. Cover loosely; refrigerate till firm for 1-2 hours.
- Melt candy coating in the microwave; mix till smooth. In coating, dip balls; let excess drip off. Put onto waxed paper-lined baking sheets then sprinkle coconut. Refrigerate for 15 minutes till firm. Keep in the fridge in an airtight container.

Nutrition Information

- Calories: 220 calories
- Total Carbohydrate: 27 g
- Cholesterol: 10 mg
- Total Fat: 13 g
- Fiber: 1 g
- Protein: 2 g
- Sodium: 32 mg

---

343. Toffee Squares

"This toffee flavor in this recipe can be upgraded by using 1/2 chopped almonds instead of toffee baking bits."
Serving: Makes 48 squares

Ingredients

- 1 cup (2 sticks) unsalted butter, at room temperature
- 1 cup firmly packed light brown sugar
- 1 large egg yolk
- 1 tsp. vanilla extract
- 1/4 tsp. salt
- 2 cups all-purpose flour
- 7 to 8 oz. milk chocolate, broken into pieces, or 1 1/2 cups milk chocolate chips
- 1 cup chopped almonds, toasted

Direction

- 1. Set the oven to 350°F and start preheating. Using parchment, line a 9-by-13-inch baking pan.
- 2. For the crust: With an electric mixer, whisk together sugar and butter on medium speed in a large bowl for about 2 minutes until light.

Whisk in salt, vanilla and egg yolk. Beat in flour gradually on low speed until just mixed. The dough should be stiff. Pat the dough evenly over the bottom of the baking pan.
- 3. Bake in the center of the oven for about 20 minutes until pale gold on top.
- 4. Take the pan out of the oven; scatter the chocolate pieces evenly over the crust. Transfer the pan back to the oven for a minute. Take the pan out again; spread the chocolate evenly over the crust with a knife. Top with almonds evenly.
- 5. Allow to completely cool in the pan on a wire rack. Cut into small squares with a sharp knife; using a small offset spatula or an icing spatula, take out of the pan carefully.

Nutrition Information

- Calories: 111
- Total Carbohydrate: 12 g
- Cholesterol: 15 mg
- Total Fat: 7 g
- Fiber: 1 g
- Protein: 1 g
- Sodium: 17 mg
- Saturated Fat: 3 g

---

344. Trail Mix Clusters

"These delicious snack with dried fruit and nuts is a heart-healthy treat."
Serving: 4 dozen. | Prep: 20m | Ready in: 25m

Ingredients

- 2 cups (12 oz.) semisweet chocolate chips
- 1/2 cup unsalted sunflower kernels
- 1/2 cup salted pumpkin seeds or pepitas
- 1/2 cup coarsely chopped cashews
- 1/2 cup coarsely chopped pecans
- 1/4 cup sweetened shredded coconut
- 1/4 cup finely chopped dried apricots
- 1/4 cup dried cranberries
- 1/4 cup dried cherries or blueberries

Direction

- Liquefy chocolate chips in a big microwave-safe bowl; mix till smooth. Mix in the rest of the ingredients.
- Onto baking sheets lined with waxed paper, drop mixture by tablespoonfuls. Chill till firm. Keep in the refrigerator in an airtight container.

Nutrition Information

- Calories: 79 calories
- Total Carbohydrate: 8 g
- Cholesterol: 0 mg
- Total Fat: 6 g
- Fiber: 1 g
- Protein: 2 g
- Sodium: 26 mg

345. Trio Of Chocolate Truffles

"Rich and smooth chocolate treats."
Serving: Makes about 30 truffles

Ingredients

- 2/3 cup whipping cream
- 1 (12-oz.) package (about 2 cups) semisweet chocolate chips
- 2 tsps. vanilla extract
- 1/4 cup unsweetened cocoa powder
- 3/4 cup (about 2 1/2 oz.) sweetened shredded coconut, toasted
- 1/2 cup (about 2 oz.) finely chopped unsalted pistachios

Direction

- Boil cream in heavy medium saucepan; take off heat. Add chocolate; whisk till smooth and melted. Whisk vanilla in; put in medium bowl and cover. Chill for about 3 hours till firm.
- Line waxed paper on baking sheet. By rounded teaspoonfuls, drop mixture on prepped baking sheet. Freeze for about 45 minutes till firm.

- Put nuts, coconut and cocoa in different bowls. Between hands, roll truffles to rounds. Roll 1/3 truffles in nuts, 1/3 in coconut and 1/3 truffles in cocoa. Use plastic to cover; chill till serving time. You can make this 2 weeks in advance, chilled.

Nutrition Information

- Calories: 95
- Total Carbohydrate: 9 g
- Cholesterol: 6 mg
- Total Fat: 7 g
- Fiber: 1 g
- Protein: 1 g
- Sodium: 9 mg
- Saturated Fat: 4 g

346. Triple Chocolate Fudge

"This recipe is good enough to be a beautiful and delicious gift."
Serving: 6-3/4 lbs.. | Prep: 20m | Ready in: 45m

Ingredients

- 4 tsps. plus 1/2 cup butter, divided
- 4-1/2 cups sugar
- 1 can (12 oz.) evaporated milk
- 1 tsp. salt
- 16 oz. German sweet chocolate, chopped
- 2 cups (12 oz.) semisweet chocolate chips
- 1 package (11-1/2 oz.) milk chocolate chips
- 2 jars (7 oz. each) marshmallow creme
- 4 cups chopped pecans or walnuts, toasted
- 2 tsps. vanilla extract

Direction

- Line foil over 2 pans of 13x9-inch; use 4 tsps. of butter to grease the foil. Combine the rest of butter with salt, milk, and sugar in a heavy Dutch oven. Boil over medium heat, whisking constantly. Cook, undisturbed, until mixture reaches soft-ball stage or a candy thermometer registers 234°.

- Take off from the heat. Whisk in chocolate chips and German sweet chocolate until no lumps remain. Fold in vanilla, pecans, and marshmallow creme. Pour mixture into the prepared pans, spread.
- Chill mixture in the fridge until set, for 60 minutes. Take fudge out of the pan using the foil. Remove the foil; divide fudge into squares about 1 inch. Place in airtight containers to store.

Nutrition Information

- Calories: 64 calories
- Total Carbohydrate: 9 g
- Cholesterol: 2 mg
- Total Fat: 3 g
- Fiber: 0 g
- Protein: 1 g
- Sodium: 17 mg

347. True Love Truffles

"A great valentine's gift."
Serving: 8 dozen. | Prep: 50m | Ready in: 50m

Ingredients

- 1 tbsp. plus 3/4 cup butter, divided
- 1-1/2 cups sugar
- 1 can (5 oz.) evaporated milk
- 2 packages (4.67 oz. each) mint Andes candies
- 1 jar (7 oz.) marshmallow creme
- 1 tsp. vanilla extract
- 22 oz. white baking chocolate, divided
- 1/2 cup semisweet chocolate chips
- Green food coloring, optional

Direction

- Use 1 tbsp. butter to butter 15x10x1-in. pan; put aside. Boil leftover butter, milk and sugar in heavy saucepan on medium heat, constantly mixing. Lower heat; mix and cook till candy thermometer reads soft-ball stage at 236°. Take off heat; mix candies in till mixture blends well and candies melt. Mix vanilla and

marshmallow crème in; spread in prepped pan. Cover; refrigerate for an hour.
- Slice to 96 pieces; roll each to ball, it'll be soft. Put onto waxed paper-lined baking sheet.
- Melt 18-oz. white chocolate and the chocolate chips in heavy saucepan/microwave-safe bowl; dip the balls into melted chocolate. Put on waxed paper; let harden. Melt leftover white chocolate; if desired, add food coloring. Drizzle on truffles; keep in airtight container.

Nutrition Information

- Calories: 161 calories
- Total Carbohydrate: 21 g
- Cholesterol: 12 mg
- Total Fat: 9 g
- Fiber: 0 g
- Protein: 1 g
- Sodium: 52 mg

348. Truffle Acorns

"Oak seed formed chocolates."
Serving: about 3 dozen. | Prep: 20m | Ready in: 20m

Ingredients

- 2 cups (12 oz.) semisweet chocolate chips
- 3 oz. cream cheese, softened
- 1 tsp. water
- 1/2 tsp. almond extract
- 1/4 cup dark chocolate candy coating (about 1/8 lb.)
- 1/3 cup finely chopped almonds, toasted
- Slivered almonds

Direction

- In the microwave, melt the chocolate chips. Mix in the extract, water and cream cheese until well mixed. Chill for an hour, until easy to manage. Form the teaspoonfuls into slightly oblong balls with 1 flatter end; put onto the baking sheet lined with waxed paper. Refrigerate until firm, about 1 to 2 hours.

- Melt the candy coating in a double boiler or microwave. Dip about 1/8 inch flat end of each acorn into the chocolate, and then dip into chopped almonds. Prick a slivered almond in the top for a stem. Bring back to waxed paper for hardening.

Nutrition Information

- Calories: 68 calories
- Total Carbohydrate: 7 g
- Cholesterol: 3 mg
- Total Fat: 5 g
- Fiber: 1 g
- Protein: 1 g
- Sodium: 8 mg

349. Truffle Cherries

"These chocolate gems can't stay long on the table in my house during the holidays."
Serving: about 2 dozen. | Prep: 20m | Ready in: 20m

Ingredients

- 1/3 cup heavy whipping cream
- 2 tbsps. butter
- 2 tbsps. sugar
- 4 oz. semisweet chocolate, chopped
- 1 jar (8 oz.) maraschino cherries with stems, well drained
- COATING:
- 6 oz. semisweet chocolate, chopped
- 2 tbsps. shortening

Direction

- Bring butter, cream and sugar in a small saucepan to a boil, stirring continuously. Take off the heat; whisk in chocolate until melted. Chill, covered for a minimum of 4 hours or until easy to handle.
- Pat dry cherries using paper towels to very dry. Form a teaspoonful of chocolate mixture around each cherry, make a ball. Chill, covered, for 2 to 3 hours or until set.

- Microwave shortening and chocolate until melted; stir until smooth. Dip cherries into melted chocolate until coated, dripping off excess. Arrange on waxed paper to firm.

Nutrition Information

- Calories: 57 calories
- Total Carbohydrate: 6 g
- Cholesterol: 7 mg
- Total Fat: 4 g
- Fiber: 0 g
- Protein: 0 g
- Sodium: 11 mg

350. Truffle Cups

"A twist on regular truffles."
Serving: 5 dozen. | Prep: 30m | Ready in: 30m

Ingredients

- 1 package (11-1/2 oz.) milk chocolate chips
- 2 tbsps. shortening
- 1 lb. white candy coating, coarsely chopped
- 1/2 cup heavy whipping cream

Direction

- Melt shortening and chips in microwave; mix till smooth then cook for 5 minutes. "Paint" chocolate mixture on inside of 1-inch foil candy cups with narrow pastry brush. Put on tray; refrigerate for 45 minutes till firm.
- 12 cups at a time, remove from the fridge; remove then throw foil cups away. Put chocolate cups back into fridge. Filling: Melt cream and candy coating; mix till smooth.
- Put into bowl; cover. Refrigerate till mixture starts to thicken or for 30 minutes. Beat filling till fluffy and light or for 1-2 minutes. Use spoon/pastry star tube to fill chocolate cups. Keep in the fridge.

Nutrition Information

- Calories: 157 calories

- Total Carbohydrate: 17 g
- Cholesterol: 8 mg
- Total Fat: 10 g
- Fiber: 0 g
- Protein: 1 g
- Sodium: 10 mg

351. Truffle Topiary

"Easy treats for any occasion."
Serving: 11 dozen. | Prep: 60m | Ready in: 01h15m

Ingredients

- 3 packages (12 oz. each) semisweet chocolate chips, divided
- 2-1/4 cups sweetened condensed milk, divided
- 1/2 tsp. orange extract
- 1/2 to 1 tsp. peppermint extract
- 1/2 tsp. almond extract
- 3/4 lb. white candy coating, coarsely chopped
- 3/4 lb. dark chocolate candy coating, coarsely chopped
- 1/2 cup ground almonds
- 1 each 6- and 8-inch Styrofoam cones or a single 12-inch cone

Direction

- Melt 1 chocolate chips package in a microwave-safe bowl. Add 3/4 cup of condensed milk; stir well. Mix orange extract in; cover. Chill till firm to shape for 45 minutes. Repeat twice more with leftover milk and chips, adding almond extract to 1 portion and peppermint extract to the other.
- Shape truffles: Form chilled mixture to 1-inch balls; put on 3 different waxed paper-lined baking sheets and chill till firm for 1-2 hours.
- In a microwave-safe bowl, melt white candy coating. In coating, dip orange-flavored balls; put on waxed paper. Let harden. Melt leftover candy coating; dip balls again to cover thoroughly. Let them harden.

- Roll almond-flavored truffles into ground almonds.
- The Tree: Brush leftover chocolate on Styrofoam cones if you want. With toothpicks, stick an end in each truffle then other end into cone, covering the whole cone with truffles.

Nutrition Information

- Calories: 83 calories
- Total Carbohydrate: 11 g
- Cholesterol: 2 mg
- Total Fat: 4 g
- Fiber: 1 g
- Protein: 1 g
- Sodium: 7 mg

352. Turtles® Candies

"A perfect dish for holidays."
Serving: 36 | Prep: 10m | Ready in: 1h30m

Ingredients

- 1/2 cup margarine
- 1 cup firmly packed light brown sugar
- 1 pinch salt
- 1/2 cup light corn syrup
- 2/3 cup sweetened condensed milk
- 1 1/2 cups chopped pecans
- 1/2 tsp. vanilla extract
- 1 (6 oz.) package semisweet chocolate chips

Direction

- Grease 2 baking sheets.
- In a saucepan, over medium heat, melt margarine; stir salt and brown sugar into melted margarine. Mix in sweetened condensed milk and corn syrup; cook while stirring occasionally for 15-20 minutes until mixture reaches 250°F (120°C). Take out of the heat; fold in pecans. Mix vanilla extract into the caramel mixture.
- Drop spoonfuls of caramel onto the greased baking sheet. Let caramels cool until firm.

- In a saucepan, over medium-low heat, cook while stirring chocolate chips for about 5 minutes until melted and smooth. Take out of the heat. Coat cooled caramels with melted chocolate; transfer back to the prepared baking sheet. Cool until chocolate has set.

Nutrition Information

- Calories: 130 calories;
- Total Carbohydrate: 16.2 g
- Cholesterol: 2 mg
- Total Fat: 7.7 g
- Protein: 1.1 g
- Sodium: 46 mg

353. Twilight Dark Chocolate Truffles

"You can add other things like coffee grounds, cinnamon, mint extract, etc."
Serving: 45 | Prep: 5m | Ready in: 1h35m

Ingredients

- 1 cup heavy cream
- 2 tbsps. butter
- 4 (1 oz.) squares baking chocolate
- 2 3/4 cups semi-sweet chocolate chips
- 2 tbsps. instant espresso powder (optional)

Direction

- Cook espresso powder, chocolate chips, baking chocolate, butter and heavy cream, constantly mixing, in saucepan on medium heat till chocolate melts to a thick and smooth mixture. Take off heat; put in bowl. Chill for about 1 hour in the fridge till mixture hardens.
- Line waxed paper on baking sheet; scoop small chocolate mixture balls onto waxed paper. Keep in the fridge till balls completely harden. Store in dry and cool place.

Nutrition Information

- Calories: 87 calories;

- Total Carbohydrate: 6.8 g
- Cholesterol: 9 mg
- Total Fat: 7.1 g
- Protein: 1.2 g
- Sodium: 6 mg

354. Vegan Almond Truffles

"Keep your vegetarian truffles and almond flour base for up to 3 days.""
Serving: 24 | Prep: 30m | Ready in: 1h30m

Ingredients

- 1 cup raw almonds
- 5 Medjool dates, pitted and chopped
- 2 tsps. coconut oil
- 1 cup raw cocoa powder
- 1/4 cup water
- 3 tbsps. agave nectar, or more to taste
- 2 tsps. chia seeds
- 2 tsps. flax seeds
- 2 tbsps. raw cocoa powder, or as needed
- Himalayan pink salt to taste

Direction

- Grind almonds finely in the bowl of a food processor. Add dates and pulse until well combined.
- Place coconut oil in a large microwaveable bowl and microwave for about 10 seconds until melted. Add flax seeds, chia seeds, agave nectar, water, 1 cup cocoa powder, and date and almond mixture; mix with a spatula or wooden spoon until a stiff dough is formed.
- Place salt and 2 tbsps. cocoa powder in shallow bowls. Line parchment paper onto a baking sheet.
- Roll dough into tbsp.-sized balls using your hands. Cover balls with cocoa powder, lightly dip in salt then place on the prepared baking sheet. Refrigerate or freeze until firm before storing them.

Nutrition Information

- Calories: 62 calories;
- Total Carbohydrate: 6.8 g
- Cholesterol: 0 mg
- Total Fat: 4.1 g
- Protein: 2.2 g
- Sodium: 3 mg

355. Vegan Chocolate Truffles

"These are vegan truffles, but you can make this with dairy ingredients too."
Serving: 60 | Prep: 10m | Ready in: 1h10m

Ingredients

- 8 oz. dairy-free cream cheese (such as Tofutti®)
- 3 cups confectioners' sugar
- 12 oz. vegan chocolate chips, melted
- 1 1/2 tsps. vanilla extract
- 1/4 cup unsweetened cocoa powder (optional)
- 1/4 cup shredded coconut (optional)
- 1/4 cup chopped almonds (optional)

Direction

- Beat cream cheese till smooth. Slowly add confectioner's sugar, beating till blended well. Add vanilla extract and melted chocolate; chill for 1 hour in the fridge.
- Form chocolate mixture to 1-in. balls. Roll in almonds/coconut/cocoa powder. Keep in the fridge.

Nutrition Information

- Calories: 38 calories;
- Total Carbohydrate: 6.6 g
- Cholesterol: 0 mg
- Total Fat: 1.2 g
- Protein: 0.3 g
- Sodium: 15 mg

356. Vegan Truffles - Toasted Coconut

"Vegan truffles! You can store this for up to three days."
Serving: 12 | Prep: 20m | Ready in: 1h30m

Ingredients

- 1 1/4 cups shredded unsweetened coconut, or to taste, divided
- 2 cups pitted Medjool dates
- 1 cup raw almonds
- 2 1/4 cups raw cocoa powder
- 1/2 cup cocoa nibs
- 1/2 cup agave nectar
- 2 tsps. vanilla extract
- 1 tsp. salt

Direction

- Preheat an oven to 175°C/350°F. Spread coconut on baking sheet; line parchment paper on another baking sheet.
- In preheated oven, bake coconut, occasionally mixing, for 7 minutes till toasted and golden.
- In food processor, blend almonds and dates till smooth; add cocoa powder. Process till incorporated completely. Put date mixture into bowl.
- Fold salt, vanilla extract, agave nectar, cocoa nibs and 1 cup toasted coconut into date mixture till truffle double is mixed evenly. Roll dough to tbsp.-sized balls.
- Put leftover toasted coconut in shallow bowl; roll the truffle balls into toasted coconut till coated. Put coated truffles onto parchment-lined baking sheet. Refrigerate the truffles for 1 hour till hardened.

Nutrition Information

- Calories: 337 calories;
- Total Carbohydrate: 50.1 g
- Cholesterol: 0 mg
- Total Fat: 17.4 g
- Protein: 7.3 g
- Sodium: 209 mg

357. White Chocolate Cranberry Fudge

"A no-bake holiday treat. Salty, crunchy almonds and chewy tart cranberries made a great pair!"
Serving: 1-1/2 lbs.. | Prep: 15m | Ready in: 15m

Ingredients

- 1 tsp. butter
- 12 oz. white baking chocolate, chopped
- 2/3 cup sweetened condensed milk
- 1 cup roasted salted almonds, coarsely chopped
- 1/2 cup dried cranberries
- 2 tsps. grated orange zest

Direction

- Using foil, line an 8-in. square pan, then coat the foil with 1 tsp. butter; put aside. Mix the milk and chocolate in a big microwaveable bowl. Microwave for 2-3 minutes at 30% power, uncovered, until chocolate is almost melted; mix until smooth. Mix in the orange zest, cranberries and almonds. Pour into the lined pan evenly.
- Cover and chill for 2 hours or until set. Lift fudge out of the pan with the foil. Remove foil; slice fudge into 1-inch squares.

Nutrition Information

- Calories: 57 calories
- Total Carbohydrate: 6 g
- Cholesterol: 2 mg
- Total Fat: 3 g
- Fiber: 0 g
- Protein: 1 g
- Sodium: 18 mg

358. White Chocolate Easter Eggs

"A favorite treat to my kids."
Serving: about 4 dozen. | Prep: 25m | Ready in: 25m

Ingredients

- 1/2 cup butter, cubed
- 3 cups confectioners' sugar
- 2/3 cup sweetened condensed milk
- 1 tsp. vanilla extract
- 2 cups finely chopped pecans
- 1 lb. white candy coating, melted
- Gel food coloring, optional

Direction

- Melt butter in a large saucepan. Mix in the vanilla, milk, and confectioners' sugar until smooth. Mix in pecans. Put into a bowl. Refrigerate while covered for 2 hours or until easy to work with. Drop onto the baking sheets that are lined with waxed papers by level tablespoonfuls. Roll into egg shapes. Refrigerate them while covered overnight.
- Dip the eggs into the candy coating. Transfer onto the waxed paper until set. Dip a crumpled, small ball of waxed paper into food coloring to create a speckled look. Press the waxed paper onto a paper plate gently to eliminate any excess food coloring, and then press the color gently onto eggs. Repeat if necessary. Use a paper towel to blot the eggs.

Nutrition Information

- Calories: 144 calories
- Total Carbohydrate: 17 g
- Cholesterol: 7 mg
- Total Fat: 9 g
- Fiber: 0 g
- Protein: 1 g
- Sodium: 25 mg

359. White Chocolate Fudge

"A white chocolate lover's dream."
Serving: 40 | Prep: 15m | Ready in: 1h25m

Ingredients

- 1 (8 oz.) package cream cheese
- 4 cups confectioners' sugar
- 1 1/2 tsps. vanilla extract
- 12 oz. white chocolate, chopped
- 3/4 cup chopped pecans

Direction

- Grease 8x8-in. baking dish; put aside.
- Beat vanilla, sugar and cream cheese till smooth in medium bowl.
- Heat white chocolate in top of double boiler above lightly simmering water, mixing till smooth and melted.
- Fold pecans and melted white chocolate into cream cheese mixture; spread in prepped baking dish. Chill for an hour; cut to 1-in. squares.

Nutrition Information

- Calories: 126 calories;
- Total Carbohydrate: 17.4 g
- Cholesterol: 8 mg
- Total Fat: 6.1 g
- Protein: 1.1 g
- Sodium: 24 mg

360. White Chocolate Grapes

"You can never go wrong with grapes and chocolates. Add peanuts, and you'll make not only a beautiful presentation, but also a delicious treat as dessert or appetizer."
Serving: 20 | Prep: 20m | Ready in: 22m

Ingredients

- 2 cups white chocolate chips
- 2 tsps. shortening
- 1 lb. seedless grapes
- 1 cup finely chopped salted peanuts

Direction

- In a microwave-safe bowl, combine the chocolate chips with the shortening. Pop it in the microwave and heat for 30-second intervals; stir between intervals until it becomes completely melted and smooth. Place the chopped peanuts on a dinner plate or a piece of waxed paper.
- Clean and dry the grapes; individually, dip them onto the melted chocolate mixture, and roll them in the peanuts. Place them on a waxed paper and set aside until they dry. To keep the chocolate mixture liquid, heat it up in the microwave oven.

Nutrition Information

- Calories: 163 calories;
- Total Carbohydrate: 15.7 g
- Cholesterol: 4 mg
- Total Fat: 10.5 g
- Protein: 3.1 g
- Sodium: 77 mg

361. White Chocolate Jingle Candy

"Perfect recipe for holidays."
Serving: 20 | Prep: 10m | Ready in: 30m

Ingredients

- 1 3/4 cups miniature marshmallows
- 1 3/4 cups corn cereal puffs (such as Kix®)
- 1 3/4 cups crispy rice cereal (such as Rice Krispies®)
- 1 3/4 cups thin pretzel sticks
- 1 3/4 cups lightly salted peanuts
- 24 oz. white chocolate candy coating
- 1 cup red and green candy-coated chocolate pieces (such as M&M's®)

Direction

- In a large bowl, mix peanuts, pretzel sticks, rice cereal, corn cereal puffs and marshmallows.
- In a microwave-safe glass or ceramic bowl at 50% power, melt white chocolate in 30-second intervals; stir for 1 1/2 minutes after each melting. Keep heating in the microwave; stir every 15 seconds, until melted. Be careful not to overheat to prevent the chocolate from scorching.
- Place melted white chocolate on top of cereal mixture; stir gently to coat; add chocolate pieces. Drop mixture onto a piece of waxed paper by large spoonfuls. Let harden for about 15 minutes.

Nutrition Information

- Calories: 367 calories;
- Total Carbohydrate: 43.2 g
- Cholesterol: 9 mg
- Total Fat: 19.7 g
- Protein: 6.4 g
- Sodium: 304 mg

---

362. White Chocolate Marshmallow Fudge

"I like to make this recipe for holiday parties or special occasions. Almost everyone finds this delicious."
Serving: 8-9 dozen. | Prep: 30m | Ready in: 30m

Ingredients

- 3 cups sugar
- 1 cup evaporated milk
- 1/2 cup butter
- 1 jar (7 oz.) marshmallow creme
- 1-2/3 cups white chocolate chips
- 1 cup chopped pecans or almonds, toasted

Direction

- Put butter, milk and sugar in a heavy saucepan; put over low heat and boil while stirring continuously. Cook until a candy thermometer reads 234 degrees, soft-ball stage.
- Take away from the heat; mix in nuts, chocolate chips and marshmallow crème to melt chocolate and marshmallow. Grease a 13x9-inch pan and spread mixture in the prepared pan. Allow to cool then cut.

Nutrition Information

- Calories: 60 calories
- Total Carbohydrate: 9 g
- Cholesterol: 4 mg
- Total Fat: 3 g
- Fiber: 0 g
- Protein: 0 g
- Sodium: 15 mg

---

363. White Chocolate Peppermint Bark

"You'll love this even if you don't like white chocolate. These can be stored for up to 1 week."
Serving: 20 | Prep: 10m | Ready in: 47m

Ingredients

- 2 (11 oz.) packages white chocolate chips (such as Ghirardelli®)
- 12 peppermint candy canes, broken into pieces
- 1/4 tsp. peppermint oil

Direction

- Using parchment paper, line an 11x17-inch baking sheet.
- In a microwaveable glass bowl, melt white chocolate chips for 3 mins on 50% power. Mix thoroughly until bowl is cooled. Keep heating for 3 more minutes; mix. Heat for 1 more minute and mix; keep heating and mixing if needed until chocolate is completely silky.
- Mix peppermint oil and candy canes into the prepared chocolate until well mixed. Put onto the lined baking sheet evenly. Smooth out using a spatula. Chill until set for half an hour

to overnight. Crack into pieces and put in an airtight container to store.

Nutrition Information

- Calories: 240 calories;
- Total Carbohydrate: 33.8 g
- Cholesterol: 7 mg
- Total Fat: 10.9 g
- Protein: 2.2 g
- Sodium: 39 mg

364. White Chocolate Peppermint Crunch

"For an easy and simple Christmas gift that is super delicious, I always confide in these crunchy candies."
Serving: about 1-1/2 lbs.. | Prep: 15m | Ready in: 20m

Ingredients

- 1 lb. white candy coating, coarsely chopped
- 1 tbsp. butter
- 1 tbsp. canola oil
- 1 cup chopped peppermint candies or candy canes

Direction

- Use waxed or parchment paper to line a baking sheet. Microwave candy coating until melted; whisk until smooth. Mix in oil and butter until combined. Mix in candies. Transfer to lined pan and spread to thickness of your choice.
- Keep chilled to firm up. Break into pieces. Keep refrigerated in a tightly sealed container to store.

Nutrition Information

- Calories: 125 calories
- Total Carbohydrate: 17 g
- Cholesterol: 1 mg
- Total Fat: 6 g
- Fiber: 0 g
- Protein: 0 g

- Sodium: 5 mg

365. White Christmas Candy

"Children love these beautiful and delicious white Christmas candies.""
Serving: 25 | Prep: 10m | Ready in: 45m

Ingredients

- 1 (12 oz.) package white chocolate chips
- 2 tbsps. creamy peanut butter
- 2 cups crispy rice cereal (such as Rice Krispies®)
- 1 cup mini marshmallows
- 1 cup lightly salted peanuts
- 1 tbsp. multi-colored sprinkles, or more to taste (optional)

Direction

- In a large microwaveable bowl, combine peanut butter and white chocolate chips.
- Microwave for 1 minute on high power; whisk using a spatula. Keep cooking in 30-second periods in the microwave; whisk until no lumps remain. Fold in peanuts, marshmallows, and rice cereal.
- Drop white chocolate mixture onto a sheet of waxed paper by spoonfuls. Scatter sprinkles over top of each mound. Put aside and allow to cool for half an hour.

Nutrition Information

- Calories: 136 calories;
- Total Carbohydrate: 13.1 g
- Cholesterol: 3 mg
- Total Fat: 8.5 g
- Protein: 2.8 g
- Sodium: 87 mg

Index

A

Allspice, 100

Almond, 3–7, 11–12, 14–15, 32–33, 39, 48, 63, 65, 71–72, 75, 77, 81, 83–84, 86–87, 94, 99,

106, 115, 117–118, 120, 122, 124, 131, 133, 135–136, 139, 144, 151, 156, 158, 161,

165–166, 168, 170–175, 177

Almond extract, 15, 39, 77, 118, 122, 165, 170, 172

Apple, 120

Apricot, 3–4, 13, 68, 70, 168

B

Bacon, 3, 5, 15, 103, 117

Baking, 11–16, 18–20, 22–25, 27–41, 45, 47–48, 50, 52–54, 56–77, 79–87, 89–98, 100–106,

109–110, 112–118, 120, 122–129, 131–133, 135–136, 138–140, 142, 144, 146–153, 156,

159–170, 172–178

Baking powder, 40, 96, 165

Banana, 3, 6, 16, 141

Beans, 4, 19, 69, 82, 110, 148–149, 153, 162

Berry, 5, 21, 28, 86, 114

Biscuits, 89

Blueberry, 3, 21, 86–87, 133, 168

Brandy, 25, 30, 39, 114

Brown sugar, 25, 27, 36–37, 40–41, 54, 58, 60, 67,

79, 83–84, 121, 131, 146, 158–159,

166, 168, 172

Butter, 3–7, 9, 11–19, 21–29, 31–34, 36–38, 40, 42–58, 60–63, 66–67, 70–71, 73, 75–80,

83–93, 95–101, 105–113, 115–124, 128–134, 136–139, 141–149, 152–155, 157–159,

162–171, 173, 175, 177–178

C

Cake, 155

Candied peel, 25

Caramel, 3–6, 25–28, 35–37, 58, 65–66, 68, 71–72, 84, 106, 109, 133, 146–147, 151, 156,

172–173

Cashew, 3, 13, 28, 133, 168

Cheddar, 79

Cheese, 3, 9, 16, 24, 37, 40–41, 43, 49, 64, 75–76, 78–80, 82–83, 85, 89–90, 92, 112–114,

116–117, 127, 129, 132, 135–136, 161–162, 165–167, 170, 174, 176

Cherry, 3–7, 29–30, 38–39, 42, 59–60, 76, 95–97, 118, 133, 161–162, 168, 171

Cherry brandy, 39

Chestnut, 3, 30, 63

Chipotle, 108

Chips, 3–4, 11–30, 32–60, 62, 64–88, 90–99, 101–103, 105–106, 108, 110–135, 138–143,

145–155, 157–159, 161–164, 166–174, 176–178

Chocolate, 1, 3–9, 11–178

Chocolate mousse, 4, 51

Chocolate truffle, 3–7, 64–65, 91, 109, 113–114, 123, 127, 135, 141, 153, 160–161, 169,

174

Cinnamon, 3, 20, 41–42, 72–73, 78, 100, 139, 143, 151, 160, 173

Cloves, 25, 100, 120, 160

Cocktail, 47, 67

Cocoa powder, 12, 16, 21, 25, 32–33, 37, 43, 46–47, 60, 63, 65, 73, 85, 97–98, 106–108,

115, 130, 132, 136, 153, 161, 163, 169, 173–174

Coconut, 3–7, 11–12, 21, 23, 38, 43, 46, 48, 55, 59–60, 73, 75–77, 86, 89–90, 94, 97, 101,

106–107, 115, 120, 128, 153, 163–164, 167–169, 173–174

Coconut cream, 4, 76

Coconut oil, 12, 55, 73, 86, 107, 115, 153, 173

Coffee, 4–5, 11, 64, 69, 78, 98, 110, 122, 127, 137, 151, 163, 173

Coffee beans, 4, 69, 110

Coffee granules, 64, 122, 127, 137

Coffee liqueur, 151

Condensed milk, 11, 21–24, 27, 33, 39, 42, 44, 49–50, 53, 58–59, 76, 78–80, 86–89,

91–92, 94, 96–97, 101–102, 106, 111, 114–115, 117, 120, 123, 125, 128–129, 131, 134, 137,

147, 152, 155–156, 163, 167, 172, 175

Corn syrup, 12–13, 27, 31–34, 36–38, 41–42, 54, 58, 60, 62–63, 70–71, 81–85, 92, 94–95,

106, 109, 117, 119–120, 126, 133–134, 136, 146, 164, 172

Crackers, 67, 85–87, 102, 158–159

Cranberry, 4, 7, 81–82, 139, 168, 175

Cream, 3–5, 14–17, 19, 21–22, 24, 26–27, 34, 36, 39–41, 43–44, 46–49, 52, 55, 62–65, 73,

75–80, 82–85, 88–90, 92, 97, 100, 106–110, 112–114, 116–118, 122, 125–129, 132,

134–136, 138–139, 141, 150, 152, 155–156, 160–162, 165–167, 169–171, 173–174, 176

Cream cheese, 16, 24, 40–41, 43, 64, 75–76, 78–80, 82–83, 85, 89–90, 112–114,

116–117, 127, 129, 135–136, 161–162, 165–167, 170, 174, 176

Cream liqueur, 110

Crisps, 4–5, 67, 86

Crumble, 85, 117, 120

Currants, 74

D

Dab, 44

Dark chocolate, 3–7, 11, 15–16, 21, 28, 33–34, 39, 49, 58, 60, 64, 68–69, 72, 74, 77, 79,

84–86, 89, 95, 99, 104, 106–110, 112, 114–115, 117, 132–133, 139–140, 146, 152–153, 159,

161, 170, 172–173

Date, 55, 173–174

Digestive biscuit, 89

Dried apricots, 13, 68, 70, 168

Dried cherries, 30, 39, 133, 168

Dried fruit, 70, 143, 168

E

Egg, 3–5, 7, 15–16, 19, 21–22, 24, 40, 43, 46–48, 57,

76, 83, 89–90, 93, 95–97, 106–107,

126, 155, 165, 168, 175

Egg yolk, 15, 47, 168

Evaporated milk, 14, 26–29, 36, 46–47, 51, 56, 60, 66, 82, 87–88, 91, 96–98, 105, 111,

116, 121–124, 128, 134, 138–139, 143, 146–149, 154, 157, 166, 169–170, 177

F

Fat, 11–70, 72–152, 154–155, 157–178

Fish, 3, 46

Flour, 15–16, 40–41, 47–48, 79, 96–97, 106, 126, 131, 151, 155, 165, 168, 173

Fruit, 6, 8, 12, 25, 70, 133, 135, 139, 143, 161, 168

Fudge, 3–7, 14, 16–17, 24–26, 28–29, 33, 37, 39–40, 46, 52–53, 56, 63, 66, 78–83, 86–89,

92–93, 95–98, 102, 105, 110–112, 115–118, 121, 123–125, 128–130, 132, 134–138, 143–145,

147–148, 152, 154, 156–159, 162, 164, 166–167, 169–170, 175–177

G

Ginger, 100, 139, 160

Gingerbread, 5, 100

Grain, 143, 156

Grapes, 7, 176

Green tea, 5, 103

Ground almonds, 151, 172

Ground ginger, 139, 160

H

Hazelnut, 3, 47–48, 65, 98–99, 161–162

Heart, 4, 14, 59–60, 101

Honey, 37, 52, 107, 115, 145, 150, 153, 155

I

Ice cream, 5, 109, 150

Icing, 97, 119, 168

J

Jam, 152

Jelly, 12, 17–19, 82

L

Lemon, 3, 5, 25, 112–113, 153

Lemon juice, 112

Liqueur, 19, 33, 86, 110, 114, 138–139, 151–152

M

Macadamia, 6, 133, 157

Macaroon, 77

Maple syrup, 12, 157, 161

Margarine, 12, 17–18, 37, 40, 56, 89–90, 108, 141, 148, 163, 172

Marshmallow, 3–7, 14, 17–19, 26–28, 36, 43, 47, 49, 59–61, 66–67, 71–73, 87–89, 91–92,

96, 98, 100–102, 105, 109, 111, 116, 118–119, 121–122, 124, 128–130, 134–135, 138–139,

143, 145, 147–148, 154–156, 158, 165–167, 169–170, 176–178

Marzipan, 5, 120–121

Mascarpone, 4, 49

Mayonnaise, 9

Meat, 8, 44

Melon, 11, 65, 100, 141

Milk, 5, 11–17, 20–37, 39, 42, 44–47, 49–53, 55–62, 64–71, 73, 75–82, 84, 86–89, 91–99,

101–103, 105–106, 108–118, 120–126, 128–131, 133–139, 141–143, 145–149, 152, 154–172,

175, 177

Milk chocolate, 5, 12–14, 16–17, 20–22, 24–27, 32, 34–37, 39, 44–46, 49, 51, 55–57, 59,

61–62, 64, 67–71, 73, 75–77, 81, 84, 88, 92–93, 96, 99, 102–103, 108–110, 112–113, 116,

122–124, 126, 128–129, 133–134, 136, 138, 141–142, 147, 160–162, 166–169, 171, 177

Mint, 4–6, 50, 59, 82, 91, 93, 111, 121, 124–126, 140, 149, 155, 170, 173

Molasses, 4, 50, 100

N

Noodles, 18–19, 41–42, 45, 47, 64

Nougat, 4–5, 71, 98

Nut, 4–6, 13–14, 17, 20, 23, 27, 30, 42, 44, 46, 48, 51–53, 62–63, 65–66, 74, 83, 87–88, 91,

93, 97–98, 101, 109–111, 121–124, 130, 132–135, 138–139, 143, 156–159, 163, 165,

168–169, 177

Nutmeg, 160

O

Oats, 55, 143, 145, 163

Oil, 12, 17, 36, 43, 55, 57–59, 67, 73–74, 85–86, 94–96, 98–99, 107, 109, 115, 130, 153, 161,

173, 177–178

Orange, 3–6, 19, 21, 25, 53, 82, 85, 104, 113–114, 121, 138–139, 172, 175

Orange juice, 19, 53, 113, 139

Orange liqueur, 19, 114, 138–139

P

Pastry, 65, 67, 71, 171

Peanut butter, 4–6, 18–19, 22–23, 26–27, 36, 38, 43, 46–47, 49, 51–52, 54–57, 73, 77,

83, 89–90, 96, 101, 108, 112, 119, 134, 137, 141–145, 154, 157, 164, 167, 178

Peanuts, 3, 11, 24–26, 36, 41–42, 45, 47, 49, 51–52, 54, 56, 59–60, 67, 71, 73, 83, 90, 92,

101–102, 109, 117, 129, 133, 135, 141–143, 150, 155–156, 163, 176–178

Pecan, 3–4, 6, 15–17, 27, 35, 44–45, 51, 53, 57–58, 60–62, 65–66, 68, 70, 77–78, 83–84, 92,

98, 120, 122, 130–131, 134–135, 137–138, 146–147, 150–151, 156–157, 162, 167–170, 172,

175–177

Peel, 3, 25, 29, 34, 53, 80, 86, 104, 108, 111, 121, 138–140

Pepper, 108

Peppercorn, 4, 74

Pie, 4, 41, 78, 81, 85, 130

Pink peppercorn, 4, 74

Pinto beans, 162

Pistachio, 3–5, 21, 28, 30, 49–50, 65, 70, 74, 104, 169

Pizza, 4, 59

Plum, 139

Pomegranate, 4, 60, 69

Popcorn, 3–4, 6, 32–33, 36–37, 44, 85, 150, 161

Potato, 3, 5–6, 44–45, 59–60, 68, 115, 150

Praline, 4, 60–61, 69

Preserves, 122, 135, 153

Prune, 139

Pulse, 14, 79–80, 109, 173

Pumpkin, 4, 6, 85–86, 121, 151, 160, 168

Pumpkin seed, 168

R

Raisins, 62, 81, 139, 143

Raspberry, 4–6, 86, 122, 129, 152–153, 155

Raspberry jam, 152

Red wine, 9

Rice, 35, 46, 48–49, 67, 83, 101, 125, 176–178

Rock salt, 153

Rum, 4, 24, 62, 107

S

Salami, 4, 63

Salt, 5, 14, 23, 27–29, 32–33, 38, 40–42, 47–48, 52, 55–57, 70–71, 73, 75, 78, 80, 86–87, 92,

96, 98, 100, 103, 106, 108, 111, 115, 118, 123–124, 126, 130, 132–134, 136–137, 143,

147–148, 152–153, 155–158, 164, 168–169, 172–174

Savory, 68

Sea salt, 5, 28–29, 55, 57, 103, 106, 133, 137, 156

Seasoning, 57, 117

Seeds, 4, 60, 69, 153, 155, 168, 173

Soda, 6, 12–13, 32, 34, 40, 54, 126, 158

Spices, 8, 25, 143, 160

Strawberry, 5–6, 72–73, 114, 129, 135, 153, 161

Sugar, 6, 11–20, 22–34, 36–38, 40–48, 50–60, 62–63, 65–72, 75–79, 82–85, 87–99, 101,

105–124, 126, 128–136, 138–139, 141, 143–149, 151, 154–159, 161–172, 174–177

Sunflower seed, 153

Swede, 163

Sweets, 111

Syrup, 12–13, 25, 27, 31–34, 36–38, 41–42, 54, 58, 60, 62–63, 70–71, 81–85, 92, 94–95, 98,

106, 109, 117–120, 124, 126, 133–134, 136, 145–146, 157, 161–162, 164, 172

T

Tea, 5, 103

Toffee, 3–5, 7, 14, 67, 92, 121, 166, 168

Truffle, 3–7, 12, 15–17, 19–20, 30–31, 39, 41, 47–49, 62–65, 78–81, 85–86, 91–92, 100,

108–110, 113–114, 122–123, 126–127, 131, 133, 135, 139, 141, 145, 150–153, 155–156,

160–161, 167, 169–174

Turkey, 3, 37, 100–101

V

Vanilla extract, 11, 14–17, 22–32, 36–37, 40–43, 45, 49–52, 54, 57–58, 60–63, 66–67,

70–71, 73, 75–76, 78–79, 82, 84–91, 93, 95–98, 105–107, 111, 113–115, 118–120, 122,

124–126, 128–132, 134, 136–137, 139, 142–149, 152, 154–156, 158–159, 161–165, 167–170,

172, 174–176

Vegan, 7, 173–174

Vegetable oil, 43, 58–59, 74, 109, 161

Vegetables, 8

Vegetarian, 173

Vinegar, 12–13, 34, 52

W

Walnut, 4–5, 15, 28–29, 35, 37–38, 42, 44, 46, 52, 62–63, 66, 76, 79–80, 83, 87–88, 93,

96–97, 101, 111, 115–116, 121–122, 128, 132, 134, 136–137, 139, 158–159, 162, 165–166,

169

Whipping cream, 15, 19, 21, 36, 39, 41, 49, 62, 84–85, 100, 106–108, 113, 122, 138,

141, 152, 160–161, 169, 171

White chocolate, 5, 7, 24, 30, 33–35, 39, 58–60, 79–82, 100, 103–105, 110–111,

113–114, 117, 127, 129, 140, 142, 150, 153, 162, 165, 170, 175–178

White sugar, 12, 14–17, 25–26, 29, 32–33, 36, 40, 46–47, 56, 60, 63, 66, 85, 88, 98, 106,

118, 121, 123, 136, 138, 145, 161, 163, 165

Wine, 9

Z

Zest, 19, 21, 53, 104, 112, 138–139, 175

Conclusion

Thank you again for downloading this book!

I hope you enjoyed reading about my book!

If you enjoyed this book, please take the time to share your thoughts and post a review on Amazon. It'd be greatly appreciated!

Write me an honest review about the book – I truly value your opinion and thoughts and I will incorporate them into my next book, which is already underway.

Thank you!

If you have any questions, **feel free to contact at:** *msingredient@mrandmscooking.com*

Ms. Ingredient

www.MrandMsCooking.com